Historical Geography
of the United States

GEOGRAPHY AND TRAVEL INFORMATION GUIDE SERIES

Series Editors: Alberta Auringer Wood, Head, Information Services Division, Library, Memorial University of Newfoundland, St. Johns, and Clifford H. Wood, Assistant Professor, Department of Geography, Memorial University of Newfoundland, St. Johns

Also in this series:

REMOTE SENSING OF EARTH RESOURCES—*Edited by M. Leonard Bryan*

TRAVEL IN ASIA—*Edited by Neal Edgar and Wendy Ma**

TRAVEL IN CANADA—*Edited by Nora T. Corley**

TRAVEL IN OCEANIA, AUSTRALIA, AND NEW ZEALAND—*Edited by Robert E. Burton*

TRAVEL IN THE UNITED STATES—*Edited by Joyce A. Post and Jeremiah B. Post*

*in preparation

The above series is part of the
GALE INFORMATION GUIDE LIBRARY

The Library consists of a number of separate series of guides covering major areas in the social sciences, humanities, and current affairs.

General Editor: Paul Wasserman, Professor and former Dean, School of Library and Information Services, University of Maryland

Managing Editor: Denise Allard Adzigian, Gale Research Company

Historical Geography
of the United States

A GUIDE TO INFORMATION SOURCES

Volume 5 in the Geography and Travel Information Guide Series

Ronald E. Grim

Gale Research Company

Book Tower, Detroit, Michigan 48226

Library of Congress Cataloging in Publication Data

Grim, Ronald E.
   Historical geography of the United States.

   (Vol. 5 in the Geography and travel information guide
series)   (Gale information guide library)
   Includes indexes.
   1. United States—Historical geography—Bibliography.
I. Title. II. Series: Geography and travel information
guide series ; v. 5)
Z1247.G74   1982   [E179.5]   016.911'73   82-15674
ISBN 0-8103-1471-1

VITA

Ronald E. Grim is bibliographer in the Geography and Map Division of the Library of Congress. Prior to this appointment he was assistant chief for reference in the Center for Cartographic and Architectural Archives, National Archives and Records Service, Washington, D.C. He began working with cartographic reference activities in the National Archives in 1972. He received his B.A. in history and geography from Muskingum College, New Concord, Ohio, and his M.A. and Ph.D. degrees in historical geography from the University of Maryland, College Park. His dissertation, which was completed in 1977, was titled, "The Absence of Towns in Seventeenth-Century Virginia: The Emergence of Service Centers in York County."

Grim is a member of the Association of American Geographers and serves on the association's Committee for Archives and History. He is secretary-treasurer of the Washington Map Society and a member of the Society for the History of Discoveries. He has published book reviews in the AMERICAN ARCHIVIST, HISTORICAL GEOGRAPHY NEWSLETTER, and JOURNAL OF HISTORICAL GEOGRAPHY.

CONTENTS

Contents

Contents

Indexes

ACKNOWLEDGMENTS

In preparing this bibliography, I have been assisted by colleagues, friends, and family. First, I would like to thank Ralph E. Ehrenberg, former chief of the Center for Cartographic and Architectural Archives, National Archives, and currently assistant chief, Geography and Map Division, Library of Congress, who originally suggested this project to me and who shared bibliographical citations, reprint articles, and special cartographic and geographical publications with me. I am also grateful to Robert D. Mitchell, associate professor of geography, University of Maryland, for lending me copies of several articles and for reading and commenting on the first draft. I owe these two colleagues, as well as Herman R. Friis, former chief of the Cartographic Archives Branch and the Center for Polar Archives, an intellectual debt. In my academic and professional associations with them, there has always been an emphasis on the use of archival and cartographic sources for research in historical geography and a particular awareness of historical geography as a unique and fascinating research interest.

I have used a number of libraries in the Washington, D.C., area in preparing this bibliography and I thank their staffs for helpful and efficient service. I would particularly like to acknowledge the aid given by James Flatness, Patrick Dempsey, and Gary Fitzpatrick of the Geography and Map Division, Library of Congress; and by Camille Simmons, Sara Strom, and Maryellen Trautman of the Library Branch, National Archives. In addition, suggestions for the chapter on "Pictorial Sources" were provided by Nancy Malan, Office of Public Programs and Exhibits, National Archives; Maygene Daniels, Office of Presidential Libraries, National Archives; and Pamela Scott, Dunlap Society.

My family and friends have also contributed to this project. Carolyn Noll graciously offered her time and typing skills in preparing the first draft, while Ann Kessler assisted with the indexing. My wife, Ottilie, and my son, Theron, have been particularly patient and understanding of the time I have spent working on this project. I not only relied on my wife's support in this project, I also depended on her expert help in proofreading and editing. Despite this assistance, I am sure there are errors of omission and interpretation, but they remain my responsibility alone.

INTRODUCTION

The historical geography of the United States, beginning with the European explorations and settlement of the sixteenth century, provides the focus for this information guide. I have generally included studies by geographers that pertain to the reconstruction of past geographies whether they emphasize spatial distributions and relationships, the regional character of specific places or areas, or the interrelationships of man with his physical environment. Equally important were studies that dealt with geographic change through time, including such processes as migration, settlement, acculturation, regionalization, industrialization, and urbanization. There is a strong emphasis on studies that use primary source material; however, studies that use relict landscape features or artifacts to interpret past settlement patterns and cultural processes are also included. These several themes are sufficiently broad to encompass the more detailed definitions and expositions that are described in the methodological statements listed in chapter 11.

Several archaic definitions of historical geography, such as the histories of cartography, political boundary changes, and exploration and discovery, are represented although not treated as prominently. For instance, works pertaining to the history of cartography are listed in the portion pertaining to cartographic sources because these studies provide background information for determining the utility of maps as historical documents. Secondly, publications, such as historical atlases, that pertain to the history of changing political boundaries are mentioned because they provide useful reference aids and research tools. Finally, works relating to the history of discoveries are treated as a separate topic because the process by which geographical knowledge is accumulated and the initial perception of the physical environment are becoming significant research themes in historical geography.

The geographical and temporal coverage of this information guide is limited almost exclusively to the United States from the beginning of the sixteenth century until the early twentieth century. In terms of subject matter, this time span represents the Europeanization of the American landscape--its exploration, settlement, and transformation through a variety of economic and cultural processes. From a methodological standpoint, it represents a time span that can be documented by a wide range of written and graphic primary source materials. The study of pre-sixteenth century aboriginal landscapes is omitted because their interpretation is based on archaeological research techniques, which are substantially different from the methodology associated with archival research. Likewise, studies of the recent past and short term changes since 1900 are generally omitted because different methodologies and sources are usually involved. In these works, there is a heavy reliance on field work and personal interpretation, while the full range of archival materials (such as manuscript census schedules) is not yet available. However, genetic or retrospective studies, which attempt to explain the current landscape as a product of past developments that started in the eighteenth or nineteenth century, are included if the studies are based on substantial archival research rather than on secondary sources.

Although the geographical coverage of this guide is limited to the United States, a listing of literature pertaining to the geographical development of this country should be considered in the context of all Anglo-America. I originally intended to include Canadian coverage, but decided to omit that portion because I quickly realized that unless I invested a substantial amount of time, I could not provide equal treatment for the archival and topical literature available on Canadian historical geography.[1] For many historical geographers this will be an unfortunate omission because Andrew H. Clark, the primary proponent of North American historical geography during the 1950s and 1960s advocated this broader context, emphasizing the parallel development of both countries within the framework of European colonization, immigration, and industrialization. In fact, much of Clark's own research, which sets the tone for many of the studies listed in this information guide, pertains to the Canadian maritime provinces and is not included here.[2]

Most of the entries included in this guide to information sources pertain to books and articles that were published or reprinted between the beginning of 1965 and the close of 1980. By emphasizing recent and current literature, my annotated listings do not duplicate the only other comprehensive bibliography of historical geography, which was compiled by Douglas R. McManis.[3] Since the publication of his bibliography in 1965, the literature on the historical geography of the United States has increased significantly. The impetus for this increased activity is closely related to the increased opportunities for historical geographers to communicate and share their research, beginning with the Conference on the National Archives and Research in Historical Geography (see entry 12-6) and followed by the institution of two periodicals (HISTORICAL GEOGRAPHY NEWS-LETTER and JOURNAL OF HISTORICAL GEOGRAPHY), and two organizations (Eastern Historical Geography Association and the Historical Geography Specialty Group of the Association of American Geographers) devoted exclusively to historical geography. The selected literature consists mainly of books and significant articles from the major journals, while articles from the lesser journals are usually mentioned in main entries by the same author. Unpublished conference papers, master's theses, and doctoral dissertations are not included because many of these studies provided the basis for later articles or monographs.

Although this bibliography was planned to complement McManis's bibliography, there are several major differences in content and organization. While McManis only listed literature related to the substance of historical geography, I am also emphasizing primary sources. Reflecting my training as a historical geographer and my professional experience in the cartographic and archival fields, I have devised a three-part organization. The first two sections deal with cartographic and archival sources which provide the basis for the topical literature described in the third section. I have placed cartographic sources first, not because they are the major source used by historical geographers, but because maps are traditionally associated with geographic studies. Rather, historical maps are used as tools in preparing base maps when determining place locations and re-creating past spatial distributions and patterns. Consequently, my listings for cartographic sources include repository guides, cartobibliographies, and analytical literature pertaining to the history of cartography.

In reality, it is the written archival or textual sources which are listed in the second section that normally provide the bulk of data used by historical geographers, particularly those following in the tradition of Andrew H. Clark. Although I use the term "archival" loosely in this second section, I am not only referring to the official written records of a government or institution, but also to other historical manuscripts and published material, as well as to other graphic sources. I have not attempted to list guides and descriptions for all the potential sources, only those that are most frequently used by historical geographers. In addition, I have listed directories and guides to archival repositories as reference aids for the creative scholar in discovering resources peculiar to his or her research interests.

Following this listing of the primary source materials, the final section provides a selection of topical literature from the field of historical geography. It is actually this last section that complements McManis's bibliography. His listing, which relies heavily on literature by historians (primarily because of limited geographical literature), is arranged geographically by broad regions and states and thereunder topically. In this guide the selected literature is arranged topically and thereunder alphabetically by name of author. The content of my annotations includes the usual bibliographical notations as well as geographic coverage, time period, and topical coverage of the study, particularly if these elements are not evident from the title. In keeping with my emphasis on sources, I usually mention the major primary sources on which the study is based. Geographical entries in the subject index allow access by region, state, or city. I have also included author and title indexes, which I found to be significant omissions from McManis's bibliography when I tried to cross check various entries for duplication.

As McManis has shown, there is a wide range of literature by historians, economists, sociologists, and anthropologists that is closely related to the interests of historical geographers. However, I have not attempted to include this literature on a systematic basis unless specific items are widely known or cited extensively by historical geographers. I have included pertinent topical bibliographies or review essays that will serve as guides to this literature. In addition, my annotations indicate whether a particular source has a good discussion of related secondary sources. It is expected that the interested scholar will pursue the footnotes of articles by individual regional or topical specialists for related historical works. In terms of future bibliographical studies, I would suggest that regional or topical bibliographies compiled by specialists in those fields would be in order.

Certainly this type of bibliography could provide a more accurate assessment of the related historical literature.

The studies included in this guide to information sources are also limited somewhat by the sources that I used in compiling the initial listing from which I made my selection. I reviewed a variety of reference aids including GEO-ABSTRACTS D and G (see entries 11-16 and 1-9), CURRENT GEOGRAPHICAL PUBLICATIONS, (see entry 11-14), footnotes from methodological statements and other key articles, and book reviews in the major geographical journals (ANNALS OF THE ASSOCIATION OF AMERICAN GEOGRAPHERS, GEOGRAPHICAL REVIEW, PROFESSIONAL GEOGRAPHER, JOURNAL OF HISTORICAL GEOGRAPHY, HISTORICAL GEOGRAPHY NEWSLETTER, and ECONOMIC GEOGRAPHY). The availability of the selected publications in the Library of Congress, National Archives, and the University of Maryland libraries was another limiting factor. If a publication was not available in one of these three institutions, it was usually omitted, based on the assumption that the publication would not be readily available in other major public or university libraries.

This latter limitation was also based on the objective that this information guide should serve a generalized audience, as well as a specialized audience of historical geographers. For the general audience, it is intended to provide an overview of the literature on the historical geography of the United States that has been published since 1965. For the historical geography community and particularly for beginning graduate students, it provides a survey of the literature pertaining to cartographic and archival sources as well as an index to the growing literature in the field. It is not intended to be a comprehensive guide to the literature on individual topics, and certainly the specialist will note numerous omissions. Rather, the volume is designed to show what sources are available to historical geographers and what historical geographers have written during the past sixteen years about the geographical development of this country.

NOTES

1.   Unfortunately, Canadian periodicals and Canadian university publications are not as readily available in the repositories in which this research was conducted. A comprehensive survey of Canada's early historical geography is found in R. Cole Harris and John Warkentin, CANADA BEFORE CONFEDERATION: A STUDY IN HISTORICAL GEOGRAPHY (New York: Oxford University Press, 1974). Each chapter is followed by a short bibliographical essay that lists pertinent secondary sources. An earlier bibliographical article by Harris was presented as "Historical Geography in Canada," CANADIAN GEOGRAPHER 11 (1967): 235-50.

2.   See Clark, THREE CENTURIES AND THE ISLAND: A HISTORICAL GEOGRAPHY OF SETTLEMENT AND AGRICULTURE IN PRINCE EDWARD ISLAND, CANADA (Toronto, 1959); and Clark, ACADIA, THE GEOGRAPHY OF EARLY NOVA SCOTIA TO 1760 (Madison, 1968).

3.   HISTORICAL GEOGRAPHY OF THE UNITED STATES: A BIBLIOGRAPHY (Ypsilanti, Mich., 1965).   See entry 11-20.

KEY TO ABBREVIATIONS

AAG ANNALS   ANNALS OF THE ASSOCIATION OF AMERICAN
GEOGRAPHERS (see entry 12-1).

AAG PROCEEDINGS   PROCEEDINGS OF THE ASSOCIATION OF
AMERICAN GOEGRAPHERS (see entry 12-24).

Part 1

CARTOGRAPHIC SOURCES

Chapter 1

CARTOGRAPHIC REFERENCE AIDS

Included in this chapter are general reference aids that can be utilized in locating and evaluating cartographic sources. The first section lists articles that discuss the utility of maps as sources for historical research. Because little has been written on this topic in the United States, there are several citations to British and Canadian publications. The second section describes a variety of publications (bibliographies, abstracts, periodicals, and collections of essays) that will serve as guides to literature on the history of cartography and map librarianship, that describe cartographic resources or collections, or that provide background material for evaluating maps as historical documents. The final section lists general guides to major map repositories (or portions thereof) that have significant collections of historical American maps.

A. MAPS AS SOURCES

1-1   De Vorsey, Louis, Jr. "Early Maps as a Source in the Reconstruction of Southern Indian Landscapes." In RED, WHITE, AND BLACK: SYMPOSIUM ON INDIANS IN THE OLD SOUTH, edited by Charles Miltudson, pp. 12-30. Southern Anthropological Society Proceedings, No. 5. Athens, Ga.: Southern Anthropological Society, 1971. viii, 142 p. Paper. Map, bibliog.

> Using two examples pertaining to mid-eighteenth century southern Indian landscapes, De Vorsey illustrates the use of maps in reconstructing past physical and cultural landscapes. In evaluating maps as sources, he advises that the researcher should consider the circumstances of the map's creation as well as its content. De Vorsey pursues the same theme in "The Virginia-Cherokee Boundary of 1771: An Example of the Importance of Maps in the Interpretation of History," East Tennessee Historical Society, PUBLICATIONS, no. 33 (1961), pp. 2-16.

1-2   Gentilcore, Louis. "The Use of Maps in Historical Geography." Association of Canadian Map Libraries. PROCEEDINGS OF THE FIFTH ANNUAL CONFERENCE, 1971, pp. 41-48. Notes.

> In addition to describing a number of Canadian maps which

3

have good research potential for historical geography, Gentilcore also mentions recent research in historical geography in which maps served as a major data source.

1-3 Harley, John Brian. "Conference Report: Mapping the Great Lakes." JOURNAL OF HISTORICAL GEOGRAPHY 4 (April 1978): 228-30.

This report is primarily a review of the conference on "Mapping the Great Lakes Region: Motive and Method," the fifth Kenneth Nebenzahl, Jr., Lectures in the History of Cartography, which were held at the Newberry Library, Chicago, August 11-13, 1977. However, Harley strongly criticizes historical geographers for their negligible participation in this and similar conferences on the history of cartography, as well as their general lack of appreciation of the historical map as a major research tool.

1-4 _____. MAPS FOR THE LOCAL HISTORIAN: A GUIDE TO THE BRIT-ISH SOURCES. London: National Council of Social Service for the Standing Conference for Local History, 1972. 94 p. Paper. Maps, notes, bibliog.

Although Harley's emphasis is on British local history, the types of maps (town plans and maps, estate maps, enclosure and tithe maps, road and canal maps, marine charts, and county maps) that he enumerates provide useful parallels for the student of American historical geography. In the chapters, each of which pertains to one type of map, he provides information about the published bibliographies and lists of maps and plans, followed with an account of the secondary literature that contains important background information.

1-5 May, Betty. "Maps as Sources of Historical Evidence." Association of Canadian Map Libraries. PROCEEDINGS OF FOURTH ANNUAL CONFERENCE, 1970, pp. 67-70. Notes.

Besides discussing reasons why maps are not used more extensively by historical researchers, May also describes three areas of historical research where maps are currently used.

1-6 "Papers Presented to the Conference on the History of Cartography, London, September 1967." IMAGO MUNDI 22 (1968): 9-84. Maps, notes.

"Early Maps as Historical Evidence" was the theme of this conference which was sponsored by the Royal Geographic Society. Eight papers are abstracted, while the remaining eight are published in full including J. B. Harley, "The Evaluation of Early Maps: Towards a Methodology," and C. Koeman, "Levels of Historical Evidence in Early Maps (with Examples)." Two of the abstracted articles were published as G. DeBoer and A. P. Carr, "Early Maps as Historical Evidence for Coastal Change," GEOGRAPHICAL JOURNAL 135 (March 1969): 17-27.

1-7   Storm, Colton. "Maps as Historical Documents." PUBLISHER'S WEEKLY
        146 (25 November 1944): 2060-65.

> Storm emphasizes the importance of maps as historical docu-
> ments, particularly as evidence of past perceptions or beliefs,
> as a supplement to a narrative description, as confirmation of in-
> formation in books, and in reconstructing past settlement patterns.

B. GUIDES TO LITERATURE ON THE HISTORY
OF AMERICAN CARTOGRAPHY

1-8   AMERICAN CARTOGRAPHER. Washington, D. C.: American Congress on
        Surveying and Mapping, 1974--. Semiannual.

> This periodical, devoted to the advancement of cartography in
> all its aspects, contains occasional articles and book reviews
> on the history of cartography. Articles of interest include:
> "Dissertations and Theses on Cartography, 1960-1977," 5 (Octo-
> ber 1978): 162-71; Fergus J. Wood, "J. G. Kohl and the 'Lost
> Maps' of the American Coast," 3 (October 1976): 107-15; David
> Woodward, "The Study of the History of Cartography: A Suggested
> Framework," 1 (October 1974): 101-15; and Herman R. Friis,
> "Statistical Cartography in the United States Prior to 1870 and the
> Role of Joseph C.G. Kennedy and the U.S. Census Office," 1
> 1 (October 1974); 131-57.

1-9   GEO ABSTRACTS G: REMOTE SENSING, CARTOGRAPHY, AND PHO-
        TOGRAMMETRY. Norwich, Engl.: University of East Anglia, Geo
        Abstracts Ltd., 1974-- . Bimonthly.

> Abstracts of articles and monographs pertaining to the history of
> cartography are included in this section of GEO ABSTRACTS.
> Although the publications that are included are international
> in scope, most of them pertain to British, American, or Cana-
> dian subjects. Prior to 1974, abstracts pertaining to the history
> of cartography were included in GEO ABSTRACTS D: SOCIAL
> GEOGRAPHY AND CARTOGRAPHY (entry 11-16).

1-10   IMAGO MUNDI. Vols. 1-26, 1935-72. Amsterdam, Holland: Nico
        Israel, 1975-- , Vol. 27-- . Lympne Castle, Kent: Imago Mundi, Ltd.,
        Annual.

> Originally founded by Leo Bagrow as an international journal
> for the study of early maps and the history of cartography up
> to the nineteenth century, the publication was taken over by
> the International Society for the History of Cartography in 1974.
> In addition to articles, it contains news notes (personal, con-
> ferences, institutions, exhibits, and acquisitions, reviews, and
> bibliographies pertaining to the history of cartography. Articles
> pertaining to the history of North American cartography that
> have been published during the last fifteen years include:

William P. Cumming, "The Montresor-Ratzer-Sauthier Sequence of Maps of New York City, 1766-76," 31 (1979): 55-65; Louis De Vorsey, "Amerindian Contributions to the Mapping of North America: A Preliminary View;," 30 (1978): 71-78; De Vorsey, "Pioneer Charting of the Gulf Stream: The Contributions of Benjamin Franklin and William Gerard DeBrahm," 28 (1976): 105-20; Coolie Verner, "Surveying and Mapping the New Federal City: The First Printed Maps of Washington, D.C.," 23 (1969): 59-72; and Verner, "The Fry and Jefferson Map," 21 (1967): 70-94. Other articles are listed in entries 2-3, 2-12, 2-13, and 2-31.

1-11 Library of Congress. Geography and Map Division. THE BIBLIOGRAPHY OF CARTOGRAPHY. 5 vols. Boston: G. K. Hall, 1973. v, 3,395 p.

The Geography and Map Division's card file, representing a bibliography of cartography of over ninety thousand entries, is reproduced in these five volumes. Although the file was begun in the late nineteenth century by Philip Lee Phillips, it has been updated to 1971 by subsequent Library of Congress staff. It includes references to cartobibliographies, mapmakers, biographies, cartographic techniques, analysis of distinctive cartographic works, and generalized and specialized books on the history of cartography. The entries, which primarily represent journal articles and monographs, are arranged alphabetically by author and subject. The two-volume FIRST SUPPLEMENT (1980) reproduces over twenty thousand cards that have been added to the card file since 1971.

1-12 THE MAP COLLECTOR. Edited by Ronald Vere Tooley. London: Map Collector Publications, Ltd., December 1977-- . Quarterly.

This publication not only contains news notes and advertisements which are primarily of interest to private map collectors, it also includes semischolarly articles on the history of cartography. Articles pertaining to North America include Conrad E. Heidenreich and Edward H. Dahl, "The French Mapping of North America in the Seventeenth Century," no. 13 (December 1980), pp. 2-11; Richard W. Stephenson, "The Millard Fillmore Map Collection," no. 12 (September 1980), pp. 10-17; and Peter J. Guthorn, "Eighteenth Century Shore and Harbor Charts Printed in America," no. 12 (September 1980), pp. 25-32. Other articles are listed in entries 2-8, 2-12, 2-16, and 9-14.

1-13 MAP COLLECTORS SERIES. Edited by Ronald V. Tooley. Vols. 1-11. London: Map Collectors' Circle, 1963-74. Ten issues per volume.

Designed for map collectors, librarians, and booksellers, most issues are cartobibliographies of maps or atlases pertaining to a particular geographic area, time period, subject, or cartographer. Even though the series is international in scope, a number of issues pertain to North American cartography: R.V. Tooley, "California as an Island," no. 8; Coolie Verner, "Maps of the Yorktown Campaign, 1780-81", no. 18; Tooley, "North American City Plans: A Selection," no. 20; Tony Campbell, "New Light on the Jansson-Visscher Maps of New England," no. 24; Tooley, "French Mapping of the Americas . . . ," no. 33; R. A. Skelton and Tooley, "The Marine Surveys of James Cook in North America, 1758-1768," no. 37; Verner, "Smith's VIRGINIA and Its Derivatives," no. 45; and Tooley, "Printed Maps of America," nos. 68, 69, 80, and 96. These articles have been reprinted in Tooley, ed., THE MAPPING OF AMERICA (London: Holland Press, 1980).

1-14 PROLOGUE: THE JOURNAL OF THE NATIONAL ARCHIVES. Vols. 1-4. 1969-72. Three issues per year. Vol. 5-- . Washington, D.C.: National Archives and Records Service, 1973-- . Quarterly.

This journal, designed as a means of communication between archivists and the academic community, is devoted mainly to articles that are based on records in the National Archives and notices of new accessions and policy changes within the National Archives. Several articles pertaining to historical maps have been included: Herman R. Friis, "The David Dale Owen Map of Southwestern Wisconsin," 1 (Spring 1969): 8-28; Ralph E. Ehrenberg, "Sketch of Parts of the Missouri and Yellowstone Rivers with a Description of the Country, etc.," 3 (Fall 1971): 73-78; and Diane M. T. Rose, "The Maps, Plans, and Sketches of Herman Ehrenberg," 9 (Fall 1977): 162-70. Other articles are listed in entries 1-34, 2-12, and 2-30.

1-15 QUARTERLY JOURNAL OF THE LIBRARY OF CONGRESS. Washington, D. C.: Library of Congress, 1943-- . Quarterly.

Since the collections, programs, and services of the Library of Congress serve as the primary focus of this publication, there are occasional articles pertaining to the holdings of the Geography and Map Division. Selected articles published before 1972 were reprinted in Ristow, A LA CARTE (see entry 1-16). Articles published since 1972 include: John A. Wolter, "The Heights of Mountains and the Lengths of Rivers," 29 (July 1972): 186-205; Richard W. Stephenson, "Maps from the Peter Force Collection," 30 (July 1973): 183-204; J. L. Sibley Jennings, Jr., "Artistry as Design: L'Enfant's Extraordinary City," 36 (Summer 1979): 225-78; and Walter W. Ristow, "Aborted American Atlases ," 36 (Summer 1979): 320-45. Other articles are cited in entries 2-12, 2-23, 3-23, 4-9, 4-17, 4-26, and 9-14.

1-16 Ristow, Walter W., comp. A LA CARTE: SELECTED PAPERS ON MAPS
AND ATLASES. Washington, D. C.: Library of Congress, 1972. x,
232 p. Maps, illus., notes, index.

Twenty articles, most of which were originally published in the
QUARTERLY JOURNAL OF THE LIBRARY OF CONGRESS,
discuss maps, atlases, and cartographers represented in the
Library of Congress holdings. All the articles were written by
former or current Library of Congress employees including Lawrence Martin, Clara Egli LeGear, Walter W. Ristow, and
Richard W. Stephenson. The essays are grouped into two sections: sixteenth- and seventeenth-century world maps and atlases
and seventeenth- through nineteenth-century American maps.
The latter section includes articles on maps of Virginia and
Maryland by John Smith, Augustine Herrman, and John Bal-
lendine; John Mitchell's map of North America and John
Melish's map of the United States; maps of the Federal City;
and the Hotchkiss Collection of Confederate maps.

1-17 _____. GUIDE TO THE HISTORY OF CARTOGRAPHY: AN ANNOTATED
LIST OF REFERENCES ON THE HISTORY OF MAPS AND MAPMAKING.
Washington, D. C.: Library of Congress, 1973. v, 96 p. Paper. Index.

Annotated bibliographical entries are listed for approximately
four hundred general reference works, monographs, and cartobibliographies relating to the history and evolution of maps
and mapmaking. Although the coverage is worldwide, there
are numerous entries pertaining to the cartographical history
of the United States and individual states during the nineteenth
and twentieth centuries. The entries are arranged alphabetically by author; however, an index provides access by subject
and geographic area. See also Ristow, "Historical Cartography
in the United States, 1959-1963," IMAGO MUNDI 17 (1963):
106-14.

1-18 Skelton, Raleigh Ashlin. MAPS: A HISTORICAL SURVEY OF THEIR
STUDY AND COLLECTING. Chicago: University of Chicago Press for
the Hermon Dunlap Smith Center for the History of Cartography at the Newberry Library, 1972. xv, 138 p. Maps, notes, index.

Four essays presented by Skelton in 1966 for the first Kenneth
Nebenzahl, Jr., Lectures in the History of Cartography at the
Newberry Library are reprinted in this volume. These essays,
which outline a conceptual framework for the history of cartog-
raphy as a discipline, are entitled: "History of Cartography:
An Introductory Survey," "The Preservation and Collecting of
Early Maps," "The Historical Study of Early Maps: Past," and
"The Historical Study of Early Maps: Present and Future." The
volume also includes a bibliography of works on the history of
cartography, published by Skelton, Superintendent of the Map
Room, British Museum.

1-19 Special Libraries Association Geography and Map Division. BULLETIN. New York: Special Libraries Association, November 1947-- . Semiannual until October 1953; thereafter quarterly.

> As the major publication of American map librarians, this bulletin includes not only a wide range of articles on the administration of map libraries, but also news of the organization and institutions; lists of new books, atlases, maps, and government publications; and reviews of atlases and related geographic literature. Issue no. 100 (June 1975) provides a list of key papers published between 1948 and 1975. Most of the articles pertaining to the history of American cartography or historical cartobibliographies are listed separately in this bibliography. Other articles of interest include: Charles A. Seavey, "Exploration and Mapping of the Grand Canyon, 1859-1903," no. 119 (March 1980), pp. 4-15; Robert C. Hansen, "The Cartographic Contributions of Matthew Fontaine Maury," no. 119, (March 1980), pp. 25-32; Andrew M. Modelski, "Introductory Essays and Commentaries for the Study of the History of Cartography from Selected Facsimile Atlases in the Library of Congress," No. 116 (June 1979), pp. 43-51; William W. Easton, "A History of Military Mapping; Its Evolution and Use," no. 109, (September 1977), pp. 40-46; Stanley D. Stevens, "Lighthouse Point: Discovery of Historical Land Use Through Maps, Photos, and Text," no. 92 (June 1973), pp. 2-11; and Jeremiah B. Post, "The Cartographic Resources of the Free Library of Philadelphia," no. 92 (June 1973), pp. 29-34.

1-20 SURVEYING AND MAPPING. Washington, D.C.: American Congress on Surveying and Mapping, 1941-- . Quarterly.

> Although most of the historical articles in this periodical pertain to surveying, several articles discuss eighteenth- and nineteenth-century maps and mapmakers: Donald A. Wise, "Surveying and Mapping the International Border in Northeast Maine: 1817-18," 40 (December 1980): 419-27; Silvio Bedini, "Andrew Ellicott, Surveyor of the Wilderness," 36 (June 1976): 113-35; John E. Walker, "The Pintado Papers," 35 (June 1975): 160-71; John A. Wolter, "The Heights of Mountains and the Lengths of Rivers," 32 (September 1972): 313-30; George E. Sites, Jr., "The Bradford Map of Nogales, Arizona," 31 (September 1971): 445-51; Arthur H. Frazier, "Whistler's Father--Topographer Extraordinary," 30 (June 1970): 289-91; and Walter W. Ristow, "Simeon De Witt, Pioneer American Cartographer," 30 (June 1970): 239-55. Other articles are listed in entries 2-25, 4-9, and 9-17.

1-21 TERRAE INCOGNITAE: THE ANNALS OF THE SOCIETY FOR THE HISTORY OF DISCOVERIES. Vols. 1-10. Amsterdam: Nico Israel, 1969-78. Vol. 11-- . Detroit: Wayne State University Press, 1979-- . Annual.

> This journal is devoted mainly to the history of geographic dis-

coveries, but it does include several articles and book reviews pertaining to the history of American cartography. Two articles of interest are Richard W. Stephenson, "The Mapping of the Northwest Boundary of Texas, 1859-1860," 6 (1974): 39-50; and John R. Hebert, "Mapping the Road to Santa Fe, 1825-1827," 7 (1976): 39-51.

1-22 Thrower, Norman J.W. MAPS AND MAN: AN EXAMINATION OF CARTOGRAPHY IN RELATIONSHIP TO CULTURE AND CIVILIZATION. Englewood Cliffs, N.J.: Prentice-Hall, 1972. vii, 184 p. Maps, notes, index.

As an overview of the development of cartography on a worldwide basis, this monograph provides the broader context in which the development of United States cartography in the nineteenth and twentieth centuries can be considered. Since this book is not intended to be a treatise on mapmaking but on map appreciation, it stresses the relationship of cartography to cultural and scientific history.

1-23 Wallis, Helen, and Zoegner, Lothar, eds. THE MAP LIBRARIAN IN THE MODERN WORLD: ESSAYS IN HONOUR OF WALTER W. RISTOW. Muenchen, Federal Republic of Germany: K.G. Saur, 1979. 295 p. Paper. Photos, diagrs., tables, notes, index.

Ristow, former chief of the Geography and Map Division, Library of Congress and a scholar in the field of map librarianship and the history of American cartography, is honored in this festschrift. Although most of the articles emphasize map librarianship, several articles describe the map collections of the American Geographical Society, the Hermon Dunlap Smith Center for the History of Cartography, the Geography and Map Division of the Library of Congress, and Departement des cartes et plans de la Bibliotheque nationale. Lists of Ristow's publications and the official publications of the Geography and Map Division are also included.

1-24 Western Association of Map Libraries. INFORMATION BULLETIN. Santa Cruz: University of California, 1969--. Three issues per year.

The administration of map libraries is the primary focus of the articles, book reviews, and association news notes in this publication. Articles pertaining to historical map collections, history of western cartography, and cartobibliographies of western maps include Philip Hoehn, "Major Cartobibliographies of the West," 2 (May 1971): 8-13; Stanley D. Stevens, "Maps in the Local History Collection," 3 (June 1973): 17-28; Richard W. Engerman, "The Map Collection of the Oregon Historical Society Library," 4 (June 1973): 40-41; David W. Schacht, "Historical Atlas and Map Collection of Oregon, Kerr Library, Oregon State University," 7 (June 1976): 13-21; Carey S. Bliss,

"Printed Maps at the Huntington Library," 7 (June 1976): 22-27; Alvin R. McLane, "Cartography of Early Nevada, 1820-1900," 10 (March 1979): 142-46; and Earl W. Kersten, "The Obsolete Topographic Maps as a Research Document," 10 (March 1979): 147-49.

1-25 Wolter, John A. "Source Materials for the History of American Cartography." Special Libraries Association Geography and Map Division. BULLE-TIN, no. 88 (June 1972), pp. 2-16. Notes.

Wolter's bibliographical essay reviews a selection of publications that deal with the history of American cartography. They are grouped in six categories: general monographs on the history of cartography, regional cartobibliographies, general carto-bibliographies and indexes, serials and publications, globes, and facsimile maps and atlases. Later versions of this essay appeared in AMERICAN STUDIES 12, no. 3 (1974): 12-27, and AMERICAN STUDIES, TOPICS AND SOURCES (Westport, Conn.: Greenwood Press, 1976), pp. 81-95.

C. GUIDES TO MAP REPOSITORIES

1-26 American Geographical Society. Map Department. INDEX TO MAPS IN BOOKS AND PERIODICALS. 10 vols. Boston: G.K. Hall, 1968. vi, 7,829 p.

The approximately 164,000 entries are arranged alphabetically by subject and geographical-political divisions. The volumes include many maps of historical interest. Additions to the index covering the period 1968 to 1971 were published in the FIRST SUPPLEMENT (1971), while additions for the period 1972 to 1975 were published in the SECOND SUPPLEMENT (1976).

1-27 California, University of. Berkeley. Bancroft Library. INDEX TO PRINTED MAPS. Boston: G.K. Hall, 1964. 521 p.

Author and area-subject entries describing the Bancroft Library's map collection are reproduced in this one-volume catalog. The emphasis of the collection is the western half of North America prior to 1900. Acquisitions since 1964 are listed in CATALOG OF MANUSCRIPT AND PRINTED MAPS IN THE BANCROFT LIBRARY (A SUPPLEMENT TO INDEX TO PRINTED MAPS), (Boston: G.K. Hall, 1975). The library's cartographic hold-ings are also described in R. Philip Hoehn, "The Bancroft Li-brary Map Collection," Western Association of Map Libraries. INFORMATION BULLETIN 8 (November 1976): 37-43.

1-28 Carrington, David K., and Stephenson, Richard W., comps. MAP COL-
LECTIONS IN THE UNITED STATES AND CANADA: A DIRECTORY.
3d ed., rev. and exp. New York: Special Libraries Association, 1978.
ix, 230 p. Paper. Index.

> This directory provides information about map collections in 743
> repositories in the United States and Canada. The entries, which
> are arranged alphabetically by state and city, usually include
> data on staff, size of collections, annual accessions, area and
> subject specialization, special collections, date coverage,
> classification systems, percentage of collections cataloged,
> service hours, reproduction facilities, and publications.

1-29 Great Britain. Public Record Office. MAPS AND PLANS IN THE PUB-
LIC RECORD OFFICE. Vol. 2: AMERICA AND WEST INDIES. Ed. by
P.A. Penfold. London: Her Majesty's Stationery Office, 1974. xv,
835 p. Index.

> Although this is not a comprehensive list, approximately forty-five
> hundred entries describe the great majority of maps of the West-
> ern Hemisphere that have been noted among the records of the
> Public Record Office. Over half of these entries pertain to
> Canada and the United States while the remainder document
> coverage of the West Indies and Bermuda, Mexico and Central
> America, and South America. The entries are arranged alpha-
> betically by province, state, island, or country within these
> sections and thereunder chronologically. A selection of these
> maps is reproduced in the microfilm publication, MANUSCRIPT
> MAPS RELATING TO NORTH AMERICA AND THE WEST IN-
> DIES, PART 1, THE REVOLUTIONARY ERA (Wakefield, Engl.:
> E.P. Microfilm Ltd., 1980); the introduction was prepared by
> John Brian Harley and Minda C. Phillips.

1-30 LeGear, Clara Egli, comp. A LIST OF GEOGRAPHICAL ATLASES IN THE
LIBRARY OF CONGRESS. 4 vols. Washington, D.C.: Library of Congress,
1958-74.

> LeGear's four volumes are a continuation of Philip Lee Phillips'
> LIST OF GEOGRAPHICAL ATLASES . . ., 4 vols. (1909-20,
> reprint, Amsterdam: Theatrum Orbis Terrarum, Ltd., 1971).
> While volumes 5 and 6 pertain to world and foreign atlases, vol-
> ume 7 describes atlases of the Western Hemisphere which were
> accessioned by the Library of Congress between 1920 and 1969,
> but none of which were published after 1967. Although this
> work repeats the 1920-50 titles found in LeGear's 1950 bibliog-
> raphy (see entry 1-31), it does provide broader coverage since
> it includes Canadian atlases and the Sanborn Map Company fire
> insurance atlases. Volume 8 is an index to volume 7.

1-31 _____ . UNITED STATES ATLASES: A LIST OF NATIONAL, STATE, COUNTY, CITY, AND REGIONAL ATLASES IN THE LIBRARY OF CONGRESS. Washington, D.C.: Library of Congress, 1950. Reprint. New York: Arno Press, 1971. viii, 445 p. Index.

> National, state, county, and city atlases of the United States which were accessioned by the Library of Congress before 1950 are described here in over 3,500 bibliographical entries. The national atlases are arranged by subject including a historical category which lists eighty-one retrospective atlases. Many of the county atlases and plat books show land ownership, while the city atlases include real estate atlases published by such firms as George W. Baist and Griffith M. Hopkins but not the Sanborn Map Company insurance atlases. This listing does include the pre-1920 atlases which were registered in Philip Lee Phillips's LIST OF GEOGRAPHICAL ATLASES IN THE LIBRARY OF CONGRESS, 4 vols. (1909-20). See entry 1-30.

1-32 Library of Congress. Geography and Map Division. THE GEOGRAPHY AND MAP DIVISION: A GUIDE TO ITS COLLECTIONS AND SERVICES. Rev. ed. Washington, D.C.: 1975. vi, 42 p. Paper. Maps, illus.

> Besides providing a general description of the organization, services, and holdings of the Geography and Map Division, the following special collections or categorizations of maps are reviewed: discovery and exploration, colonial America and revolutionary war, post-revolutionary war, pre-Civil War, Civil War, post-Civil War, United States official maps and charts, foreign surveys, Oriental map collection, atlases, and globes.

1-33 Michigan, University of. William L. Clements Library. RESEARCH CATALOG OF MAPS OF AMERICA TO 1860 IN THE WILLIAM L. CLEMENTS LIBRARY. Edited by Douglas W. Marshall. 4 vols. Boston: G.K. Hall, 1972. xi, 2,086 p.

> The card catalog pertaining to approximately ten thousand pre-1860 printed and manuscript maps of America in the Division of Maps in the William L. Clements Library is reproduced in these four volumes. The maps included in this listing will be of interest to historical researchers in the fields of cartography, discovery and exploration, the American colonies, the revolutionary war, the War of 1812, and the opening of the West. The first two volumes provide an alphabetical arrangement of the cards by author (cartographer, publisher, engraver, or seller) and title, while the last two volumes are arranged by geographic area and subject (canals, forts, Indians, and railroads). Volume 4 also includes a separate listing of atlases. This catalog supercedes two earlier publications which served as guides to smaller portions of the collections: Randolph G. Adams, BRITISH HEADQUARTERS MAPS AND SKETCHES USED BY SIR HENRY CLIN-

TON (1928) and Christian Brun, GUIDE TO THE MANUSCRIPT MAPS IN THE WILLIAM L. CLEMENTS LIBRARY (1959).

1-34 National Archives and Records Service. GUIDE TO CARTOGRAPHIC RECORDS IN THE NATIONAL ARCHIVES. Washington, D.C.: 1971. xi, 444 p. Index.

Approximately 1.5 million maps and over 2 million aerial photographic images which represent the holdings of the National Archives' Cartographic Branch (currently Center for Cartographic and Architectural Archives) as of 1966 are briefly described in this comprehensive guide. Because these cartographic items were derived from the records of 134 federal agencies, the entries are arranged administratively. Although these records date from the eighteenth century, they pertain primarily to nineteenth- and twentieth-century United States. A brief overview of these cartographic records is found in A. Philip Muntz, "Federal Cartographic Archives: A Profile," PROLOGUE 1 (Spring 1969): 3-7.

1-35 New York (City). Public Library. Map Division. DICTIONARY CATALOG OF THE MAP DIVISION. 10 vols. Boston: G.K. Hall, 1971. iii, 8,898 p.

Over 165,000 cards are reproduced listing maps and other cartographic publications in the New York Public Library. Included are entries for printed government maps (Navy Hydrographic Office, Coast and Geodetic Survey, Army Topographic Command), manuscript maps from the Manuscript Division, early printed maps from the Rare Book Division, six thousand atlases, and eleven thousand volumes pertaining to the history and techniques of mapmaking. Additions to the catalog are included in BIBLIOGRAPHIC GUIDE TO MAPS AND ATLASES: 1979 (Boston (Boston: G.K. Hall, 1980).

1-36 Noe, Barbara R., comp. FACSIMILES OF MAPS AND ATLASES: A LIST OF REPRODUCTIONS FOR SALE BY VARIOUS PUBLISHERS AND DISTRIBUTORS. 4th ed. Washington, D.C.: Library of Congress, Geography and Map Division, 1980. iv, 35 p. Paper. Index.

Approximately five hundred facsimile maps and atlases that were available from 145 distributors as of November 1978 are listed in this booklet. The previous edition, which was compiled by Walter W. Ristow in 1968, was entitled FACSIMILES OF RARE HISTORICAL MAPS. Ristow also prepared a review on the same topic, "Recent Facsimile Maps and Atlases," QUARTERLY JOURNAL OF THE LIBRARY OF CONGRESS 24 (July 1967): 213-29.

1-37 Perry, Alan. "Geographers, Cartographers, and Regional Federal Archives."
Special Libraries Association Geography and Map Division. BULLETIN,
no. 115 (March 1979), pp. 2-6.

> The eleven Federal Archives and Records Centers of the Na-
> tional Archives and Records Service are introduced as a re-
> gional source for historical cartographic records.

1-38 "Resources in France for the American Historian." QUARTERLY JOURNAL
OF THE LIBRARY OF CONGRESS 30 (October 1973): 244-67. Maps,
notes.

> Four short articles describe the map holdings of four French
> repositories (Archives nationale, Bibliotheque nationale, Bibli-
> otheque de l' Inspection du Genie, and Library of the ministere
> d'Etat charge de la Defense nationale) which pertain primarily
> to the American War of Independence.

1-39 Ristow, Walter W., ed. WORLD DIRECTORY OF MAP COLLECTIONS.
International Federation of Library Associations Publications, 8. Muenchen,
Germany: Verlag Dokumentation, Publishers, 1976. 326 p.

> Compiled by the Geography and Map Literature Subsection of
> the International Federation of Library Associations, this direc-
> tory lists 285 major map collections in forty-five countries.
> Forty percent of the entries describe selected collections in
> Canada, Federal Republic of Germany, United Kingdom, and
> the United States. Each entry includes a summary statement
> about the institution's holdings, as well as selected references
> to published guides and finding aids.

1-40 Stanley, William A. "A Cartographic Treasure: National Ocean Survey's
Map Collection." Special Library Association Geography and Map Division. BULLETIN, no. 91 (March 1973), pp. 11-17.

> The historical cartographic holdings of the National Ocean Sur-
> vey (formerly Coast and Geodetic Survey) are reviewed. This
> collection of approximately twenty-four thousand items includes
> not only a complete set of the Coast and Geodetic Survey's pub-
> lished charts, but also privately published nautical charts and
> atlases from the eighteenth and nineteenth centuries, Civil War
> maps, and Washington, D.C., maps.

1-41 Warren, Katherine F. "Introduction to the Map Resources of the British
Museum." PROFESSIONAL GEOGRAPHER 17 (November 1965): 1-9.
Notes.

> In introducing the cartographic resources of the British Museum,
> Warren describes the holdings of the Map Room, the principal
> map catalogs, and the maps and topographical materials in the

major manuscript collections. Since the primary coverage of the holdings is the British Empire, there are some maps pertaining to the exploration and colonization of North America. Two published catalogs, which include entries for North America, United States, or individual colonies and states are British Museum, Department of Printed Books, Map Room, CATALOG OF PRINTED MAPS, CHARTS, AND PLANS: PHOTOLITHOGRAPHIC EDITION COMPLETE TO 1964, 15 vols. (London: British Museum, 1967); and British Museum, Department of Manuscripts, CATALOG OF THE MANUSCRIPT MAPS, CHARTS, AND PLANS AND OF THE TOPOGRAPHICAL DRAWINGS IN THE BRITISH MUSEUM, 3 vols. (London: British Museum, 1844-61, reprinted 1962). The history of the map collections is described by Helen Wallis, "The Map Collections of the British Museum Library," in Helen Wallis and Sarah Tyacke, eds., MY HEAD IS A MAP: ESSAYS AND MEMOIRS IN HONOUR OF R.V. TOOLEY (London: Frances Edwards and Carta Press, 1973), pp. 3-20.

Chapter 2
TEMPORAL LISTINGS

Cartobibliographies, collections of facsimile reproductions, and analytical books and articles that pertain to a specific time period, event, or topic are listed in this chapter which is divided into three sections: comprehensive histories of American mapping; pre-1800 maps (concentrating on the revolutionary war); and post-1800 maps (highlighting the mapping of Civil War and the mapping activities of the federal government).

A. GENERAL HISTORIES

2-1 Kish, George. THE DISCOVERY AND SETTLEMENT OF NORTH AMERICA, 1500-1865: A CARTOGRAPHIC PERSPECTIVE. New York: Harper and Row, 1979. 61 p. Paper. 203 slides.

> A collection of slide reproductions of approximately two hundred maps from numerous libraries, including the Clements Library, Library of Congress, National Archives, and Public Record Office, illustrate the exploration and settlement of North America. Brief descriptions of each slide discuss the cartographic background and content of the maps.

2-2 Schwartz, Seymour I., and Ehrenberg, Ralph E. THE MAPPING OF AMERICA. New York: Harry N. Abrams, Inc., 1980. 363 p. Maps, illus., bibliog., index.

> Written for the general reader, the text, along with 223 map reproductions, documents the history of American cartography. Schwartz wrote the first seven chapters which cover the period 1500-1800, while Ehrenberg contributed the last three chapters which trace the cartographic developments after 1800.

B. PRE-1800

2-3 Black, Jeannette D., ed. THE BLATHWAYT ATLAS. Vol. 1: THE MAPS. Vol. 2: COMMENTARY. Providence, R.I.: Brown University Press, 1970, 1975. Vol. 1, boxed, 48 maps; Vol. 2, xx, 235 p. Notes, index.

This facsimile atlas reproduces forty-eight maps brought together
in 1683 for the use of the Office of Lords of Trade and Plantations by the office's secretary William Blathwayt. This collection of thirty-five engraved maps and thirteen manuscript maps,
which is now in the John Carter Brown Library, represents the
first atlas that depicts the various British colonies in North
America and the West Indies. Black's commentary describes
each map putting it in its historical context and discussing its
relationship to the Office of Lords of Trade and Plantations.
Black also discusses this facsimile project in "The Blathwayt
Atlas: Maps Used by British Colonial Administrators in the
Time of Charles II," IMAGO MUNDI 22 (1968): 20-29.

2-4   Cappon, Lester J. "Geographers and Mapmakers, British and American,
       from about 1750 to 1789." PROCEEDINGS OF THE AMERICAN ANTI-
       QUARIAN SOCIETY 81 (October 1971): 243-71. Notes.

       In describing the state of the geographic science in Britain and
       North America during the last half of the eighteenth century,
       Cappon concentrates on topographers (miscellaneous writers of
       an uncritical nature) and mapmakers.

2-5   Capps, Marie T., and Stroup, Theodore G. UNITED STATES MILITARY
       ACADEMY LIBRARY MAP COLLECTION: THE PERIOD OF THE AMERICAN
       REVOLUTION, 1753-1800. West Point, N.Y.: United States Military
       Academy, 1971. viii, 82 p. Paper. Maps, bibliog., index.

       West Point's map holdings which pertain to the American revo-
       lutionary war period, 1753-1800, are described in 185 entries.
       The entries which are grouped by seven geographical regions
       (North America, Canada, New England, Middle Atlantic, West
       Point and vicinity, South Atlantic, and west of the Appalachians),
       include maps from four atlases, engraved maps, and photorepro-
       ductions of maps from other collections.

2-6   Clark, David Sanders. INDEX TO MAPS OF THE AMERICAN REVOLU-
       TION IN BOOKS AND PERIODICALS. Westport, Conn.: Greenwood
       Press, 1974. xiv, 301 p. Index, bibliog.

       Maps in books and periodicials that illustrate the American
       revolutionary period, 1763-89, are indexed in over fifty-seven
       hundred entries. While most of the maps depict military opera-
       tions, references to maps showing social, economic, and polit-
       ical conditions are also included. The entries are arranged by
       region and colony and thereunder chronologically. A subject
       and name index is provided as well as full bibliographical entries
       from which these maps were selected.

2-7   _____. INDEX TO MAPS OF THE FRENCH AND INDIAN WAR IN BOOKS
       AND PERIODICALS. Fayetteville, N.C.: By the Author, 1974. x, 118 p.
       Paper. Index, bibliog.

Similar in format to the previous work, this index lists maps which illustrate the background of the French and Indian War, British and French military operations in North America, the Cherokee War, the Havana Campaign, and postwar boundaries. There are 785 references to reproductions of maps compiled during or shortly after the war and maps reconstructed since the war.

2-8   Colles, Christopher. A SURVEY OF THE ROADS OF THE UNITED STATES OF AMERICA, 1789. Ed. by Walter W. Ristow. Cambridge, Mass.: Harvard University Press, 1961. xii, 227 p. Maps, illus., notes, bibliog., index.

In addition to a facsimile reproduction of Colles's 1789 SURVEY OF THE ROADS . . ., Ristow includes a biography of Colles, emphasizing his engineering and cartographic activities. Colles's survey of the roads from New York to Virginia was one of the earliest American road guides. Ristow also discusses the brief career of Colles's daughter in "Eliza Colles, America's First Female Map Engraver," MAP COLLECTOR, no. 10 (March 1980), pp. 14-17.

2-9   Cumming, William P. BRITISH MAPS OF COLONIAL AMERICA. Chicago: University of Chicago Press, 1974. xii, 114 p. Maps, notes, bibliog., index.

Cumming surveys British cartography of colonial North America in four essays which deal with the mapping of southern and northern colonies, charting the coasts, and mapping related to the French and Indian and revolutionary wars. These essays, which were originally presented as the second series of the Kenneth Nebenzahl, Jr., Lectures in the History of Cartography at the Newberry Library in April 1970, examine the mapmakers, their methods, the historical background giving rise to the production of the maps, and the maps themselves. Two appendixes and a bibliographical essay list maps, cartobibliographies, and repositories relevant to the study of the mapping of colonial America.

2-10   Fite, Emerson D., and Freeman, Archibald. A BOOK OF OLD MAPS DELINEATING AMERICAN HISTORY FROM THE EARLIEST DAYS TO THE CLOSE OF THE REVOLUTIONARY WAR. Cambridge, Mass.: Harvard University Press, 1926. Reprint. New York: Arno Press, 1969; New York: Dover Publications, 1969. xv, 299 p. Maps, notes, index.

The original 1926 edition of this atlas contains seventy-four black and white facsimile reproductions of maps of regions, colonies, and cities within North America as well as early world maps which include North America. These maps date from 1474 to 1825 with seventeen dated in the 1770s. Each map is accompanied by several pages of text which describe the contents and historical background of the map. The Arno Press reprint also includes a reproduction and discussion of the Vinland map (see entry 2-24).

2-11 Greenwood, W. Bart, comp. THE AMERICAN REVOLUTION, 1775-1783: AN ATLAS OF 18TH CENTURY MAPS AND CHARTS. Intro. by Louis De Vorsey, Jr. Washington, D.C.: Department of the Navy, Naval History Division, 1972. Folio, 20 maps. Book, vii, 85 p. Paper. Index, bibliog.

Prepared as a complement to the Naval History Division's multi-volume series NAVAL DOCUMENTS OF THE AMERICAN REVOLUTION, this portfolio reproduces twenty late eighteenth-century maps and charts that are particularly useful for illustrating the British and American naval operations during the revolutionary war. The accompanying booklet includes an index to the geographic names found on the maps as well as an introductory essay by Louis De Vorsey, Jr., entitled "A Background to Surveying and Mapping at the Time of the American Revolution; An Essay on the State of the Art." Greenwood describes the atlas and its sources in "The United States Navy's Atlas of the American Revolution," Special Libraries Association Geography and Map Division, BULLETIN, no. 91 (March 1973), pp. 18-24.

2-12 Guthorn, Peter J. AMERICAN MAPS AND MAP MAKERS OF THE REVO-LUTION. Monmouth Beach, N.J.: Philip Freneau Press, 1966. 48 p. Maps, index. BRITISH MAPS OF THE AMERICAN REVOLUTION. Monmouth Beach, N.J.: Philip Freneau Press, 1972. 79 p. Maps, index.

Using the same format, these two volumes list maps created during or shortly after the American Revolution. The map listings are arranged by mapmaker and accompanied by brief biographies of those individuals. The first volume covers maps compiled primarily by Americans, although a few French officers in the American Army are also included. The latter work concentrates on manuscript maps produced by British officers although some published maps are included. Guthorn identifies six broad categories of maps: military geographical surveys, fortification and encampment drawings, sketch maps, public information news maps, formal documentary battle or campaign maps, and finely finished artistic renderings. Other articles by Guthorn pertaining to mapping during the revolutionary war period include: "Revolutionary War Mapmakers," PROLOGUE 9 (Fall 1977): 171-77; "Kosciuszko as Military Cartographer and Engineer in America," IMAGO MUNDI 29 (1977): 49-53; "Military Mapping During the American Revolution," THE MAP COLLECTOR, no. 2 (March 1978), pp. 8-21; and "A Hessian Map from the American Revolution: Its Origin and Purpose," QUARTERLY JOURNAL OF THE LIBRARY OF CONGRESS 33 (Summer 1976): 219-31.

2-13 Harley, John Brian; Petchenik, Barbara Bartz; and Towner, Lawrence W. MAPPING THE AMERICAN REVOLUTIONARY WAR. Chicago: University of Chicago Press, 1978. viii, 187 p. Maps, diagrs., notes, bibliog., index.

> The military cartography associated with the American Revolution is analyzed in five essays that were originally presented as part of the fourth Kenneth Nebenzahl, Jr., Lectures in the History of Cartography at the Newberry Library, November 1974. The first three essays by Harley deal with the contemporary eighteenth-century mapping of the war. After developing a classification scheme for the contemporary maps, Harley discusses the training of the mapmakers and the nature of the map users. The retrospective mapping of the nineteenth and twentieth centuries are reviewed by Towner and Petchenik, respectively. Other articles by Harley dealing with the mapping of the last half of the eighteenth century are "Specifications for Military Surveys in British North America, 1750-75," in INTERNATIONAL GEOGRAPHY, 1972, edited by W. Peter Adams and Frederick M. Helleiner (Toronto: Toronto University Press, 1972), 1: 424-25; "George Washington Map Maker," GEOGRAPHICAL MAGAZINE 48 (July 1976): 588-94; and "The Bankruptcy of Thomas Jeffreys: An Episode in the Economic History of Eighteenth Century Map Making." IMAGO MUNDI 20 (1966): 27-48.

2-14 Jeffreys, Thomas. THE AMERICAN ATLAS. 1776. Facsimile ed. Intro. by Walter W. Ristow. Amsterdam: Theatrum Orbis Terraum, 1974. xv, 30 map plates.

> Jeffreys's 1776 atlas, which is a collection of twenty-three maps originally published by Jeffreys in the preceding two decades, represents British America prior to the outbreak of the revolutionary war. Ristow's introduction to the bicentennial facsimile edition presents a biographical sketch of Jeffreys and his role in the British mapping of North America in the middle of the eighteenth century, as well as a bibliographical discussion of the atlas.

2-15 Klemp, Egon. AMERICA IN MAPS DATING FROM 1500 to 1856. New York: Holmes and Meier, 1976. 239 p. Maps, notes, index.

> A selection of seventy-six maps of North and South America produced from the time of Columbus's discovery of America to the mid-nineteenth century, ending with the initial exploration and mapping of North America, are reproduced in this volume. Accompanying commentary discusses bibliographical sources and content of each map. Included are seven maps of New France and Canada, nineteen maps of eastern North America and New England, and four maps of the west and northwest coasts of North America.

2-16 Lewis, G. Malcolm. "The Indigenous Maps and Mapping of North American Indians." MAP COLLECTOR, no. 9 (December 1979), pp. 25-32. Maps, notes.

In conjunction with his research on a proposed cartobibliography of Indian and Inuit maps, Lewis prepared this introduction to selected seventeenth-, eighteenth-, and nineteenth-century maps drawn by Indians. See also Lewis, "Towards a Cartobibliography of North American Indian Maps and Mapping," Special Libraries Association Geography and Map Division, BULLETIN, no. 106 (December 1976), pp. 3-10.

2-17 McLaughlin, Patrick D., comp. PRE-FEDERAL MAPS IN THE NATIONAL ARCHIVES: AN ANNOTATED LIST. Special List No. 26. Rev. ed. Washington, D.C.: National Archives and Records Service, 1975. ix, 49 p. Paper. Maps, index.

Maps in the National Archives which were compiled, published, or portray events prior to 1790 are described in this list. These 221 maps, portfolios, and atlases, which were selected from the records of twelve federal government agencies, cover primarily the eastern portion of the United States. McLaughlin also reviewed six publications pertaining to the mapping of the revolutionary war in "American Revolution in Maps," AMERICAN ARCHIVIST 37 (January 1974): 43-49.

2-18 Margary, Harry. NORTH AMERICA AT THE TIME OF THE REVOLUTION: A COLLECTION OF EIGHTEENTH CENTURY MAPS. 3 parts. Lympne Castle, Kent: By the author, 1972-75.

Margary, a noted publisher of facsimile maps, has produced a three-part series of fifteen maps pertaining to North America at the time of the American Revolution. Part 1 is a reproduction of Henry Popple's 1733 map of the British Empire. The map is reproduced on twenty sheets with an introduction by William P. Cumming and Helen Wallis. Part 2 consists of five maps on nineteen sheets (North America, Virginia and Maryland, Hudson River, New Jersey and New York, and New England) with introductory notes by Louis De Vorsey, Jr. Part 3 includes nine maps of the remaining colonies on twenty sheets with introductory notes by William P. Cumming and Douglas W. Marshall.

2-19 Marshall, Douglas W., and Peckham, Howard H. CAMPAIGNS OF THE AMERICAN REVOLUTION: AN ATLAS OF MANUSCRIPT MAPS. Ann Arbor: University of Michigan Press; Maplewood, N.J.: Hammond, 1976. v, 138 p. Maps, notes, index.

This bicentennial atlas, consisting of fifty-eight facsimile map reproductions and accompanying text, portrays the various battles and campaigns of the American Revolution in the context of a large-scale pacification effort, rather than concentrating on a few major battles. The British cartographic effort is emphasized, since fifty of these maps were drawn by British participants, and includes thirty from the Sir Henry Clinton papers at the University of Michigan. The lack of accurate maps available at the time of the battle is evident since thirty-two of these illustrations were commemorative maps drawn after the battle.

2-20   Nebenzahl, Kenneth. A BIBLIOGRAPHY OF PRINTED BATTLE PLANS OF THE AMERICAN REVOLUTION, 1775-1795. Chicago: University of Chicago Press, 1975. xiv, 159 p. Bibliog., index.

Prepared in conjunction with his ATLAS OF THE AMERICAN REVOLUTION (see entry 2-21), this cartobibliography describes over two hundred maps printed between 1775 and 1795 that pertain to the military activities associated with the revolutionary war. Consequently, these detailed entries represent maps prepared and published by eyewitnesses rather than by historians and historical cartographers of the war.

2-21   Nebenzahl, Kenneth, and Higginbotham, Don. ATLAS OF THE AMERICAN REVOLUTION. Chicago: Rand McNally, 1974. 218 p. Maps, illus., index.

The primary emphasis of this bicentennial publication is the fifty-four color reproductions of eighteenth-century engraved maps, which illustrate the major military activities of the American Revolution. While the maps were selected by map collector Kenneth Nebenzahl from various repositories, the accompanying narrative text by historian Don Higginbotham recounts the story of the Revolution.

2-22   Rice, Howard C., Jr., and Brown, Anne S.K., eds. and trans. THE AMERICAN CAMPAIGNS OF ROCHAMBEAU'S ARMY, 1780, 1781, 1782, 1783. Vol. 1: THE JOURNALS OF CLERMONT-CREVECOEUR, VERGER, AND BERTHIER. Vol. 2: ITINERARIES, MAPS AND VIEWS. Princeton, N.J.: Princeton University Press; Providence, R.I.: Brown University Press, 1972. Vol. 1, xxviii, 351 p.; vol. 2, vi, 362 p. Maps, illus., notes, index.

This collection of selected documents presents a comprehensive survey of the campaigns of the French army under Rochambeau during the American Revolution. The first volume contains the journals of Clermont-Crevecoeur, Verger, and Berthier, which were translated from the original French manuscripts held by the Rhode Island Historical Society, Brown University Library, and Princeton University Library. The second volume includes translations from the Berthier papers of the army's itinerary (detailed mile-by-mile descriptions of the route taken between Rhode Island and Williamsburg) as well as 177 maps and views which illustrate the campaigns. These illustrations, some of which are in color, were selected from scattered depositories in the United States and France. Most were drawn during or shortly after the war by French officers.

2-23 Ristow, Walter W. "Maps of the American Revolution: A Preliminary Survey." QUARTERLY JOURNAL OF THE LIBRARY OF CONGRESS 28 (July 1971): 196-215. Maps, notes.

Ristow reviews the mapping activities before, during, and after the revolutionary war, with particular emphasis on those maps which are in the holdings of the Library of Congress. These maps are described in more detail in John R. Sellers and Patricia Molen Van Ee, MAPS AND CHARTS OF NORTH AMERICA AND THE WEST INDIES, 1750-1789: A GUIDE TO THE COLLECTIONS IN THE LIBRARY OF CONGRESS (Washington, D.C.: Library of Congress, 1981).

2-24 Skelton, Raleigh Ashlin; Marston, Thomas E.; and Painter, George D. THE VINLAND MAP AND THE TARTAR RELATION. New Haven: Yale University Press, 1965. xii, 291 p. Maps, notes, bibliog., index.

Yale University's acquisition of the Vinland map is introduced in this publication. The map contained what was thought to be the earliest cartographic representation still extant of the New World, proving that Norsemen had explored North America before its discovery by Columbus. Challenges to the map's authenticity were numerous, some of which are presented in Wilcomb E. Washburn, ed., PROCEEDINGS OF THE VINLAND MAP CONFERENCE (Chicago: University of Chicago Press for the Newberry Library, 1971). In 1974 Yale University announced that chemical analysis of the inks suggested that the map was a forgery.

2-25 Snyder, John P. "The Erskine-DeWitt Maps." SURVEYING AND MAPPING 39 (March 1979): 33-48. Maps, notes.

The subject of this article is the background, content, and coverage of a series of approximately three hundred manuscript road maps prepared by Robert Erskine and Simeon DeWitt for the Continental army. These maps, which were prepared between 1777 and 1781, provide primary documentation of the road network of the Middle Atlantic colonies at the time of the Revolution. Four index maps were prepared to show the coverage of these maps which extend from Yorktown, Virginia, to Connecticut, but with a major emphasis on northern New Jersey and southern New York. Most of these maps are in the custody of the New York Historical Society.

2-26 Thrower, Norman J.W., ed. THE COMPLEAT PLATTMAKER: ESSAYS ON CHART, MAP, AND GLOBE MAKING IN THE SEVENTEENTH AND EIGHTEENTH CENTURIES. Berkeley and Los Angeles: University of California Press, 1978. xvii, 241 p. Maps, illus., notes, index.

Reprinted here are six essays which resulted from various activities of the William Andrews Clark Memorial Library of the University of California, Los Angeles, which is dedicated to the study of British culture in the seventeenth and eighteenth centuries. The essays include: Helen M. Wallis, "Geographie is Better than Divinitie: Maps, Globes, and Geography in the Days of Samuel Pepys"; Thomas R. Smith, "Manuscript and Printed Sea Charts in the Seventeenth Century London: The Case of the Thames School "; Jeannette D. Black, "Mapping the English Colonies in North America: The Beginnings"; Coolie Verner, "John Seller and the Chart Trade in Seventeenth Century England"; David Woodward, "English Cartography, 1650-1750: A Summary"; and Norman J.W. Thrower, "Edmund Halley and Thematic Geocartography." Although these essays emphasize the development of cartography in England in the seventeenth and eighteenth century, they contribute to the context for studying the formative period of American cartography.

2-27 Wheat, James C., and Brun, Christian F. MAPS AND CHARTS PUBLISHED IN AMERICA BEFORE 1800: A BIBLIOGRAPHY. New Haven: Yale University Press, 1969. Rev. ed. Holland Press Cartographica 3. London: Holland Press, 1978. xxiv, 215 p. Maps, bibliog., index.

This annotated listing is the first attempt to list all maps published in America prior to 1800. Over nine hundred maps are described, including not only maps and charts published separately, but also maps used as illustrations in books, pamphlets, atlases, gazetteers, almanacs, and magazines. The detailed entries, which are a model of cartobibliographical research, are arranged geographically by continent, region, and colony and thereunder chronologically by date of publication.

C. POST-1800

2-28 Claussen, Martin P., and Friis, Herman R. DESCRIPTIVE CATALOG OF MAPS PUBLISHED BY CONGRESS, 1817-43. Washington, D.C.: 1941. xiii, 104 p. Index.

Approximately five hundred maps published in the Congressional Serial Set from 1817 to 1843 are described and indexed in this catalog. Many of these maps accompanied the annual reports of the contemporary mapping agencies, including the General Land Office, the Bureau of Topographical Engineers, and the Coast Survey. The authors plan to publish an expanded version of this catalog as AMERICAN AND FOREIGN MAPS PUBLISHED BY THE U.S. CONGRESS, 1789-1861: HISTORICAL CATALOG AND INDEX. Other entries pertaining to the Congressional Serial Set are 2-48, 6-15, and 7-13.

2-29 Ehrenberg, Ralph E. GEOGRAPHICAL EXPLORATION AND MAPPING IN THE NINETEENTH CENTURY: A SURVEY OF THE RECORDS IN THE NATIONAL ARCHIVES. Reference Information Paper, No. 66. Washington, D.C.: National Archives and Records Service, 1973. vii, 22 p. Paper. Notes.

> Ehrenberg analyzes the cartographic and textual records of the major federal mapping and surveying agencies in terms of their research potential for historical geographers. His footnotes provide a good source for finding aids and articles that relate to these records.

2-30 _____. "Taking the Measure of the Land." PROLOGUE 9 (Fall 1977): 128-50. Maps, notes.

> Ehrenberg discusses the mapping activities of the federal government prior to 1900, concentrating on four types of maps: jurisdictional (township, state, and national boundary surveys), topographic maps and hydrographic charts, military reconnaissance and campaign maps and plans, and thematic or special purpose maps, and thematic or special purpose maps (population, geology, land classification, weather, and postal routes). His research is based on the cartographic holdings of the National Archives.

2-31 Friis, Herman R. "Highlights in the First Hundred Years of Surveying and Mapping and Geographical Exploration of the United States by the Federal Government, 1775-1880." SURVEYING AND MAPPING 18 (April-June 1958): 186-206.

> This article is the first of a number of articles prepared by Friis in which the major theme is the role of the federal government in exploring, surveying, and mapping the United States. These articles include: "A Brief Review of the Development and Status of Geographical and Cartographical Activities of the United States Government, 1776-1818," IMAGO MUNDI 19 (1965): 68-80; "Highlights of the Geographical and Cartographical Activities of the Federal Government in the Southeastern United States, 1776-1864," SOUTHEASTERN GEOGRAPHER 6 (1966): 41-57; "Highlights of the Geographical and Cartographical Contributions of Graduates of the U.S. Military Academy with a Specialization as Topographical Engineers Prior to 1860," PROCEEDINGS OF THE EIGHTH ANNUAL MEETING OF THE NEW YORK-NEW JERSEY DIVISION OF THE ASSOCIATION OF AMERICAN GEOGRAPHERS 1 (April 1968): 10-29; and "The Role of the United States Topographical Engineers in Compiling a Cartographic Image of the Plains Region," in IMAGES OF THE PLAINS, edited by Brian W. Blouet and Merlin P. Lawson, pp. 59-74 (Lincoln: University of Nebraska Press, 1975). Most of these articles were originally presented orally with numerous slide illustrations. His map descriptions highlight the nineteenth-century cartographic holdings of the National Archives,

while his detailed footnotes provide an excellent guide to the literature on this topic. Two articles dealing with more specific aspects of federally sponsored exploration of the West include: "Cartographic and Geographic Activities of the Lewis and Clark Expedition," JOURNAL OF THE WASHINGTON ACADEMY OF SCIENCES 44 (November 1954): 338-51, and "Stephen H. Long's Unpublished Manuscript Map of the United States Compiled in 1820-22(?)," CALIFORNIA GEOGRAPHER 8 (1967): 75-87. Two exhibit catalogs of the National Archives, which were prepared under the direction of Friis, describe numerous maps which illustrate this theme: GEOGRAPHICAL EXPLORATION AND TOPOGRAPHICAL MAPPING BY THE UNITED STATES GOVERNMENT (Washington, D.C.: National Archives, 1952) and FEDERAL EXPLORATION OF THE AMERICAN WEST BEFORE 1880 (Washington, D.C.: National Archives, 1963).

2-32 Hargett, Janet L., comp. LIST OF SELECTED MAPS OF STATES AND TERRITORIES. Special List, No. 29. Washington, D.C.: National Archives and Records Service, 1971. viii, 113 p. Paper. Index.

Approximately nine hundred state and territorial maps dating from the late eighteenth to the early twentieth century are described in this list. These maps, which were selected from the records of twelve federal agencies, can serve primarily as general reference aids but are also useful for showing changing place name locations and county boundaries during the nineteenth century.

2-33 Hecht, Arthur, and Heynen, William J. RECORDS AND POLICIES OF THE POST OFFICE DEPARTMENT RELATING TO PLACE NAMES. Reference Information Paper, No. 72. Washington, D.C.: National Archives and Records Service, 1975. vii, 16 p. Paper. Illus.

Besides describing records of the Post Office Department now in the National Archives, which are useful for place name studies, this paper also lists nineteenth-century state postal route maps. See also Hecht, "Route Maps of the U.S. Postal Service of the 18th and 19th Centuries." AMERICAN PHILATELIST 93 (November 1979): 981-86.

2-34 Heynen, William J., comp. AGRICULTURAL MAPS IN THE NATIONAL ARCHIVES OF THE UNITED STATES, CA. 1860-1930. Reference Information Paper, No. 75. Washington, D.C.: National Archives and Records Service, 1976. vii, 25 p. Paper. Maps.

This paper provides a survey of several significant map series that are oriented toward agricultural history and such related topics as rural land use, vegetation, and climate.

2-35 _____ . CARTOGRAPHIC RECORDS OF THE BUREAU OF AGRICULTUR-
AL ECONOMICS. Special List, No. 28. Washington, D.C.: National
Archives and Records Service, 1971. viii, 110 p. Paper. Maps, index.

> Over four thousand maps from the records of the Bureau of Agri-
> cultural Economics, an agency which collected and published a
> wide variety of information about agriculture and rural conditions
> in the United States, are described in this list. Although most
> of these maps were created between 1902 and 1953, some, such
> as those prepared for the ATLAS OF AMERICAN AGRICULTURE,
> pertain to nineteenth-century agricultural and land use patterns.
> Also included among these records are the cartographic works
> of O.E. Baker and F.J. Marschner.

2-36 _____ . UNITED STATES HYDROGRAPHIC MANUSCRIPT CHARTS IN THE
NATIONAL ARCHIVES, 1838-1980. Special List, No. 43. Washington, D.C.:
National Archives and Records Service, 1978. xi, 250 p. Paper. Maps,
index.

> The U.S. Navy Hydrographic Office's pre-1908 manuscript
> maps which number about five thousand items, are described in
> this list. These maps show primarily hydrographic data but also
> show limited topographic information for coastal areas. Although
> the coverage is worldwide, several hundred items pertain to the
> coastal areas of the United States and Canada.

2-37 Kelsay, Laura E., comp. CARTOGRAPHIC RECORDS IN THE NATIONAL
ARCHIVES OF THE UNITED STATES RELATING TO AMERICAN INDIANS.
Reference Information Paper, No. 71. Washington, D.C.: National Ar-
chives and Records Service, 1974. v, 35 p. Paper. Notes.

> Maps from the records of seven federal agencies dealing with
> Indian activities and affairs are briefly described in terms of
> exploration of Indian country, Indian land cessions, establish-
> ment of reservations, and population, transportation, and indus-
> try on the reservations. Also included are two appendixes which
> describe specific maps depicting Indian activities and population.

2-38 _____ . CARTOGRAPHIC RECORDS OF THE BUREAU OF INDIAN AF-
FAIRS. Special List, No. 13. Rev. ed. Washington, D.C.: National
Archives and Records Service, 1977. vii, 187 p. Paper. Index.

> Approximately 294 cubic feet of cartographic records from the
> Bureau of Indian Affairs now in the National Archives are des-
> cribed in this list. These maps, which date from the early 1800s
> to the 1960s, reflect the U.S. government's involvement with
> the Indians, including land cessions and the establishment and im-
> provement of reservations.

2-39 _____ . LIST OF CARTOGRAPHIC RECORDS OF THE GENERAL LAND
OFFICE. Special List, No. 19. Washington, D.C.: National Archives and
Records Service, 1964. v, 202 p. Paper. Index.

Although this publication does not describe all the cartographic
records of the former General Land Office now in the National
Archives, it does provide full annotated descriptions of individual maps from four important cartographic series. The records
include manuscript and annotated maps dating from 1790 to
1946 which show the progress of surveys and the disposal of lands
in the public land states, maps and field notes from the survey
of boundaries of public land states and special reservations, and
published territorial, state, and national maps of the General
Land Office.

2-40 Ladd, Richard S., comp. MAPS SHOWING EXPLORERS' ROUTES, TRAILS,
AND EARLY ROADS IN THE UNITED STATES: AN ANNOTATED LIST.
Washington, D.C.: Library of Congress, 1962. vi, 137 p. Paper. Map,
index.

This annotated bibliography lists three hundred selected maps
from the Library of Congress holdings which show explorers'
routes, trails, and early roads. The entries are arranged alphabetically by author or publisher, but the index provides
access by geographic area or significant route.

2-41 LeGear, Clara Egli, comp. THE HOTCHKISS MAP COLLECTION: A LIST
OF MANUSCRIPT MAPS, MANY OF THE CIVIL WAR PERIOD, PREPARED
BY MAJ. JED. HOTCHKISS, AND OTHER MANUSCRIPT AND ANNOTA-
TED MAPS IN HIS POSSESSION. Washington, D.C.: Library of Congress,
1951. 90 p. Paper. Index.

The map collection of Jedediah Hotchkiss, a topographical en-
gineer in the Confederate army, is itemized. Most of these
341 maps pertain to Civil War Virginia. The journal which
Hotchkiss kept as he was preparing these maps, is reprinted in
Archie P. McDonald, ed., MAKE ME A MAP OF THE VALLEY:
THE CIVIL WAR JOURNAL OF STONEWALL JACKSON'S TO-
POGRAPHER (Dallas: Southern Methodist University Press, 1973).

2-42 McLaughlin, Patrick D., comp. TRANSPORTATION IN NINETEENTH-
CENTURY AMERICA: A SURVEY OF THE CARTOGRAPHIC RECORDS
IN THE NATIONAL ARCHIVES OF THE UNITED STATES. Reference
Information Paper, No. 65. Washington, D.C.: National Archives and
Records Service, 1973. vii, 15 p. Paper. Notes.

Nine series of maps that document the nineteenth-century development of the transportation network in the United States are
reviewed in this paper.

2-43 Moak, Jefferson M. PHILADELPHIA MAPMAKERS. Philadelphia: Shack-
amaxon Society, 1976. 32 p. Paper. Maps, notes, bibliog.

Besides describing the mapmaking industry of Philadelphia, which
was the mapping capital of the United States during the last
half of the nineteenth century, Moak provides a list of map-

makers, addresses, and specific occupations (engraver, lithographer, publisher, surveyor, colorist, etc.). For additional articles by Moak about Philadelphia mapmakers, see, "Historic Mapmakers of Philadelphia, A Partial List of Mapmakers from 1850-1900," Special Libraries Association Geography and Map Division, BULLETIN, no. 104 (June 1976), pp. 42-45, and "The All-American Mapmaker," MAPLINE 14 (1979): 5-6.

2-44 Modelski, Andrew M., comp. RAILROAD MAPS OF THE UNITED STATES: A SELECTIVE ANNOTATED BIBLIOGRAPHY OF ORIGINAL 19TH-CENTURY MAPS IN THE GEOGRAPHY AND MAP DIVISION OF THE LIBRARY OF CONGRESS. Washington, D.C.: Library of Congress, 1975. v, 112 p. Paper. Maps, notes, index.

Full bibliographical entries, along with descriptions of maps' contents, are provided for 622 nineteenth-century railroad maps in the holdings of the Library of Congress. These maps, which were produced for various reasons, are categorized by their geographic coverage: national, regional, state, or individual railroad. An introductory essay discusses the development of nineteenth-century railroad mapping.

2-45 National Archives and Records Service. CIVIL WAR MAPS IN THE NATIONAL ARCHIVES. Washington, D.C.: General Services Administration, 1964. xi, 127 p. Paper. Maps, index.

Over eight thousand maps and fortifications plans which pertain to the Civil War are described in this publication. These cartographic records were selected from the records of fourteen federal government agencies which are now in the National Archives. The first section provides a succinct collective description of all of items, while the second section provides a full description of the more significant maps of individual states, campaigns, and battles. These maps are also described briefly in A. Philip Muntz, "Union Mapping in the America Civil War," IMAGO MUNDI 17 (1963): 90-94.

2-46 Ristow, Walter W. MAPS FOR AN EMERGING NATION: COMMERCIAL CARTOGRAPHY IN NINETEENTH-CENTURY AMERICA. Washington, D.C.: Library of Congress, 1977. v, 66 p. Paper. Maps, bibliog.

Prepared as an exhibit catalog, this booklet provides an overview of the development of American commercial cartography during the nineteenth century. The introductory essay discusses the various types of maps produced in the context of three periods: the engraving era, 1785-1830; the beginning of the lithographic era, 1830-1865; and the post-Civil War era, 1865-1900. Descriptions of the 112 maps in the exhibit are also included.

2-47 Seavey, Charles A. "Maps as Documents/Documents as Maps." Special Libraries Association Geography and Map Division. BULLETIN, no. 112 (June 1978), pp. 2-18. Notes.

After reviewing the federal government's map publishing activities in the nineteenth and early twentieth centuries, Seavey discusses the bibliographical controls and finding aids that are available for these maps.

2-48 _____. "Maps of the AMERICAN STATE PAPERS." Special Libraries Association Geography and Map Division. BULLETIN, no. 107, March 1977, pp. 28-35; and no. 110, December 1977, pp. 3-11.

A full annotated entry is provided for each map found in the AMERICAN STATE PAPERS, a published collection of federal government documents dating from 1789 throught the 1830s. These maps reflect the government's early activities in foreign relations, military and naval affairs, and public lands. See also entries 2-28, 6-15, and 7-13 for other works pertaining to published federal government documents.

2-49 Stephenson, Richard W., comp. CIVIL WAR MAPS: AN ANNOTATED LIST OF MAPS AND ATLASES IN MAP COLLECTIONS OF THE LIBRARY OF CONGRESS. Washington, D.C.: Library of Congress, 1961. v, 138 p. Paper. Index.

Seven hundred entries describe maps and atlases that pertain to military activities and fortifications during the Civil War. Except for maps of the United States or maps of more than one state, which are arranged chronologically, the other entries are arranged geographically by state and thereunder by battle site.

2-50 U.S. National Ocean Survey. Scientific Services Division. Physical Science Services Branch. Map Library. NATIONAL OCEAN SURVEY CARTOBIBLIOGRAPHY, CIVIL WAR COLLECTION. Rockville, Md.: 1980. v, 64 p. Paper.

Civil War maps in the National Ocean Survey's historical map collection are described. Many of these maps were produced by the U.S. Coast Survey and the Office of Topographical Surveys.

2-51 U.S. War Department. THE OFFICIAL MILITARY ATLAS OF THE CIVIL WAR. Intro. by Richard Sommers. 1891-95. Reprint. New York: Arno Press, Crown Publishers, 1978. 29 p., 178 plates. Maps, illus., index.

This facsimile reprint of the ATLAS TO ACCOMPANY THE OFFICIAL RECORDS OF THE UNION AND CONFEDERATE ARMIES (Washington, D.C.: 1891-95), includes 821 battle, campaign, and regional maps. In addition, there are 106 engravings, mainly of fortifications, and 209 drawings of weapons, equipment, uniforms, and flags. The manuscript maps, which were collected while preparing the original edition, are in the National Archives among the records of the Adjutant General's Office (Record Group 94).

Chapter 3
GEOGRAPHICAL LISTINGS

Cartobibliographies, collections of facsimile reproductions, and analytical books and articles pertaining to a particular region, state, or place are listed here. The first section deals with broad national regions covering more than one state, while the second section focuses on individual states or areas within states. Several entries published before 1965 have been included in order to provide a broader geographical coverage.

A. REGIONAL

3-1 Brown, Lloyd A. EARLY MAPS OF THE OHIO VALLEY: A SELECTION OF MAPS, PLANS, AND VIEWS MADE BY INDIANS AND COLONIALS FROM 1673 TO 1783. Pittsburgh: University of Pittsburgh Press, 1959. xiv, 132 p. Maps, illus., bibliog.

> The cartographical history of the upper Ohio River Valley up to 1783 is illustrated with reproductions of overy fifty maps selected from the holdings of numerous American, British, and French libraries. Descriptions of the individual maps not only indicate the specific depository in which the map is located, but also explain the map's significance and relevance to the Ohio Valley.

3-2 Cumming, William P. THE SOUTHEAST IN EARLY MAPS WITH AN ANNO-TATED CHECKLIST OF PRINTED AND MANUSCRIPT REGIONAL AND LO-CAL MAPS OF SOUTHEASTERN NORTH AMERICA DURING THE COLONIAL PERIOD. 2d ed. Chapel Hill: University of North Carolina Press, 1962. ix, 284 p., 67 map plates. Notes, bibliog., index.

> The history of cartography in southeastern North America before the American Revolution is discussed in an introductory essay in terms of discovery, early exploration and settlement, and the eighteenth-century expansion of the frontier and subsequent land surveys. Facsimile reproductions of sixty-one maps dated between 1507 and 1773 illustrate this discussion. In addition,

annotated descriptions of 450 regional maps of the Southeast
and local maps exclusive of Virginia and Maryland are included.
First published in 1958 by Princeton University Press, subsequent
impressions in 1962, 1966, and 1973 have noted minor correc-
tions and added eight additional map descriptions.

3-3 "Early Mapping of the Southeast." SOUTHEASTERN GEOGRAPHER 6 (1966):
1-57. Maps, notes.

This entire issue is devoted to four papers which were originally
presented at the annual meeting of the Southeastern Division,
Association of American Geographers, November 25, 1965. The
four papers include William P. Cumming, "Mapping of the Southeast: The First Two Centuries"; Louis De Vorsey, Jr., "The Colonial Southeast on 'An Accurate General Map'"; Walter Ristow,
"State Maps of the Southeast to 1833"; and Herman R. Friis,
"Highlights of the Geographical and Cartographical Activities
of the Federal Government in the Southeastern United States,
1776-1865."

3-4 Newberry Library. Chicago. CHECKLIST OF PRINTED MAPS OF THE MID-
DLE WEST TO 1900. 11 vols. Boston: G.K. Hall, 1980.

Descriptions of approximately 26,600 printed maps found in 127
different collections are reproduced in this catalog. Cards are
included for individual states (Illinois, Indiana, Iowa, Kansas,
Michigan, Minnesota, Missouri, Nebraska, North and South
Dakota, Ohio, and Wisconsin) as well as for broader regions
(Great Lakes and Northern Great Plains). This project was
described in "The Catalog of Maps of the North Central States
Project," MAPLINE, Special No. 2 (December 1978), 6 p.

3-5 Wagner, Henry R. THE CARTOGRAPHY OF THE NORTHWEST COAST OF
AMERICA TO THE YEAR 1800. 2 vols. Berkeley: University of California Press, 1937. Reprint. 2 vols. in 1. Amsterdam: Nico Israel, 1968.
xi, 543 p. Maps, bibliog., index.

In the first volume, Wagner discusses individual maps which
document the exploration and related development of cartography of the northwest coast of North America (lower California
to Alaska) from the beginning of the sixteenth century until the
end of the eighteenth century. The second volume includes a
chronological listing of the maps, place names still in use, obsolete place names, and a bibliography. See also Ronald F.
Lockmann, "Some Eighteenth Century Maps of Pacific North
America: The La Perouse Expedition in California," HISTORI-
CAL GEOGRAPHY NEWSLETTER 5 (Spring 1975): 16-24.

3-6   Wheat, Carl I. MAPPING THE TRANSMISSISSIPPI WEST, 1540-1861.
       5 vols. San Francisco: Institute of Historical Cartography, 1957-63.
       lxxi, 1,641 p. Maps, notes, index.

       Using a chronological and topical approach, Wheat provides a
       detailed history of the mapping of the American West. Although
       the title indicates a terminal date of 1861, the final volume ex-
       tends the coverage into the 1860s and 1870s. The five volumes
       are titled separately: Vol. 1, THE SPANISH ENTRADA TO THE
       LOUISIANA PURCHASE (1957); Vol. 2, FROM LEWIS AND
       CLARK TO FREMONT, 1804-1845 (1958); Vol. 3, FROM THE
       MEXICAN WAR TO THE BOUNDARY SURVEYS, 1846-1854
       (1959); Vol. 4, FROM THE PACIFIC RAILROAD SURVEYS TO THE
       ONSET OF THE CIVIL WAR, 1855-1860 (1960); Vol. 5 (in two
       parts), FROM THE CIVIL WAR TO THE GEOLOGICAL SUR-
       VEY (1963). Each volume contains numerous facsimile repro-
       ductions of selected maps discussed in the text and concludes
       with a "bibliocartography," which lists title, author, medium,
       dimensions, and repository for each map mentioned in the text.
       For further bibliographical details which pertain to those maps
       that were selected from federal government publications, see
       Charles A. Seavey, "A Bibliographical Addendum to Carl I.
       Wheat's MAPPING THE TRANSMISSISSIPPI WEST, 1540-1861,"
       Special Libraries Association Geography and Map Division.
       BULLETIN, no. 105, September 1976, pp. 12-19.

B. INDIVIDUAL STATES

3-7   Baughman, Robert W. KANSAS IN MAPS. Topeka: Kansas State Histori-
       cal Society, 1961. 104 p. Maps.

       Over eighty facsimile map reproductions illustrate the history of
       Kansas. Most of the maps were selected from the author's pri-
       vate collection and the Kansas State Historical Society.

3-8   Becker, Robert H. DESIGNS ON THE LAND: DISENOS OF CALIFOR-
       NIA RANCHOS AND THEIR MAKERS. San Francisco: Book Club of
       California, 1969. 161 p. Maps.

       Becker reproduces sixty-four disenos (rough sketch maps of Span-
       ish and Mexican land grants in California), which were selected
       from the records of the U.S. District Court and are now in the
       custody of the Bancroft Library, University of California, Berke-
       ley. These facsimile reproductions are arranged by mapmaker or
       cartographer. Brief biographies of the twenty-five cartographers
       that could be identified are included as well as brief descriptions
       of the various ranchos that are depicted. Cross references in-
       dicate the location of other copies of the disenos in the Na-
       tional Archives and the California State Archives. Facsimile
       reproductions and descriptions of thirty-seven disenos were
       included in Becker, DISENOS OF CALIFORNIA RANCHOS:

MAPS OF THIRTY-SEVEN LAND GRANTS, 1822-1846, FROM THE RECORDS OF THE U.S. DISTRICT COURT, SAN FRANCISCO (San Francisco: Book Club of California, 1964).

3-9　Birmingham Public Library (Alabama). A LIST OF NINETEENTH CENTURY MAPS OF THE STATE OF ALABAMA. Compiled by Sara Elizabeth Mason. Birmingham: 1973. ix, 116 p. Paper. Index.

Nineteenth-century Alabama state maps in six Alabama libraries or archival institutions are described in this bibliography and union list. While the entries are arranged chronologically, there is also an author index. Pre-statehood (1819) maps and maps of individual counties or parts of the state are not included.

3-10　Blake, Janice G., comp. PRE-NINETEENTH CENTURY MAPS IN THE COLLECTION OF THE GEORGIA SURVEYOR GENERAL DEPARTMENT. Atlanta: State Printing Office, 1975. xx, 173 p. Paper. Notes, bibliog., index.

After reviewing the history of Georgia's Surveyor General Office, Blake presents descriptions of approximately three hundred pre-nineteenth-century maps, most of which pertain to Georgia.

3-11　Clark, David Sanders. INDEX TO MAPS OF NORTH CAROLINA IN BOOKS AND PERIODICALS ILLUSTRATING THE HISTORY OF THE STATE FROM THE VOYAGE OF VERRAZZANO IN 1524 TO 1975. Fayetteville, N.C.: 1976. viii, 229 p. Paper. Index, bibliog.

Clark lists 3,300 references to maps illustrating North Carolina's history found in 590 publications. The entries are arranged by subject under six major categories (land and resources; exploration, settlement, and development; government and politics; economy; services and amenities; and military history) and numerous subheadings.

3-12　Clark, Thomas D. HISTORIC MAPS OF KENTUCKY. Lexington: University Press of Kentucky, 1979. Folio, 10 maps. Book, vi, 90 p. Paper. Maps, photos, notes.

The cartographical representation of Kentucky from the late eighteenth century until the Civil War is illustrated with ten facsimile maps, with seven in color. The accompanying booklet describes the historical background of these maps as well as of other notable Kentucky maps.

3-13　Cobb, David A. "Vermont Maps Prior to 1900: An Annotated Cartobibliography." VERMONT HISTORY 39 (Summer and Fall 1971): 169-317. Maps, bibliog., index.

Approximately five hundred manuscript and published maps are described in thirteen chapters which are arranged chronologically by decade. Appendixes also list U.S. Geological Survey topographic quadrangles, Sanborn Fire Insurance maps, and town boundary maps that pertain to Vermont.

3-14 Creek, Alma Burner. MAPS OF THE GENESEE VALLEY AND FINGER LAKES REGION, 1776-1950. Rochester, N.Y.: Rochester Regional Research Library Council, 1977. iii, 145 p. Maps, bibliog.

Printed and manuscript maps and county atlases found in nine Rochester area libraries are described in this union list. The maps, which date from 1776 to 1950, pertain to Rochester and vicinity, the Genesee Valley, the Finger Lakes Region, and western New York state.

3-15 Cumming, William P. NORTH CAROLINA IN MAPS. Raleigh, N.C.: State Department of Archives and History, 1966. Folio, 15 maps. Book, vii, 36 p. Paper. Maps, notes.

Facsimile reproductions of fifteen maps dated from 1585 to 1896 illustrate the advance of geographic knowledge and the expansion of settlement in North Carolina. Two to three pages of text discuss the historical background and significance of each map.

3-16 Day, James, et al., comp. MAPS OF TEXAS, 1527-1900: THE MAP COLLECTION OF THE TEXAS STATE ARCHIVES. Austin, Tex.: Pemberton Press, 1964. 182 p. Maps, index.

Detailed bibliographical entries (title, publisher, date, scale, dimensions, and short description) are listed for over two thousand catalogued maps in the Texas State Archives. This is a revision of THE MAP COLLECTION OF THE TEXAS STATE ARCHIVES, 1527-1900 (Austin, 1962), which was a reprint from the SOUTHWESTERN HISTORICAL QUARTERLY 65 (January and April 1962): 399-439, 539-74; and 66 (July and October 1962): 103-32, 271-303.

3-17 Hafstad, Margaret R. "The Society's Map Collection." WISCONSIN MAGAZINE OF HISTORY 52 (Spring 1969): 223-38. Maps, notes.

Hafstad describes the map collection of the State Historical Society of Wisconsin, which is not limited to but emphasizes historical maps of Wisconsin, including county land ownership atlases, Sanborn Fire Insurance maps, and panoramic views.

3-18 Karpinski, Louis C. MAPS OF FAMOUS CARTOGRAPHERS DEPICTING NORTH AMERICA: AN HISTORICAL ATLAS OF THE GREAT LAKES AND MICHIGAN, WITH BIBLIOGRAPHY OF THE PRINTED MAPS OF MICHIGAN TO 1880. 2d ed. Amsterdam, Holland: Meridian Publishing Co., 1977. 539 p. Maps, index.

Originally published as BIBLIOGRAPHY OF THE PRINTED MAPS OF MICHIGAN, 1804-80 (1931), this work attempts to list all the maps of Michigan printed between 1805 and 1880, as well as the pre-1805 maps of North America that depict the Great Lakes region. The revised title of the reprint edition reflects the latter coverage. Photocopies of 123 of the listed maps are included.

3-19 Kelsay, Laura E., and Ashby, Charlotte M., comps. CARTOGRAPHIC RECORDS RELATING TO THE TERRITORY OF WISCONSIN, 1836-48. Special List, No. 23. Washington, D.C.: National Archives and Records Serivce, 1970. vii, 41 p. Paper. Maps, index.

Cartographic records pertaining to Wisconsin's territorial period (1836-48) are described in this list. These maps and field notes were selected from the cartographic records of six federal agencies and are now in the National Archives.

3-20 Kelsay, Laura E., and Pernell, Frederick W., comps. CARTOGRAPHIC RECORDS RELATING TO THE TERRITORY OF IOWA, 1838-46. Special List, No. 27. Washington, D.C.: National Archives and Records Service, 1971. vi, 29 p. Paper. Diagrs., index.

Individual maps pertaining to Iowa's territorial period (1838-46), which are found among the records of seven federal government agencies now in the National Archives, are described in this list.

3-21 Miles, William, comp. MICHIGAN ATLASES AND PLAT BOOKS: A CHECKLIST, 1872-1973. Lansing: Michigan Department of Education, State Library Services, 1975. ix, 178 p. Paper. Index.

This checklist itemizes 876 Michigan state and county atlases and plat books found in thirteen Michigan libraries and the Library of Congress. The entries, which date from 1872 to 1973, are arranged geographically by state and county and thereunder chronologically. Many of the county plat books show land ownership.

3-22 Miller, Ruby M. PENNSYLVANIA MAPS AND ATLASES IN THE PENNSYLVANIA STATE UNIVERSITY LIBRARIES. Bibliographical Series, No. 5. University Park: Pennsylvania State University Libraries, 1972. xii, 682 p. Maps.

Maps and atlases in the Pennsylvania State University Libraries that pertain to Pennsylvania are listed in this bibliography. Although many of these items are dated after 1940, there are some items of historical interest, including Sanborn Fire Insurance atlases and scattered nineteenth and early twentieth-century state, county, and city maps. The entries are arranged both topically and geographically.

3-23 [Mills, Robert]. MILLS' ATLAS OF SOUTH CAROLINA: AN ATLAS OF THE DISTRICTS OF SOUTH CAROLINA IN 1825. Fascimile ed. Introd. by Charles E. Lee. Columbia, S.C.: Wilkins and Keels, 1965. 32 p. Maps.

Reproduced from the original engravings of Mills's 1825 atlas, this limited full-scale facsimile edition includes an introduction by Charles E. Lee of the South Carolina Archives, which discusses the creation of the original atlas. A more detailed discussion of the background of the original atlas is presented by Walter W. Ristow, "Robert Mills' Atlas of South Carolina," QUARTERLY JOURNAL OF THE LIBRARY OF CONGRESS 34 (January 1977): 52-66.

3-24 Preston, Ralph N. EARLY WASHINGTON. Corvallis, Oreg.: Western Guide Publishers, 1974. 68 p. Paper. Maps, photos.

Washington's nineteenth and early twentieth-century history is illustrated with reproductions of eighteen historical maps and numerous photographs.

3-25 _____. HISTORICAL MAPS OF OREGON. Corvallis, Oreg.: Western Guide Publishers, 1972. 64 p. Paper. Maps, photos.

Reproductions of seventeen historical maps, as well as numerous photographs, illustrate Oregon's nineteenth and early twentieth-century history. In addition, a series of eleven maps show Oregon's changing county boundaries from 1843 to 1941.

3-26 Princeton University Library. NEW JERSEY ROAD MAPS OF THE 18TH CENTURY. 1964. Reprint. Princeton, N.J.: 1970. 48 p. Maps.

Three manuscipt and one published series of maps which show roads in eighteenth-century New Jersey are reproduced here. Each group of these road or strip maps, which were selected from the Princeton University Library collections, is accompanied by a brief commentary.

3-27 Sames, James W., III, comp. INDEX OF KENTUCKY AND VIRGINIA MAPS, 1562 TO 1900. Ed. by Lewis C. Wood, Jr. Frankfort: Kentucky Historical Society, 1976. xi, 288 p. Maps.

Over five thousand maps of Kentucky and Virginia found in ten repositories are described. The list is cumbersome to use because the entries are arranged chronologically and there is no geographical, subject, or author index.

3-28 Sanchez-Saaveda, E.M. A DESCRIPTION OF THE COUNTRY: VIRGINIA'S CARTOGRAPHIES AND THEIR MAPS, 1607-1881. Richmond: Virginia State Library, 1975. Folio, 9 maps. Book, xi, 130 p. Paper. Maps, illus., photos., bibliog.

Nine facsimile maps representing "landmarks" in the history of

Virginia's cartography are included in the portfolio. The accompanying booklet provides a history of Virginia's cartography
with each chapter devoted to a discussion of the creation of
one of the nine maps, as well as related maps from the same
time period. Other facsimile reproductions of Virginia maps
include THE JOHN HENRY COUNTY MAP OF VIRGINIA,
1770, introduction by Louis B. Wright (Charlottesville: University Press of Virginia, 1977), and THE FRY AND JEFFERSON
MAP OF VIRGINIA AND MARYLAND: FACSIMILES OF THE
1754 AND 1794 PRINTINGS WITH AN INDEX, introduction by
Dumas Malone (2d ed.; Charlottesville: University Press of
Virginia, 1966). The latter publication also includes a checklist by Coolie Verner enumerating the eighteenth-century editions of the map.

3-29 Simonetti, Martha L., comp. DESCRIPTIVE LIST OF THE MAP COLLECTION
IN THE PENNSYLVANIA STATE ARCHIVES. Harrisburg: Pennsylvania
Historical and Museum Commission, 1976. 178 p.

The maps in the principal map collection (MG 11) in the Division of Archives and Manuscripts are described in this finding
aid. These maps, which were accumulated over the years from
the inception of the state archives in 1903, pertain to Pennsylvania dating from 1681 to the present. The seven hundred
entries, some describing multiple sheet maps, represent a wide
variety of maps including county, township, city, borough,
boundary, topographic, geological, military, and "bird's-eye
view" maps. There are maps in other manuscript and record
groups in the state archives. Those found among the records
of the Board of Canal Commissioners (RG 17) are described in
Simonetti, comp., INVENTORY OF CANAL COMMISSIONERS'
MAPS IN THE PENNSYLVANIA STATE ARCHIVES (Harrisburg:
Pennsylvania Historical and Museum Commission, Bureau of
Archives and History, 1968).

3-30 Smith, Thomas H. THE MAPPING OF OHIO. Kent, Ohio: Kent State
University Press, 1977. xiii, 252 p. Maps, notes, bibliog., index.

The development of Ohio's cartography is discussed and illustrated
with approximately eighty maps. The themes which are covered
include pre-nineteenth-century maps of North America depicting
the exploration and growing knowledge of the Ohio country;
nineteenth-century maps of pre-historic Indian mounds, fortification plans and battle maps reflecting military activities in
Ohio from the late eighteenth century until the Civil War; land
survey maps of various grants and land districts; published state
maps; selected early ninteenth-century city plans; and internal
improvement maps. An appendix lists county atlases published
in the late nineteenth and early twentieth centuries.

3-31 Snyder, John P. THE MAPPING OF NEW JERSEY: THE MEN AND THE ART. New Brunswick, N.J.: Rutgers University Press, 1973. xiv, 234 p. Maps, photos., notes, bibliog., index.

> Snyder reviews the history of private, local, state, and federal mapping activities in New Jersey, focusing on four periods: pre-1750, 1750-1800, 1800-1880, and post-1888. This survey includes discussions of numerous topics including eighteenth-century cartographers Robert Erskine, John Hills, Christopher Colles, and Thomas Hutchins; the establishment of the New Jersey Geological Survey and the completion of a topographical survey of the entire state in 1888; and New Jersey's twentieth-century mapping firms, General Drafting Co., and Hammond, Inc. The book is illustrated with examples of seventeenth through twentieth-century maps, as well as with various index maps prepared by Snyder.

3-32 Wells, Ann Harwell. "Early Maps of Tennessee, 1794-1799." TENNESSEE HISTORICAL QUARTERLY 35 (Summer 1976): 123-43. Maps, notes.

> Eight maps of Tennessee published between 1794 and 1799 are reproduced and described in this article.

Chapter 4

URBAN MAPS

The availability, history, and research potential of urban maps provide the focus for this chapter. The first two sections describe very specific types of maps, fire insurance maps and panoramic or bird's-eye views of cities. The broader category of urban plans and maps constitutes the third section, while the final section is concerned with city maps showing changing ward boundaries and related city and county directories, both of which have provided the basis for many recent historical urban studies. Two other publications listing fire insurance atlases are described in entries 1-30 and 1-31.

A. FIRE INSURANCE MAPS

4-1   Gibson, Lay James. "Tucson's Evolving Commercial Base, 1883-1914: A Map Analysis." HISTORICAL GEOGRAPHY NEWSLETTER 5 (Fall 1975): 10-17. Maps, notes.

> Gibson uses Sanborn Fire Insurance maps from 1883, 1904, and 1914 to map and describe the changing composition and spatial pattern of the commercial activities of Tucson, Arizona.

4-2   Hoehn, R. Philip. "Fire Insurance Maps in the Bancroft Library, University of California, Berkeley." Western Association of Map Libraries. INFORMATION BULLETIN 3 (March 1972): 31-35.

> Hoehn provides a listing of the fire insurance maps in the Bancroft Library, most of which pertain to California communities. He also reviews the publishing history of a San Francisco firm in "The Dakin Publishing Company and its Fire Insurance Maps," Western Association of Map Libraries. INFORMATION BULLETIN 7 (June 1976): 47-59. For a listing of fire insurance maps of Santa Cruz County, see Stanley D. Stevens, "Color Microfilming of Sanborn Maps for a Local History Collection," Western Association of Map Libraries. INFORMATION BULLETIN 1 (June 1970): 2-8.

4-3 Hoehn, R. Philip, et al. UNION LIST OF SANBORN FIRE INSURANCE MAPS HELD BY INSTITUTIONS IN THE UNITED STATES AND CANADA. 2 vols. Western Association of Map Libraries, Occasional Paper, Nos. 2-3. Santa Cruz, Calif.: Western Association of Map Libraries, 1976-77. Vol. 1, xvii, 178 p.; vol. 2, xv, 201 p. Paper. Maps, bibliog.

> This union list covers twenty-five thousand fire insurance maps and atlases held by American and Canadian institutions, excluding the Library of Congress and California State University of Northridge (see entries 1-30 and 4-7). The entries, which are arranged alphabetically by state and community, include the name of the county, available editions, and institutions holding these volumes. The first volume, which was compiled by Hoehn, covers Alabama to Missouri; the second volume, compiled by William S. Peterson-Hunt and Evelyn L. Woodruff, covers Montana to Wyoming, Canada, and Mexico.

4-4 Library of Congress. Geography and Map Division. Reference and Bibliography Section. FIRE INSURANCE MAPS IN THE LIBRARY OF CONGRESS: PLANS OF NORTH AMERICAN CITIES AND TOWNS PRODUCED BY THE SANBORN MAP COMPANY. Washington, D.C.: 1981. x, 773 p. Paper. Maps, illus., index.

> The entire collection of Sanborn Company fire insurance maps in the Library of Congress is described in this checklist. The entires are arranged alphabetically by state and city. This is the largest extant collection of Sanborn Company maps. The introduction was prepared by Walter W. Ristow (see entry 4-9).

4-5 Moody, Eric N. "Urban History in Fire Insurance Maps: Nevada as a Case Study." Western Association of Map Libraries. INFORMATION BULLETIN 10 (March 1979): 129-38.

> Besides demonstrating the usefulness of fire insurance maps in studying urban development on the mining frontier, Moody also provides a union list of fire insurance maps for Nevada communities which are available at a number of institutions.

4-6 Radford, John P. "A Note on the Spatial Analysis of Sets of Highly Disaggregated Data." HISTORICAL METHODS NEWSLETTER 5 (June 1972): 115-17. Notes.

> Radford discusses the use of fire insurance maps to plot the spatial characteristics of highly disaggregated data which can be associated with street addresses, such as data obtained from city directories or census schedules.

4-7 Rees, Gary, and Hoeber, Mary. A CATALOGUE OF SANBORN ATLASES AT CALIFORNIA STATE UNIVERSITY, NORTHRIDGE. Western Association of Map Libraries, Occasional Paper, No. 1. Santa Cruz, Calif.: Western Association of Map Libraries, 1973. xxi, 122 p. Paper. Maps, bibliog., index.

Department, California State University, Northridge, are listed
in this catalog. This collection includes 4,311 maps or volumes
of maps for 1,631 communities, primarily in the western United
States. The book also includes a bibliography of sources pertaining to Sanborn Atlases. This collection is also described
by Ralph D. Vicero, "The Sanborn Map Collection of the
Western United States at San Fernando Valley State College,"
HISTORICAL GEOGRAPHY NEWSLETTER 2 (Spring 1972): 49-
60.

4-8   Reynolds, Regina, and Ruwell, Mary Elizabeth. "Fire Insurance Records:
A Versatile Resource." AMERICAN ARCHIVIST 38 (January 1975): 15-21.
Maps, illus.

The contents and utility of the fire insurance records in the archives of the Insurance Company of North America Corporation
are described. Included are textual records (blotters, policies,
surveys, and proofs of loss) as well as maps and architectural
drawings which can be a versatile resource for the reconstruction of urban landscapes and personal wealth.

4-9   Ristow, Walter W. "United States Fire Insurance and Underwriters Maps,
1852-1968." QUARTERLY JOURNAL OF THE LIBRARY OF CONGRESS
25 (July 1968): 194-218. Maps, photos., notes.

The accession by the Library of Congress of 1,840 volumes of
Sanborn Fire Insurance maps from the U.S. Census Bureau is
described. Ristow also discusses the development of fire insurance maps including how the maps were created, how they
were used, and a brief history of the Sanborn Map Company.
A similar article by Ristow is "U.S. Fire Insurance Maps, 1852-
1968," SURVEYING AND MAPPING 30 (March 1970): 19-41.

4-10 Ross, Stanley H. "The Central Business District of Mexico City as Indicated on the Sanborn Maps of 1906." PROFESSIONAL GEOGRAPHER
23 (January 1971): 31-39. Maps, notes.

Ross demonstrates the utility of Sanborn maps in reconstructing
the urban morphology and land use of Mexico City in 1906.

B. PANORAMIC VIEWS

4-11 Beckman, Thomas. MILWAUKEE ILLUSTRATED: PANORAMIC AND BIRD'S
EYE VIEWS OF A MIDWESTERN METROPOLIS, 1844-1908. Milwaukee:
Milwaukee Art Center, 1978. 68 p. Paper. Maps, illus., notes, index.

Forty-eight panoramic and bird's-eye views of Milwaukee, which
were included in a 1978 exhibit in the Milwaukee Art Center
and Wisconsin State Historical Society, are described in this

catalog. The introductory essay reviews the production of these lithographic views in Milwaukee, which became a center for this industry in the last third of the nineteenth century.

4-12 Cumming, John, comp. A PRELIMINARY CHECKLIST OF 19TH CENTURY LITHOGRAPHS OF MICHIGAN CITIES AND TOWNS. Mount Pleasant: Central Michigan University, Clarke Historical Library, 1969. vi, 24 p. Paper.

After reviewing the development of bird's-eye and panoramic views in Michigan, Cumming lists 160 views of approximately one hundred Michigan communities.

4-13 Hebert, John R. PANORAMIC MAPS OF ANGLO-AMERICAN CITIES: A CHECKLIST CF MAPS IN THE COLLECTIONS OF THE LIBRARY OF CONGRESS, GEOGRAPHY AND MAP DIVISION. Washington, D.C.: Library of Congress, 1974. v, 118 p. Paper. Maps, illus., index.

Entries which list the name of the city, date, artist, publisher, printer, and dimensions are provided for 1,117 panoramic maps, primarily of U.S. cities. The introductory essay reviews the panoramic map industry in the United States and highlights some of the more prominent firms in the business. A preview of this work appeared as "Panoramic Maps of American Cities," SPECIAL LIBRARIES 63 (December 1972): 554-62.

4-14 Maule, Elizabeth Singer. BIRD'S EYE VIEWS OF WISCONSIN COMMUNITIES: A PRELIMINARY CHECKLIST. Madison: State Historical Society of Wisconsin, 1977. 76 p. Paper.

Maule lists 193 panoramic or bird's-eye views of Wisconsin cities and towns. The depositories of known copies are listed. Most are available at the State Historical Society of Wisconsin or the Library of Congress.

4-15 Reps, John W. CITIES ON STONE: NINETEENTH CENTURY LITHOGRAPH IMAGES OF THE URBAN WEST. Fort Worth, Tex.: Amon Carter Museum of Western Art, 1976. 99 p. Maps, notes, bibliog.

Although originally intended as an exhibit catalog of bird's-eye and panoramic views of western cities, Reps's introductory essay is considered the standard text on the historical origins and production of bird's-eye city views. Reps also evaluates the accuracy of these pictorial views as historical documents. In addition to the 143 views that are exhibited, the catalog also includes color reproductions of fifty-one city views.

4-16 Warren, James R., Sr. "Thaddeus Mortimer Fowler, Bird's-Eye-View Artist." Special Libraries Association Geography and Map Division. BULLETIN, no. 120, June 1980, pp. 27-35. Notes.

A brief biography of T.M. Fowler, one of the major producers of bird's-eye views from 1869 to 1922, is presented in addition to a list of maps drawn or published by Fowler.

C. CITY MAPS AND PLANS

4-17 Ehrenberg, Ralph E. "Mapping the Nation's Capital: The Surveyor's Office, 1791-1818." QUARTERLY JOURNAL OF THE LIBRARY OF CONGRESS 36 (Summer 1979): 279-319. Maps, diagrs., notes.

Ehrenberg reviews the early cartographic history of Washington, D.C., from surviving documents in the Library of Congress and the National Archives. The cartographic products of these planning, surveying, and mapping activities were prepared by the personnel of the Surveyor's Office which included Pierre L'Enfant, Andrew Ellicott, James Dermott, Nicholas and Robert King, and Benjamin Latrobe. See also Herman R. Friis and Ehrenberg, "Nicholas King and His Wharfing Plans of the City of Washington, 1797," RECORDS OF THE COLUMBIA HISTORICAL SOCIETY, 1966-68 (Washington, D.C.: 1969): 34-46; and Ehrenberg, "Nicholas King: First Surveyor of the City of Washington, 1803-1812," RECORDS OF THE COLUMBIA HISTORICAL SOCIETY, 1969-70 (Washington, D.C.: 1971): 31-65.

4-18 _____, comp. CARTOGRAPHIC RECORDS IN THE NATIONAL ARCHIVES OF THE UNITED STATES USEFUL FOR URBAN STUDIES. Reference Information Paper, No. 68. Washington, D.C.: National Archives and Records Service, 1973. vii, 14 p. Paper. Notes.

Various series of maps which are useful for historic urban studies are surveyed in this paper. These series include city and town-site plans, census enumeration district maps and descriptions, real property surveys, and aerial photographs.

4-19 Gutheim, Frederick, and Washburn, Wilcomb E. THE FEDERAL CITY: PLANS AND REALITIES. Washington, D.C.: Smithsonian Institution Press, 1976. xvi, 170 p. Paper. Maps, illus., photos., bibliog., index.

Prepared as a catalog for an exhibit that was sponsored by the Smithsonian Institution in cooperation with the National Capital Planning Commission and the Commission of Fine Arts, this publication focuses on the planning and physical development of Washington, D.C., and particularly its monumental core. The catalog is well-illustrated with reproductions of maps, drawings, still and aerial photographs, and three-dimensional models that were included in the exhibit.

4-20 Harlow, Neal. MAPS AND SURVEYS OF THE PUEBLO LANDS OF LOS ANGELES. Los Angeles: Dawson's Book Shop, 1976. xvii, 169 p. Maps, notes, bibliog., index.

Fourteen facsimile reproductions of maps and surveys of the pueblo lands of Los Angeles, dated from 1781-1881, provide the basis for tracing the legal growth of the town from its original organization through the final adjudication providing legitimate title to the city's land. See also William W. Robinson, MAPS OF LOS ANGELES FROM ORD'S SURVEY OF 1849 TO THE END OF THE BOOM OF THE EIGHTIES (Los Angeles: Dawson's Book Shop, 1966), which provides a catalog of 127 maps of Los Angeles and vicinity, dating from 1849 to 1888. Twenty-seven of these are reproduced as facsimiles. The narrative in both books is well-documented, while the map descriptions include the repositories of the respective maps.

4-21 _____ . THE MAPS OF SAN FRANCISCO BAY FROM THE SPANISH DISCOVERY IN 1769 TO THE AMERICAN OCCUPATION. [San Francisco]: Book Club of California, 1950. xii, 140 p. Maps, notes, bibliog.

Facsimile reproductions and catalog descriptions of thirty-nine maps of San Francisco Bay area are included in this limited edition. The maps, which do not include disenos of the ranchos in this area, are dated from 1769 to 1847.

4-22 Koerner, Alberta G. Auringer, comp. DETROIT AND VICINITY BEFORE 1900: AN ANNOTATED LIST OF MAPS. Washington, D.C.: Library of Congress, 1968. vi, 84 p. Paper. Maps, index.

Bibliographical entries with descriptive notes are provided for 237 maps and atlases pertaining to Detroit and vicinity. The original or photocopies of most of these maps are in the Library of Congress.

4-23 McCauley, Lois B. MARYLAND HISTORICAL PRINTS, 1752 TO 1889. Baltimore: Maryland Historical Society, 1975. xvi, 259 p. Maps, illus., notes, bibliog., index.

Lithographs and engravings printed between 1752 and 1889 provide a visual documentary of Baltimore and other Maryland communities in this well-illustrated publication. This cartographic and pictorial record is discussed in terms of three groupings: views of Maryland (maps, panoramic views, and landscape scenes); landmarks in Maryland (views of buildings and architectural drawings); and events in Maryland (views of people, historic events, and military activities). Also included is a listing of Maryland printmakers, along with a brief biography of each. The work of one of these firms is illustrated in an exhibit catalog prepared by McCauley, A. HOEN ON STONE: LITHOGRAPHS OF E. WEBER & CO., AND A. HOEN & CO., BALTIMORE, 1835-1969 (Baltimore: Maryland Historical Society, 1969). This firm was a major publisher of federal government maps and landscape scenes, particularly those appearing in the Congressional Serial Set. See entries 2-28, 6-15, and 7-13.

4-24 Reps, John W. CITIES OF THE AMERICAN WEST: A HISTORY OF FRONTIER URBAN PLANNING. Princeton: Princeton University Press, 1979. xiii, 827 p. Maps, illus., photos., bibliog., index.

In Reps's most recent volume on the history of urban planning, the primary focus (as in the earlier works) is the planning of the physical pattern of the towns in terms of street orientation, block size, and public reservations. The regional emphasis in this volume is the trans-Mississippi West until the end of the nineteenth century. Over five hundred reproductions consisting of maps, plans, plats, bird's-eye views, and landscape scenes are used to illustrate this volume. Similar studies by Reps which not only pertain to the history of urban planning but also serve as a guide to numerous historical urban plans started with THE MAKING OF URBAN AMERICA, A HISTORY OF CITY PLANNING (Princeton: Princeton University Press, 1965), which was reprinted in an abridged paperback format as TOWN PLANNING IN FRONTIER AMERICA (Princeton: Princeton University Press, 1969). Studies of a more regional nature include MONUMENTAL WASHINGTON: THE PLANNING AND DEVELOPMENT OF THE CAPITAL CENTER (Princeton: Princeton University Press, 1967); and TIDEWATER TOWNS: CITY PLANNING IN COLONIAL VIRGINIA AND MARYLAND (Charlottesville: University Press of Virginia for Colonial Williamsburg Foundation, 1972). Another article by Reps appears in entry 12-6.

4-25 Snyder, Martin P. CITY OF INDEPENDENCE: VIEWS OF PHILADELPHIA BEFORE 1800. New York: Praeger Publishers, 1975. 304 p. Maps, illus., notes, index.

The graphic sources (maps, architectural drawings, and landscape scenes) documenting Philadelphia's growth and physical appearance from 1680 to 1800 are reproduced (195 figures, some in color) and discussed.

4-26 Stephenson, Richard W. "The Delineation of a Grand Plan." QUARTERLY JOURNAL OF THE LIBRARY OF CONGRESS 36 (Summer 1979): 207-24. Maps, notes.

Stephenson reviews the provenance of Pierre Charles L'Enfant's original manuscript plan of Washington, D.C., in terms of its creation in the early 1790s, its subsequent disposition during the nineteenth and twentieth centuries, and its current restoration by the Library of Congress.

4-27 Thomas, Samuel W., ed. VIEWS OF LOUISVILLE SINCE 1766. Louisville, Ky.: Courier-Journal Lithographing Co., 1971. Maps, illus., photos., notes, index.

Primarily a pictorial history of Louisville, this well-illustrated book includes numerous nineteenth-century maps and panoramic views of the city.

D. WARD MAPS AND DIRECTORIES

4-28 Conzen, Michael P. "State Business Directories in Historical and Geographical Research." HISTORICAL GEOGRAPHY NEWSLETTER 2 (Fall 1972): 1-14. Map, diagrs., table, notes.

> State business directories are reviewed in terms of their content, publishing history, accuracy, and research potential. These directories, which were published primarily during the second half of the nineteenth century, usually contained a gazetteer providing a geographical listing of businesses and a classified business section listing businesses by functional categories.

4-29 Kirkham, E. Kay. A HANDY GUIDE TO RECORD-SEARCHING IN THE LARGER CITIES OF THE UNITED STATES. Logan, Utah: Everton Publishers, 1974. vi, 137 p.

> Entries for over three hundred of the largest cities in the United States list city directories available in the Library of Congress and the Genealogical Society Library, city newspapers, genealogical libraries, sources of vital statistics (birth, death, and marriage records), and the first federal census for each city. Also included are reproductions of thirty-eight maps with ward boundaries and street indexes. See also Kirkham, "A Selected Bibliography of Available Maps and Cities' Directories of Some of the Larger Cities of the U.S.," in RESEARCH IN AMERICAN GENEALOGY (Salt Lake City: Deseret Book Company, 1956), pp. 96-107.

4-30 Knights, Peter R. "City Directories as Aids to Ante-Bellum Urban Studies: A Research Note." HISTORICAL METHODS NEWSLETTER 2 (September 1969): 1-10. Tables, notes.

> In reviewing Boston's city directories for the 1830-60 period, Knights makes some general comments about the compilation, contents, biases, and research potential of city directories.

4-31 LeFurgy, William G. "Baltimore's Wards, 1797-1978: A Guide." MARYLAND HISTORICAL MAGAZINE 75 (June 1980): 145-53. Notes.

> After describing the function of wards, LeFurgy provides a chronology of Baltimore's ward changes with references to pertinent laws and a list of extant maps which show Baltimore's wards.

4-32 Shelley, Michael H., comp. WARD MAPS OF UNITED STATES CITIES: A SELECTIVE CHECKLIST OF PRE-1900 MAPS IN THE LIBRARY OF CONGRESS. Washington, D.C.: Library of Congress, 1975. v, 24 p. Paper.

> Included in this checklist are selected nineteenth-century ward maps for the twenty-five most populous cities (according to the 1880 census) as well as for ten other cities often researched by

demographers and genealogists. These maps provide a graphic
index to nineteenth-century federal and state censuses which
are usually arranged by ward. Each entry lists the date the
map was published as well as the census year for which the
ward boundaries are valid.

4-33 Spear, Dorothea N. BIBLIOGRAPHY OF AMERICAN DIRECTORIES
THROUGH 1860. Worcester, Mass.: American Antiquarian Society, 1961.
Reprint. Westport, Conn.: Greenwood Press, 1978. 389 p.

The 1,647 entries primarily describe city directories, although
some county directories are included. The entries include title,
annotations as to contents (maps, advertisements, illustrations),
and repositories holding individual volumes. Most of the directories are available in the American Antiquarian Society.

4-34 Weinberg, Allen, and Fields, Dale, comps. WARD GENEALOGY OF THE
CITY AND COUNTY OF PHILADELPHIA. [Philadelphia]: Department of
Records, [1958]. 42 p. Paper. Maps.

Philadelphia's ward boundary changes between 1705 and 1958
are depicted on thirty-three maps. Streets within the individual
wards are not shown, although those streets which served as
ward boundaries are indicated. This booklet was republished
as GENEALOGY OF PHILADELPHIA COUNTY SUBDIVISIONS,
compiled by John Daly and Allen Weinberg, [2d ed.], Philadelphia: Department of Records, [1966].

Chapter 5

HISTORICAL ATLASES

The atlases listed in this chapter are secondary or retrospective compilations based on current research which reconstructs past geographical patterns. Atlases and maps showing changing political boundaries (state, county, minor civil division, or congressional district) are emphasized. These atlases serve not only as a reference aid for general audiences but also as research tools for further historical-geographical studies. Historical or retrospective atlases that were published before 1967 are listed in entries 1-30 and 1-31. This chapter provides separate listings for atlases pertaining to the entire nation and for those atlases pertaining to individual states.

A. BIBLIOGRAPHIES

5-1 Cappon, Lester J. "The Historical Map in American Atlases." AAG AN-NALS 69 (December 1979): 622-34. Notes.

Cappon traces the development of the historical map in American atlases by reviewing the creation and contents of various histori-cal atlases which have been published since the last quarter of the nineteenth century. Three of these atlases, described elsewhere in this chapter, are William R. Shepherd's HISTORICAL ATLAS (entry 5-27), Charles O. Paullin and John K. Wright's ATLAS OF THE HISTORICAL GEOGRAPHY OF THE UNITED STATES (entry 5-24), and THE ATLAS OF EARLY AMERICAN HISTORY: THE REVOLUTIONARY ERA, 1760-90 (entry 5-6).

5-2 Stephenson, Richard W. "Atlases of the Western Hemisphere: A Summary Survey." GEOGRAPHICAL REVIEW 62 (January 1972): 92-119. Notes.

Stephenson provides summary reviews of 147 atlases pertaining to the Western Hemisphere which were published from 1962 to 1971. There are numerous references to United States and Canadian atlases as well as to state and provincial atlases, in-cluding thirteen historical atlases and ten with historical sections.

This work supplements Ena L. Yonge's review of pre-1962 atlases, "Regional Atlases: A Summary Review," GEOGRAPHICAL RE- VIEW 52 (1962): 429-31, which includes six historical atlases. Each of the historical atlases mentioned in these two articles is listed separately in the following section of this bibliography as well as historical atlases and state atlases with historical sections published since 1972. Fifty-five state and provincial thematic atlases (including several with historical sections) are reviewed in Richard W. Stephenson and Mary Galneder's "Anglo-American State and Provincial Thematic Atlases: A Survey and Bibliography," CANADIAN CARTOGRAPHER 6 (June 1969): 15-45.

B. NATIONAL ATLASES

5-3   Andriot, John L. TOWNSHIP ATLAS OF THE UNITED STATES. McLean, Va.: Andriot Associates, 1979. xxxix, 1,184 p. Maps, index.

The current minor civil divisions of all fifty of the United States are mapped and indexed in this volume. The maps portray minor civil divisions and/or census county divisions, urbanized areas, and public land survey townships. This edition replaces an earlier work by Andriot, TOWNSHIP ATLAS OF THE UNITED STATES: NAMED TOWNSHIPS (McLean, Va.: Andriot Associates, 1977), which mapped and indexed the minor civil divisions for the twenty-two states with named townships. Although both publi- cations are based on 1970 Bureau of the Census state maps which show minor civil divisions, the Bureau of the Census has also published similar maps for each state for each census year since 1930. Copies of these maps are available among the cartographic records of the Bureau of the Census (Record Group 29) in the National Archives.

5-4   Bennett, Sari, and Earle, Carville. THE GEOGRAPHY OF AMERICAN LABOR AND INDUSTRIALIZATION, 1865-1908: AN ATLAS. GALI Working Paper, No. 2. Catonsville: University of Maryland, Baltimore County, Department of Geography, 1980. xiii, 82 p. Maps.

Forty color maps illustrate the geography of labor activity in the northeastern United States during the late nineteenth and early twentieth centuries. Topics include strike frequency and success rate, diffusion of strike activity, spatial patterns of skilled and unskilled wages, and growth of union membership.

5-5   Birdsall, Stephen S., and Florin, John W. A SERIES OF COUNTY OUT- LINE MAPS OF THE SOUTHEASTERN UNITED STATES FOR THE PERIOD, 1790-1860. Map Study, No. 2. Chapel Hill: University of North Caro- lina, Department of Geography, 1973. Folio, 8 maps. Book, 27 p. Paper.

Eight maps depict the changing county boundaries in the southeastern United States (including Maryland, West Virginia, Kentucky, Missouri, Arkansas, and Texas) from 1790 to 1860. Since these maps are fairly general, they are not intended to provide precise information about specific boundary changes. Rather, these maps will be most useful for historical geographers plotting statistical data at decennial intervals.

5-6 Cappon, Lester J.; Petchenik, Barbara Bartz; and Long, John H., eds. ATLAS OF EARLY AMERICAN HISTORY: THE REVOLUTIONARY ERA, 1760-1790. Princeton, N.J.: Published for the Newberry Library and the Institute of Early American History and Culture by Princeton University Press, 1976. xvi, 157 p. Maps, notes, index.

Compiled by a staff of nine historians and cartographers, this atlas is composed of seventy-four pages of maps which depict the revolutionary war period from 1760 to 1790. The remainder of the volume is devoted to text which explains the content, rationale, and sources for the individual maps. Besides general reference maps which show county boundaries, towns, and roads in the American colonies in 1775, other maps depict city plans, population and cultural activities before the war and in 1790, economic activities, British administration, military activities associated with the war, and post-war conditions including the Confederation and settlement of the West. The original proposal and goals for the atlas were presented by the editor-in-chief, Lester J. Cappon, in "The Case for a New Historical Atlas of Early America," WILLIAM AND MARY QUARTERLY, 3d ser., 28 (1971): 121-27. Cappon also reviewed the atlas, as well as earlier historical atlases, when comparing the relation of geography and cartography with history in "Cartography and History: The Atlas of Early American History as a Case Study," Special Libraries Association Geography and Map Division, BULLETIN, no. 94, December 1973, pp. 9-19. The cartographic editor, Barbara Bartz Petchenik, discussed the experiences and problems encountered in developing this atlas in "Cartography and the Making of an Historical Atlas: A Memoir," AMERICAN CARTOGRAPHER 4 (April 1977): 11-28 and "Atlas of Early American History Review," AMERICAN CARTOGRAPHER 5 (April 1978): 70-72.

5-7 Cole, Donald B. ATLAS OF AMERICAN HISTORY. Boston: Ginn and Company, 1967. viii, 151 p. Paper. Maps, diagrs., index.

Historical maps with accompanying text illustrate major geographical themes in the history of the United States in this atlas.

5-8 Darby, H.C., and Fullard, Harold, eds. THE NEW CAMBRIDGE MODERN HISTORY. VOLUME XIV, ATLAS. London: Cambridge University Press, 1970. xxiv, 319 p. Maps, index, bibliog.

Designed to meet the needs of the readers of the NEW CAM-

BRIDGE MODERN HISTORY, this historical atlas pertains primarily to Europe, but also includes sections on North America,
Latin America, Africa, the Far East, and Australasia. The North
American section treats the broad outlines of the political,
military, demographic and economic history of the United States.

5-9 Esposito, Vincent J., ed. THE WEST POINT ATLAS OF AMERICAN WARS.
2 vols. 1959. Reprint. New York: Frederick A. Praeger, 1978. [774 p.]
Maps, bibliog.

Compiled by the Department of Military Art and Engineering,
U.S. Military Academy, West Point, this atlas portrays the
details of the significant battles in American history. The first
volume, which covers the time period 1689 to 1900, consists of
158 maps pertaining primarily to the Civil War but also including the revolutionary war, War of 1812, Mexican War, and Span-
ish-American War. The second volume, which spans the period
1900 to 1953, contains 71 maps of World War I, 170 maps of
World War II, and 15 maps of the Korean conflict. The maps,
many of which depict daily or hourly movements, are accompanied by a page of text explaining the particular situation
that is depicted.

5-10 Fox, Edward W., ed. ATLAS OF AMERICAN HISTORY. New York: Oxford University Press, 1964. xvi, 48 p. Maps, gazetteer.

The major political, military, and demographic themes of U.S.
history are portrayed in this atlas. Most of these maps were prepared on a physical base in order to emphasize the geographical
environment of the historical events.

5-11 Friis, Herman R. "A Series of Population Maps of the Colonies and the
United States, 1625-1790." Mimeographed and Offset Publication, No. 3.
Rev. ed. New York: American Geographical Society, 1968. 65 p.
Maps, diagrs., table, notes.

The changing population distribution of the Atlantic Seaboard
from 1625 to 1790 is depicted in ten population dot maps reconstructed by Friis. In the accompanying text and footnotes,
he describes and evaluates the pertinent census and cartographic
sources for plotting colonial population distributions. He also
reviews settlement in terms of migration routes and rural and
urban settlement patterns. Originally published under the same
title in GEOGRAPHICAL REVIEW 30 (July 1940): 463-70, this
version has been revised primarily to update footnote references.

5-12 Gaustad, Edwin S. HISTORICAL ATLAS OF RELIGION IN AMERICA. 1962.
Rev. ed. New York: Harper and Row, 1976. xiv, 189 p. Maps, diagrs.,
notes, index.

The religious history of the United States is represented geographically and statistically by utilizing 132 maps and graphs. The maps show the distribution of churches for individual denominations in 1750 and the distribution of denominational membership in 1850 and 1950. The graphs show the growth of denominational membership during the colonial period and from 1800 to 1975.

5-13 Gilbert, Martin. AMERICAN HISTORY ATLAS. London: Weidenfeld and Nicholson, 1968; New York: Macmillan, 1969. 119 p. Maps.

This small atlas provides a visual guide to American history employing 112 black and white maps, each with a two or three sentence description. The maps portray various topics ranging from Indian origins and distributions to black-white relations in the 1950s and 1960s. Several themes that are repeated at various intervals include exploration, military activities, transportation networks, and social and political issues.

5-14 Hammond, Inc. MAN AND HISTORY. Maplewood, N.J.: 1971. 192 p. Maps, diagrs., tables, index.

This unique reference tool combines a chronological listing of dates and events with historical maps. Although the coverage is worldwide, approximately half of the book (62 pages) is devoted to the history of the United States.

5-15 _____. UNITED STATES HISTORY ATLAS. Maplewood, N.J.: 1977. 64 p. Paper. Maps, diagrs., index.

This atlas illustrates various topics (exploration, population and settlement, military activities, boundaries, electoral votes, economic and social patterns, and natural resources) in the history of the United States.

5-16 Historical Records Survey. New York (City). THE ATLAS OF CONGRESSIONAL ROLL CALLS. Vol. 1: THE CONTINENTAL CONGRESSES AND THE CONGRESSES OF THE CONFEDERATION, 1777-1789. Ed. by Clifford L. Lord. Cooperstown, N.Y.: New York State Historical Association, 1943. ix, [310] p. Maps, notes, bibliog., index.

Compiled as a project of the New York and New Jersey Historical Records Surveys' staffs, this atlas was the first and only volume in a contemplated series of forty-two volumes which would map all the yea-nay roll-call votes in Congress from 1777 to 1937, representing many of the controversial issues before the various Congresses. Although this volume pertains only to the Continental and Confederation Congresses, the manuscript maps prepared for later Congresses are in the National Archives among the records of the Work Projects Administration (Record Group 69) in the Center for Cartographic and Architectural Archives. These manuscript materials also include maps depicting state and county boundaries which were used to compile the congressional district boundaries. Among the bibliographical entries in this introductory volume are citations to secondary works on county boundaries.

5-17 Jackson, Kenneth T., and Adams, James Truslow, eds. ATLAS OF AMERICAN HISTORY. 1943. Rev. ed. New York: Charles Scribner's Sons, 1978. xv, 294 p. Maps, index.

This revised edition adds 51 new maps to the original 147 maps. The original maps emphasized frontier topics including exploration and settlement, American Revolution and Civil War battles, boundary disputes, and American Indians. The new maps concentrate on twentieth-century developments, especially demographic, social, and economic patterns and the worldwide involvement of the United States. Although there are no footnotes or narrative, the original maps were noted for their accurate scholarship since they were compiled under the direction of sixty-four historians.

5-18 Kagan, Hilde Heun, et al. AMERICAN HERITAGE PICTORIAL ATLAS OF UNITED STATES HISTORY. New York: American Heritage Publishing Co., 1966. 424 p. Maps, illus., index.

A wide range of topics in U.S. history are illustrated in this atlas, including Indian cultures and land cessions, exploration and territorial explansion, military operations, foreign involvements, population density, ethnicity, religion, voting patterns, agriculture, industry, natural resources, and transportation. The 210 maps, which are supplemented by extensive narrative, but no footnotes, include numerous reproductions of contemporary maps. However, the majority are modern reconstructions published in color. A special feature is four portfolios of panoramic views of revolutionary and Civil War battles, nineteenth-century cities, and U.S. National Parks.

5-19 Kirkham, E. Kay. A GENEALOGICAL AND HISTORICAL ATLAS OF THE UNITED STATES OF AMERICA. Logan, Utah: Everton Publishers, 1976. xi, 328 p. Maps, bibliog., index.

Prepared as an aid for genealogical research, the primary emphasis is changing state and county boundaries which are depicted on reproductions of state maps from ten atlases dated 1804 to 1909. There is also an 1886 place name index with entries arranged alphabetically under state.

5-20 Long, John H. "Historical Boundary Data File." MAPLINE, Special No. 3 (April 1979), 6 p.

This short article describes the background and status of the Historical Boundary Data File Project, which is being sponsored by the Newberry Library and funded by the National Endowment for the Humanities. The purpose of this project is to map all the changes in the boundaries, seats of government, and relevant geographic names of the territories, states, and counties of the United States since 1788, by using a combination of traditional historical research and computer cartography. At the time of publication of this article, the research and appropriate maps for Pennsylvania, Maryland, New Jersey, and Delaware were completed, while those for Ohio, Indiana, Illinois, Michigan, and Wisconsin were in progress. Similar research is proposed for Missouri, Iowa, Minnesota, Kansas, Nebraska, South Dakota, and North Dakota. This project is also described in "U.S. Historical County Boundary Data File," JOURNAL OF HISTORICAL GEOGRAPHY 2 (July 1976): 206.

5-21 Lord, Clifford Lee, and Lord, Elizabeth H. HISTORICAL ATLAS OF THE UNITED STATES. 1944. Rev. ed. New York: Henry Holt and Co., 1953. Reprint. New York: Johnson Reprint Corp., 1972. xv, 238 p. Maps, tables, index.

Lords's atlas differs significantly from other atlases produced by the major map publishers. The 312 maps, many of which were selected from federal government publications and other secondary sources, are not accompanied by an explanation. Besides the usual themes of military activities and population densities and characteristics, other themes covered which are not normally found in other atlases include political topics (boundary disputes, voting patterns, and district and federal court boundaries), economic patterns (agriculture, industry, and transportation), and social issues (abolition, prohibition, education, and child labor).

5-22 Miller, Theordore R. GRAPHIC HISTORY OF THE AMERICAS. New York: John Wiley, 1969. viii, 61 p. Paper. Maps.

Although the major emphasis of this atlas is the political, military, economic, and cultural history of the United States, it does include sixteen maps of the Americas, placing U.S. developments in the context of the entire Western Hemisphere. There are also several maps of Western Europe and the Pacific Basin reflecting the U.S. involvement in those areas during World Wars I and II. These black and white maps show considerable historical and geographical detail, but there is little narrative and no indication of sources.

5-23 Parson, Stanley B., et al. UNITED STATES CONGRESSIONAL DISTRICTS, 1788-1841. Westport, Conn.: Greenwood Press, 1978. xvi, 416 p. Maps, bibliog., index.

The boundaries of individual congressional districts and the counties encompassed therein for the early national period, 1788-1841, are depicted in this atlas. There is a single map for each state for the first two congresses as well as for the subsequent redistricting during each of the succeeding decades from 1792 to 1841. Each map is accompanied by a list which includes name, address, and dates of service of the respective representatives; the county composition of each district; and the total population, slave population, area, and density of each county founded between 1788 and 1841, while the bibliography lists the statutes which define the composition of each state's congressional district. This atlas is designed to be used with the congressional roll-call data which is available from the Inter-University Consortium for Social and Political Research (ICPSR), Ann Arbor, Michigan (see entry 6-33).

5-24 Paullin, Charles O., and Wright, John K. ATLAS OF THE HISTORICAL GEOGRAPHY OF THE UNITED STATES. Washington, D.C.: Carnegie Institution; New York: American Geographical Society, 1932. Reprint. Westport, Conn.: Greenwood Press, 1975. xv, 162 p. 166 map plates. Tables, notes, index.

This was the first major historical atlas of the United States and remains the standard for evaluating others published since. In addition to facsimile reproductions of maps representing early cartography, exploration, land surveys, and city plans, the major topics covered by reconstructed maps include Indians, land disposal and survey, evolution of territorial and state boundaries, international and state boundary disputes, population and settlements, politics and reforms, economic patterns (agriculture, manufacturing, transportation, and trade), and military history. The accompanying text provides a critical evaluation of the sources of information on which the maps are based. All the maps are reproduced in black and white in the reprint edition, although the color maps are reproduced on color microfiche.

5-25 Rand McNally. THESE UNITED STATES: ATLAS OF AMERICAN HISTORY. Chicago: 1974. 64 p. Maps, illus., diagrs., tables, index.

This atlas includes the usual topics of exploration, military activities, territorial expansion, transportation, and twentieth-century foreign involvement.

5-26 Sale, Randall D., and Karn, Edwin D. AMERICAN EXPANSION: A BOOK OF MAPS. Homewood, Ill.: Dorsey Press, 1962. Reprint. Lincoln: University of Nebraska Press, 1979. ii, 28 p. Paper. Maps.

Twelve maps, one for each decade between 1790 and 1900, depict the advance of the settlement frontier as indicated by population density and the longevity of land offices. The maps also show changing state and territorial boundaries, explorers' routes, and major trails, roads, and railroads.

5-27 Shepherd, William R. SHEPHERD'S HISTORICAL ATLAS. 9th ed. New York: Barnes and Noble, 1964, reprinted with revisions, 1976. xii, 226 map plates, 115 p. Maps, index.

Primarily a world historical atlas, this classic atlas first published in 1911 includes twenty-four plates pertaining to U.S. history.

5-28 U.S. Geological Survey. THE NATIONAL ATLAS OF THE UNITED STATES OF AMERICA. Edited by Arch C. Gerlach. Washington, D.C.: 1970. xiii, 417 p. Maps, diagrs., tables, index.

The twenty-three page historical section in this national atlas includes maps pertaining to Indian distributions, exploration and settlement, territorial growth, battle and historic sites, and presidential election results. Also included are a series of maps by Herman R. Friis depicting nineteenth- and twentieth-century world geographic expeditions and polar regions exploration. Sources for most historical maps are indicated.

5-29 Van Zandt, Franklin K. BOUNDARIES OF THE UNITED STATES AND THE SEVERAL STATES. Geological Survey Professional Paper 909. Washington, D.C.: Government Printing Office, 1976. ix, 191 p. Paper. Maps, photos., notes, bibliog., index.

This professional paper, which is based on several earlier Geological Survey Bulletins, outlines the historical development of the international boundaries of the United States, as well as the boundaries of the individual states. In describing these boundaries, reference is made to the treaty, statute, and/or survey relating to the individual boundaries. Numerous maps depict many of the significant boundary changes.

5-30 Wesley, Edgar B. OUR UNITED STATES: ITS HISTORY IN MAPS. 3d ed. Chicago: Denoyer-Geppert, 1965. 96 p. Paper. Maps, index.

The history of the United States from discovery and early exploration through twentieth-century involvement overseas is depicted on forty-two color maps. Each of these maps, which are adapted from the publisher's wall map series, is accompanied by a page of text explaining the historical events depicted on the respective map.

C. INDIVIDUAL STATE ATLASES

5-31 Abbott, Newton Carl, and Carver, Fred E. THE EVOLUTION OF WASH-INGTON COUNTIES. Compiled by J.W. Helm. Yakima, Wash.: Published jointly by Yakima Valley Genealogical Society and Klickitat County Historical Society, 1978. 169 p. Paper. Maps, notes, index.

Based on Abbott's 1927 master's thesis, this revised and expanded work traces the changes in the county boundaries in the territory and state of Washington during the nineteenth and early twentieth century through the use of approximately fifty maps. An appendix provides the text of the laws creating the counties and defining their boundaries.

5-32 Arbingast, Stanley A., et al. ATLAS OF TEXAS. 5th ed. Austin: University of Texas, Bureau of Business Research, 1976. Paper. xii, 179 p. Maps, photos., illus., tables.

Although the emphasis of this atlas is on current physical, demographic, and economic patterns, this edition does include a new section on culture and history. This section, which is based primarily on work by Terry G. Jordan, includes maps showing population and culture origins and distributions, voting patterns, land surveys, military activities, and exploration and transportation routes.

5-33 Beck, Warren A., and Haase, Ynez D. HISTORICAL ATLAS OF CALIFORNIA. Norman: University of Oklahoma Press, 1974. viii, 227 p. Maps, notes, index.

A historian and cartographer collaborated to produce 101 maps of California's history and geography from the Indian era to the present. The subjects portrayed include physical characteristics; Spanish and Mexican exploration and settlement; Mexican land grants on a county level; Anglo-American exploration, military activities, and settlement; changing state and county boundaries; and various twentieth-century topics such as agriculture, mineral and forest resources, and natural disasters.

5-34 _____. HISTORICAL ATLAS OF NEW MEXICO. Norman: University of Oklahoma Press, 1969. 145 p. Maps, notes, index.

Sixty-two maps depict various aspects of New Mexico's history and geography including physical characteristics and mineral resources, Indian lands and settlements, Spanish and Mexican exploration and settlement, changing territorial and county boundaries, nineteenth-century military activities, and principal towns, trails, and roads at selected intervals during the nineteenth and twentieth centuries. Each map is accompanied by a page of text explaining the map.

5-35 Bryant, Pat, comp. GEORGIA COUNTIES: THEIR CHANGING BOUNDARIES. Atlanta: State Printing Office, 1977. xiv, 162 p. Paper. Maps, notes.

Besides discussing the general development of Georgia's counties, Bryant provides a chronological listing of the counties by date of creation and an alphabetical listing of counties indicating the various dates of boundary changes, as well as references to the respective laws. This publication also includes nineteen maps prepared by Borden Dent, Georgia State University, which show county boundaries at ten-year intervals from 1790 to 1970.

5-36 Colorado Water Conservation Board. BASIC MAPS OF COLORADO AND HISTORY OF CHANGES IN COUNTY BOUNDARIES. Denver: 1939. 16 p. Paper. Maps.

Eight maps depict Colorado's changing county boundaries between 1876 and 1930.

5-37 Corbitt, David L. FORMATION OF NORTH CAROLINA COUNTIES, 1663-1943. 2d ed. Raleigh: North Carolina State Department of Archives and History, 1969. xxix, 323 p. Maps, index.

Twelve maps show North Carolina's changing county boundaries from 1700 to 1912. In addition, an alphabetical listing of the counties includes the derivation of the name, date of formation, description of boundaries, and references to the pertinent laws for each county.

5-38 Dexter, Lincoln A., comp. MAPS OF EARLY MASSACHUSETTS: PRE-HISTORY THROUGH THE SEVENTEENTH CENTURY. Wilbraham, Mass.: Dexter, 1979. Paper. vii, 116 p. Maps, illus., notes, bibliog., index.

Reconstructed maps pertaining to the early history of Massachusetts are grouped under five topics: geology, archaeology, seventeenth-century Indian tribes, sixteenth and seventeenth-century exploration, and seventeenth-century settlements. Each section has a selected bibliography of secondary sources.

5-39 Dodd, Donald B., and Dent, Borden. HISTORICAL ATLAS OF ALABAMA. University: University of Alabama Press, 1974. xiii, 160 p. Maps, index.

Alabama's history is portrayed in this atlas by means of coordinated maps and text. The initial chapters depict pre-statehood exploration and settlement; military sites and activity in the Creek and Indian Wars (1813-14) and the Civil War; and county boundary changes (1819-1974). The remaining chapters, which are arranged by chronological periods (antebellum, Civil War, Reconstruction, early twentieth century, Depression, and post-World War II), show various thematic distributions (total population, black population, urbanization, transportation, industry, education, personal wealth, cotton production, and selected election results).

5-40 Donley, Michael W., et al. ATLAS OF CALIFORNIA. Culver City, Calif.: Pacific Book Center, 1979. v, 191 p. Maps, diagrs., tables, index.

The maps in this attractive, colorful state atlas are divided into
four sections: the human imprint, economic patterns, physical
environment, and reference. The first grouping, which pertains
to cultural and historical geography, includes approximately thirty
maps of historical interest: Indian distributions, missions, Mexican land grants, mining, evolution of county boundaries, urban
development particularly in the Los Angeles and San Francisco
areas, population growth and density, immigration and ethnic
groups, and voting patterns. Some of the maps are based on
those found in Beck and Haase's atlas (see entry 5-33), while
the remainder represent new topics.

5-41 Durrenberger, Robert W. PATTERNS ON THE LAND: GEOGRAPHICAL,
HISTORICAL AND POLITICAL MAPS OF CALIFORNIA. 4th ed. Palo
Alto, Calif.: National Press Books, 1972. vi, 102 p. Paper. Maps,
illus., photos., diagrs., tables, index.

Devoted primarily to current geographical patterns (physical,
demographic, resource utilization, economic), this attractive
state atlas does have a twenty-four page historical section focusing on exploration and Indian, Spanish, Mexican, and American settlements.

5-42 Farmer, Judith A., and Holmes, Kenneth L. AN HISTORICAL ATLAS OF
EARLY OREGON. Portland, Oreg.: Historical Cartographic Publications,
1973. 63 p. Maps, bibliog., index.

Twenty-two color maps, each with accompanying text, reconstruct Oregon's early history prior to 1850. The maps are
grouped in four categories: Indians; early exploration; maritime
fur trade and exploration; and overland exploration, fur trade,
and settlement.

5-43 Hale, John S. A HISTORICAL ATLAS OF COLONIAL VIRGINIA. [Staun-
ton, Va.]: Old Dominion Publications, 1978. [100] p. Maps, bibliog.,
index.

Virginia's colonial history is illustrated with twenty maps. Three
of these are facsimile reproductions of seventeenth-century maps,
while the remainder are pictorial maps compiled by the author.

5-44 Hiden, Martha W. HOW JUSTICE GREW. VIRGINIA COUNTIES: AN
ABSTRACT OF THEIR FORMATION. Jamestown 350th Anniversary Historical Booklet, No. 19. Williamsburg: Virginia 350th Anniversary Celebration
Corp., 1957. Reprint. Charlottesville: University Press of Virginia, 1973.
101 p. Paper. Maps, photos, bibliog., index.

The development of Virginia's counties is presented through the
use of a chronological narrative. The utility of this booklet for
historical geographers is limited because it includes only two
maps. The classic work on the development of Virginia's counties remains Morgan P. Robinson, "Virginia Counties: Those

Resulting from Virginia Legislation," BULLETIN OF THE VIR-
GINIA STATE LIBRARY 9 (1916): 1-283.

5-45 Illinois Secretary of State. COUNTIES OF ILLINOIS: THEIR ORIGIN
AND EVOLUTION. [Springfield, Ill.: 1972.] Paper. 65 p. Maps.

Besides providing a chronological description of the origins and
evolution of the counties in Illinois, this state publication also
includes twenty-three maps which show county boundaries at
selected dates superimposed over the current boundaries.

5-46 Loy, William G., et al. ATLAS OF OREGON. Eugene: University
of Oregon Books, 1976. vii, 215 p. Maps, illus., diagrs., tables,
index.

In the same format as Donley et al., ATLAS OF CALIFORNIA
(see entry 5-40), this atlas contains scattered historical maps
depicting Indian cultures, donation land claims, public land
surveys, county boundaries, population growth and immigration,
voting patterns , and urban development, especially for Portland.
The maps are explained in accompanying text and references
cited.

5-47 Miller, David E. UTAH HISTORY ATLAS. 2d ed. Salt Lake City:
Smith Secretarial Service, 1968. [100] p. Maps.

Forty-seven black and white maps portray Utah's history, concentrating on such topics as physical features, explorers' routes
and trails, Mormon migration, and changing territorial, state
and county boundaries. Each map is accompanied by a page of
explanation.

5-48 Morris, Gerald E., and Kelly, Richard D., Jr., eds. THE MAINE BICEN-
TENNIAL ATLAS: AN HISTORICAL SURVEY. Portland: Maine Historical
Society, 1976. [xii], 20 p., 69 map plates. Notes.

Three types of maps are included in this state historical atlas:
thirty-five maps reconstructing Maine's history and past geography; twenty-seven maps depicting Maine's current physical,
cultural, and political conditions; and seven facsimile reproductions. The topics covered by the reconstructed maps include
early explorations, settlements, land grants, military activities,
international boundary disputes, population densities, congressional districts, railroads, and economic conditions.

5-49 Morris, John W.; Goins, Charles R.; and McReynolds, Edwin C. HISTORI-
CAL ATLAS OF OKLAHOMA. 2d ed. Norman: University of Oklahoma
Press, 1976. xxvi, [166] p. Maps, notes, index.

Oklahoma's historical and geographical development is reconstructed by utilizing eighty-three maps. Important topics include

Spanish and French claims, explorers' routes, and the evolution of the boundaries of the various Indian nations, as well as important places and political divisions within the individual nations, military activities, and twentieth-century county, congressional, and judicial district boundaries.

5-50 Mottaz, Stan. "County Evolution in Nevada." NEVADA HISTORICAL SOCIETY QUARTERLY 21 (Spring 1978): 25-50. Maps, notes.

Using legislative records, Mottaz has recreated twenty-one maps which show Nevada's changing county boundaries from 1852 to 1973.

5-51 Nimmo, Sylvia. MAPS SHOWING COUNTY BOUNDARIES, NEBRASKA, 1854-1925. Papillion, Nebr.: By the Author, 1978. 38 p. Paper. Maps.

Thirty-four maps depict the changing boundaries of Nebraska's counties between 1854 and 1925.

5-52 Pool, William C. A HISTORICAL ATLAS OF TEXAS. Austin: Encino Press, 1975. xi, 190 p. Maps, notes, index.

Various topics illustrating the history of Texas are depicted in this atlas. Included are maps showing archaeology and Indians, early exploration, American settlement and associated military activities, early town plans, frontier expansion and territorial growth, voting patterns, Mexican and Civil War activities, ethnic distributions, and the development of the cattle and oil industries. Each of the seventy-one maps is accompanied by an explanation and a list of selected references.

5-53 Raymond, Parrish, Pine and Plavnick, Inc. MARYLAND HISTORICAL ATLAS. [Annapolis]: State of Maryland, Department of Economic and Community Development, 1973. ix, 61 p. Paper. Maps, illus., photos., notes.

The maps in this atlas review the significant events in Maryland's history emphasizing the resultant historic sites and landmarks. The maps pertain to several themes: original boundaries, Indians, early settlers, black population, town planning, domestic architecture, institutions, economy, transportation, and military activities.

5-54 Snyder, John P. THE STORY OF NEW JERSEY'S CIVIL BOUNDARIES, 1606-1968. Trenton: Bureau of Geology and Topography, 1969. xiii, 294 p. Maps, notes, index.

Based on extensive research of legal statutes, Snyder has prepared thirty-seven maps and a detailed narrative which describe New Jersey's changing county and minor civil division boundaries. Also included are reproductions of five historical maps and five deeds.

5-55 Socolofsky, Homer E., and Self, Huber. HISTORICAL ATLAS OF KAN-
SAS. Norman: University of Oklahoma Press, 1972. xxxii, 140 p.
Maps, notes, index.

> Various topics of the history and geography of Kansas are de-
> picted on seventy maps. Topics covered include physical fea-
> tures; early explorers' routes; Indian reservations, trails, and
> settlements; trails and railroads; changing territorial, state,
> and congressional district boundaries; and forts and military
> activities. Each map is accompanied by a page of text explain-
> ing the map.

5-56 Sommers, Lawrence M., ed. ATLAS OF MICHIGAN. Lansing: Michigan
State University Press, 1977. xi, 242 p. Maps, photos., diagrs., bibliog.,
index.

> Although this colorful state atlas deals primarily with contempo-
> rary spatial distributions, it does include a section on history and
> culture (pp. 99-134). This section includes over forty maps that
> deal with such historical topics as the Indian, French, and Brit-
> ish occupation of the area; the progression of nineteenth-century
> settlement; the evolution of territorial, state, and county bounda-
> ries; mid to late nineteenth-century immigration and industry;
> and presidential and gubernatorial politics.

5-57 Walker, Henry P., and Bufkin, Don. HISTORICAL ATLAS OF ARIZONA.
Norman: University of Oklahoma Press, 1979. [152] p. Maps, notes,
index.

> The historical development of Arizona is depicted in sixty-five
> maps. The topics covered include physical characteristics, pre-
> history, Spanish exploration and settlement, territorial and county
> boundary changes, development of Indian reservations, transporta-
> tion (trails, supply routes, stagecoach routes, and railroads),
> mining activities, military posts, federal and private land owner-
> ship, population growth, and historic sites. Each map is accom-
> panied by a short narrative and a list of references.

5-58 Welch, Richard W. COUNTY EVOLUTION IN MICHIGAN, 1790-1897.
State Library Services Occasional Paper, No. 2. Lansing: Michigan Department of Education, 1972. v, 44 p. Paper. Maps, notes, bibliog.

> Changing county boundaries from 1790 to 1897, as well as In-
> dian land cessions and territorial boundaries, are shown on
> twenty-two maps. An alphabetical listing of counties includes
> date of formation, description of boundary changes, and refer-
> ences to pertinent laws.

Part 2

ARCHIVAL AND OTHER HISTORICAL SOURCES

Chapter 6

ARCHIVAL REFERENCE AIDS

General reference aids describing the availability and utility of archival and other historical sources are included in this chapter. The first section focuses on articles by geographers which discuss the geographical significance of particular historical sources. Several British and Canadian references are included as examples because literature on this topic is rather minimal. The second section lists directories to archival and manuscript repositories and general discussions of several broad categories of records that are common to a number of institutions. The final section consists of guides to individual archival repositories with emphasis on the National Archives and the Library of Congress. Several other major repositories that are noted for their collections of historical materials pertaining to exploration, Western settlement, business and industry, history of cartography, and social statistics are also included. In this final section no attempt was made to be comprehensive, but those entries that are included will serve as a guide to the types of finding aids that are available for similar repositories.

A. HISTORICAL SOURCES FOR GEOGRAPHERS

6-1 Baker, Alan R.H.; Hamshere, John D.; and Langton, John, eds. GEO-GRAPHICAL INTERPRETATIONS OF HISTORICAL SOURCES: READINGS IN HISTORICAL GEOGRAPHY. London: David and Charles; New York: Barnes and Noble, 1970. 458 p. Maps, photos., diagrs., tables, notes, index.

> Although this collection of twenty articles, originally published in the 1950s and 1960s, pertains to the historical geography of England and Wales, the articles were selected for their geographical interpretation and analysis of particular historical source materials. These articles, which are based on sources ranging from the Domesday Inquest of 1086 and other medieval taxation accounts to nineteenth-century industrial and population censuses, are arranged chronologically by the date of the pertinent source material rather than by similar categories of documents.

6-2   Brayshay, Mark. "Using American Records to Study Nineteenth-Century
       Emigrants from Britain." AREA 11, no. 2 (1979): 156-60. Illus., diagrs.,
       notes.

       Brayshay describes the content of nineteenth-century U.S. Cus-
       toms' passenger lists and shows how they can be used in trans-
       Atlantic migration studies.

6-3   Ehrenberg, Ralph E. "Appendix A: Bibliography to Resources on Historical
       Geography in the National Archives." In his PATTERN AND PROCESS:
       RESEARCH IN HISTORICAL GEOGRAPHY, pp. 315-49. Washington, D.C.:
       Howard University Press, 1975.

       Ehrenberg's bibliography lists approximately 260 published and
       internal finding aids, microfilm publications, and articles in
       scholarly periodicals which describe textual, audiovisual, and
       cartographic records in the National Archives that are potentially
       useful for research in historical geography. The entries are
       arranged geographically (national, regional, and state) and
       thematically within the national category (exploration and
       settlement, population characteristics, agriculture, trade and
       commerce, manufacturing and industry, transportation and com-
       munication, urban development, and natural resources and clima-
       tology). Selected entries from this listing are included in the
       present bibliography.

6-4   Ernst, Joseph A., and Merrens, Harry Roy. "Praxis and Theory in the
       Writing of American Historical Geography." JOURNAL OF HISTORICAL
       GEOGRAPHY 4 (July 1978): 277-90. Notes.

       This essay examines the use of the more literary or qualitative
       primary sources such as contemporary travel accounts, topogra-
       phies, and geographies in the writing of American historical geog-
       raphy. Although the subjectivity of individual's perception in
       these accounts is emphasized, it is also pointed out that the
       latter-day scholar cannot use these data objectively because of
       his own personal biases. Consequently, objectivity in understand-
       ing past geographies should be sought in the collective effort of
       subjective scholars engaging in contemporary dialogue.

6-5   Meinig, Donald W. "Railroad Archives and the Historical Geographer."
       PROFESSIONAL GEOGRAPHER 7 (May 1955): 7-10.

       Based on his research in the archives of the Northern Pacific
       and Union Pacific Railroad Companies, Meinig reviews the types
       of records that are available in these private corporations' ar-
       chives for research in the historical geography of railroads.

6-6   Merrens, Harry Roy. "The Physical Environment of Early America: Images
       and Image Makers in Colonial South Carolina." GEOGRAPHICAL REVIEW 59
       (October 1969): 530-56. Notes.

       Merrens categorizes the seventeenth- and eighteenth-century

narrative accounts of South Carolina's physical environment into five classes: promotional literature, official reports, travel accounts, natural history accounts, and settlers' statements. His analysis of the writers' motivations in interpreting the landscape provides the framework for evaluating similar colonial period sources useful for environmental description.

6-7 _____. "Source Materials for the Geography of Colonial America." PROFESSIONAL GEOGRAPHERS 15 (January 1963): 8-11. Notes.

Merrens describes various types of primary sources (taxable lists, customs statistics, merchant records, newspapers, estate inventories, land surveys, local court minutes, travel accounts, maps) which are available for reconstructing the historical geography of the original thirteen colonies.

6-8 _____, ed. THE COLONIAL SOUTH CAROLINA SCENE: CONTEMPORARY VIEWS, 1697-1774. Tricentennial Edition, No. 7. Columbia: University of South Carolina Press, 1977. xi, 295 p. Notes, index.

The purpose of this volume is to convey a picture of colonial South Carolina through the use of contemporary documents and to illustrate the variety of sources that are available for the study of past geographical patterns. More than thirty edited documents are reproduced, including a natural historian's account of the physical environment, merchants' and family letters, reports of government and church officials, estate inventories, and a few travel accounts.

6-9 Moodie, D.W. "The Hudson's Bay Company's Archives: A Resource for Historical Geography." CANADIAN GEOGRAPHER 21 (Fall 1977): 268-74. Notes.

The archives of the Hudson Bay Company which are deposited in the Provincial Archives of Manitoba, are primarily a Canadian source; however, several historical geographers have utilized these records and have written about their utility for geographical research. Their analyses provide an example of the types of information that are available in business records for historical and geographical research. The archives include maps, ships' logs, Indian trade accounts, meteorological observations, explorers' journals, and the company's administrative and business records. These records are also described by another geographer, Arthur J. Ray, in "The Early Hudson's Bay Company Account Books as Sources for Historical Research: An Analysis and Assessment," ARCHIVARIA 1 (Winter 1975-76): 3-38; and "The Hudson's Bay Company Account Books as Sources for Comparative Economic Analysis of the Fur Trade: An Examination of Exchange Rate Data," WESTERN CANADIAN JOURNAL OF ANTHROPOLOGY 6 (1976): 44-50.

6-10 Morgan, Michael A. HISTORICAL SOURCES IN GEOGRAPHY. Sources and Methods in Geography. London: Butterworths, 1979. 153 p. Paper. Maps, illus., diagrs., tables, bibliog., index.

> Although this study pertains primarily to British sources, it is one of the few book-length studies that discusses historical sources that are useful for geographical research. The author discusses the content, format, and availability of various types of records and makes suggestions through the use of case studies for appropriate research and analysis by historical geographers. The narrative is organized topically in six chapters, emphasizing a variety of sources: "Domesday Book"; "Middle Ages" (lay subsidies, poll taxes, inquisitions, legal cases, land grants); "Agriculture" (manorial court records, enclosure awards and maps, tithe maps and apportionments, agricultural censuses, probate inventories); "Population" (parish registers, churchwarden's accounts, partial counts, and censuses); "Directories, Rate Books, and Newspapers"; and "Transport" (roads, canals, railways).

6-11 Trindell, Roger T. "The Geographer, the Archives and American Colonial History." PROFESSIONAL GEOGRAPHER 20 (March 1968): 98-102. Map, diagr., notes.

> Using examples from American colonial history, Trindell discusses the role of archives and manuscripts as primary source materials, in place of field work, in historical geographical research. He also reviews the major guides to archival and manuscript collections, such as Hamer, A GUIDE TO ARCHIVES AND MANUSCRIPTS IN THE UNITED STATES (see entry 6-22) and NATIONAL UNION CATALOG OF MANUSCRIPT COLLECTIONS (see entry 6-19), as well as earlier publications which these two guides have replaced.

B. DIRECTORIES AND COLLECTIVE FINDING AIDS

6-12 AMERICAN ARCHIVIST. Washington, D.C.: Society of American Archivists, 1938-- . Quarterly.

> In addition to society news notes, institutional accessions, and book reviews of archival literature, this journal's articles pertain primarily to the administration, preservation, and description of archival holdings. The annual classified bibliography, "Writings on Archives, Current Records, and Historical Manuscripts," includes references to published guides of state and local archives and manuscript collections. Articles describing the content and problems of municipal archives include: Richard J. Cox, "The Plight of American Municipal Archives: Baltimore, 1729-1979," 42 (July 1979): 281-92; Maygene Daniels, "District of Columbia Building Permits," 38 (January 1975) 23-30;

and Dale A. Somers et al., "Surveying the Records of a City: The History of Atlanta Project," 36 (July 1973) 353-59. Archival materials useful for migration studies are described in Robert M. Warner and Francis X. Blouin, Jr., "Documenting the Great Migrations and a Century of Ethnicity in America," 39 (July 1976): 319-28; and Richard N. Juliani, "The Use of Archives in the Study of Immigration and Ethnicity," 39 (October 1976): 469-77. Other articles of interest include Charles E. Dewing, "The Wheeler Survey Records: A Study in Archival Anomaly," 27 (April 1964): 219-27; and Clyde M. Collier, "The Archivist and Weather Records," 26 (October 1963): 477-85.

6-13 American Association for State and Local History. DIRECTORY: HISTORICAL SOCIETIES AND AGENCIES IN THE UNITED STATES AND CANADA. Compiled and edited by Donna McDonald. 11th ed. Nashville: 1978. vi, 474 p. Paper. Index.

The eleventh edition of this directory provides an updated and fairly comprehensive listing of the historical societies and agencies in the United States and Canada. Although no attempt is made to suggest the quality or quantity of a society's records holdings, the directory does list address, telephone, staff, publications, major programs, and date range of collections for each institution.

6-14 Brooks, Philip C. RESEARCH IN ARCHIVES: THE USE OF UNPUBLISHED PRIMARY SOURCES. Chicago: University of Chicago Press, 1969. xi, 127 p. Notes, bibliog.

A useful guide for beginning researchers, this monograph explains the use of archival and unpublished primary sources. Some of the topics covered include types of repositories, finding aids, relationship between researcher and archivist, limitations on access and use, footnotes, and copying.

6-15 Congressional Information Service. C.I.S. U.S. SERIAL SET INDEX, 1789-1969. 36 vols. Washington, D.C.: 1975-79.

A comprehensive, retrospective index is provided for the U.S. Congressional Serial Set, which is an ongoing collection of publications compiled under the direction of the Congress including the American State Papers; congressional journals, reports, directories and manuals; and the annual reports of federal executive agencies. The main index is a subject and keyword index derived from the publications' titles. There is also an index of personal names and organizations affected by private relief legislation and a numerical list of reports and documents. The Serial Set has been published on microfiche under the title of C.I.S. U.S. SERIAL SET ON MICROFICHE. The original and reprint editions of the American State Papers and the Serial Set are reviewed in Martin P. Claussen, "Revisiting America's State Papers, 1789-1861: A Clinical Examination and Prognosis," AMERICAN ARCHIVIST 36 (October 1973): 523-36. The maps associated with the American State Papers and the Serial Set are described in entries 2-28 and 2-48, while the value of these publications for exploration accounts is reviewed in entry 7-13.

6-16 Davis, Richard C., comp. NORTH AMERICAN FOREST HISTORY: A GUIDE TO ARCHIVES AND MANUSCRIPTS IN THE UNITED STATES AND CANADA. Santa Barbara, Calif.: Clio Books for Forest History Society, 1977. xxi, 376 p. Bibliog., index.

Archival and manuscript records relating to forest history (lumber and forest products industries, forestry, conservation politics, national and state parks movements, and wilderness preservation) in 358 repositories in the United States and Canada are described in this guide. Detailed entries are arranged by state, city, and repository. The bibliography lists guides to state archival and historical society collections.

6-17 Freidel, Frank, ed. HARVARD GUIDE TO AMERICAN HISTORY. Rev. ed. 2 vols. Cambridge, Mass.: Belknap Press of Harvard University Press, 1974. 1,346 p. Index.

Primarily a bibliography of secondary literature on American history, this guide does include several chapters that discuss historical sources, particularly printed public documents (federal, state, and local), unpublished primary sources (National Archives, state and local archives, manuscript collections, foreign archives), microfilm materials and printed historical works (government documents, magazines, newspapers, almanacs), and travel literature.

6-18 Hale, Richard W., ed. GUIDE TO PHOTOCOPIED HISTORICAL MATERIALS IN THE UNITED STATES AND CANADA. Ithaca, N.Y.: Cornell University Press for the American Historical Association, 1961. xxxiv, 241 p. Bibliog., index.

Basic bibliographical information pertaining to photocopied manuscripts is provided in this guide. The entries are listed by author, compiler, or holder of the original material and include the title of the material, date range, and repository of the microfilmed copy. The photocopied materials for most states and provinces include census, government, county, local, church, personal, and business records. Microfilm copies of many of the county and local records are available through the Genealogical Society of the Church of Jesus Christ of Latter-Day Saints, Salt Lake City. A bibliography of finding aids to photocopied materials is also included.

6-19 Library of Congress Catalogs. NATIONAL UNION CATALOG OF MANU-
SCRIPT COLLECTIONS. Ann Arbor, Mich.: J.W. Edwards, 1959-61;
Hamden, Conn.: Shoe String Press, 1962; Washington, D.C.: Library of
Congress, 1963/64-- .

> By 1980 this ongoing catalog included published descriptions
> (in 18 volumes) of approximately 46,640 manuscript collections
> located in 1,122 repositories throughout the United States. The
> entries are normally arranged alphabetically by repository in each
> volume, corresponding to the year in which the information was
> submitted. Indexes, which are cumulated for 1963-66, 1967-69,
> 1970-74, and after 1975 at five-year intervals, provide approxi-
> mately 487,600 references in one alphabet to personal names,
> places, subjects, and named historical periods. Because the
> entries are based on information prepared and submitted by the
> various public or quasi-public repositories (colleges and univer-
> sities, historical societies, religious institutions, state libraries
> and archives, museums, national government institutions, presi-
> dential libraries, and public libraries) the coverage is neither
> uniform nor comprehensive.

6-20 Main, Gloria A. "Probate Records as a Source for Early American History."
WILLIAM AND MARY QUARTERLY, 3d series, 32 (January 1975): 89-99.
Table, notes.

> Based on her research in Massachusetts and Maryland records,
> Main describes the content and degree of coverage of probate
> records (wills, inventories, and accounts of administration).
> She shows that these records are a useful quantifiable source
> for studies of economic development, evolving social structure,
> and cultural change. The biases and defects of these records
> are explained in this article, as well as in another article by
> Main, "The Correction of Biases in Colonial American Probate
> Records," HISTORICAL METHODS NEWSLETTER 8 (December
> 1974): 10-28. See also Daniel Scott Smith, "Underregistration
> and Bias in Probate Records: An Analysis of Data from
> Eighteenth-Century Hingham, Massachusetts," WILLIAM AND
> MARY QUARTERLY, 3d series, 32 (January 1975): 100-110;
> and Lois Green Carr and Lorena S. Walsh, "Inventories and
> the Analysis of Wealth and Consumption Patterns in St. Mary's
> County, Maryland, 1658-1777," HISTORICAL METHODS 13
> (Spring 1980): 81-104.

6-21 National Archives and Records Service. NATIONAL HISTORICAL PUBLI-
CATIONS AND RECORDS COMMISSION PUBLICATIONS CATALOG,
1976. Washington, D.C.: 1976. vii, 87 p. Paper.

> Over two hundred letterpress and microfilm publications spon-
> sored by the National Historical Publications and Records Com-
> mission are listed in this catalog. Although these publications

pertain primarily to the papers of prominent Americans and corporate bodies important in American history, some projects such
as the papers of John C. Fremont, Benjamin Latrobe, Stephen H.
Long, Frederick Law Olmsted, Zebulon M. Pike, Henry R.
Schoolcraft, or Isaac I. Stevens will be of interest to some
historical geographers.

6-22 National Historical Publications and Records Commission. DIRECTORY OF
ARCHIVES AND MANUSCRIPT REPOSITORIES IN THE UNITED STATES.
Washington, D.C.: National Archives and Records Service, 1978. 905 p.
Index.

Prepared as a revision to Philip M. Hamer's A GUIDE TO AR-
CHIVES AND MANUSCRIPTS IN THE UNITED STATES (New
Haven: Yale University Press, 1961), this directory describes
the historical records holdings of over 2,600 institutions (federal
agencies, state and local archives and historical societies, museums, and corporate, organizational, and university archives
and libraries) in the United States and several territories. Each
full entry includes address, hours, user services, summary statement of holdings, and bibliographical references to guides and
finding aids, as well as cross references to pertinent entries in
the NATIONAL UNION CATALOG OF MANUSCRIPT COL-
LECTIONS (see entry 6-19). While the entries are arranged
alphabetically by state and city, each state's entries are pre-
ceded by a brief description of that state's program for the disposition of county and local government records.

6-23 Raimo, John W., ed. A GUIDE TO MANUSCRIPTS RELATING TO AMERICA
IN GREAT BRITAIN AND IRELAND. Rev. ed. Westport, Conn.: Meckler
Books for the British Association for American Studies, 1979. xxv, 467 p.
Notes, index.

A revision of the GUIDE edited by B.R. Crick and Miriam Alman
(Oxford University Press for the British Association for American
Studies, 1961), this publication provides brief descriptions of
all manuscripts in Great Britain and Ireland relating to the his-
tory and literature of the American colonies and the United
States. It is supplemented by the various volumes published by
the Carnegie Institution of Washington, D.C.: Charles M.
Andrews, GUIDE TO THE MATERIALS FOR AMERICAN HISTORY,
TO 1783, IN THE PUBLIC RECORD OFFICE OF GREAT BRITAIN,
2 vols. (1912, 1914); Charles M. Andrews and Francis G. Daven-
port, GUIDE TO THE MANUSCRIPT MATERIALS FOR THE HIS-
TORY OF THE UNITED STATES TO 1783, IN THE BRITISH MU-
SEUM, IN MINOR LONDON ARCHIVES, AND THE LIBRARIES
OF OXFORD AND CAMBRIDGE (1908); and Charles O. Paullin
and Frederic L. Paxson, GUIDE TO THE MATERIALS IN LONDON

ARCHIVES FOR THE HISTORY OF THE UNITED STATES SINCE
1783 (1914). See also Grace Gardner Griffin, A GUIDE TO
MANUSCRIPTS RELATING TO AMERICAN HISTORY IN BRITISH
DEPOSITORIES REPRODUCED FOR THE DIVISION OF MANU-
SCRIPTS OF THE LIBRARY OF CONGRESS (Washington, D.C.:
Library of Congress, 1946).

6-24 Schmeckebier, Lawrence F., and Eastin, Roy B. GOVERNMENT PUBLICA-
TIONS AND THEIR USE. 1936. 2d rev. ed. Washington, D.C.: Brook-
ings Institution, 1969. xi, 502 p. Notes, index.

Designed as a guide to both nineteenth- and twentieth-century
federal government publications, this volume describes the pertinent catalogs, lists, and bibliographies. Nineteenth-century
publications of particular interest include congressional documents, annual reports of executive departments and bureaus,
reports of exploring expeditions, and maps. An appendix lists
depository libraries.

6-25 Society of American Archivists. DIRECTORY OF BUSINESS ARCHIVES IN
THE UNITED STATES AND CANADA. Chicago: Society of American
Archivists, 1980. 51 p. Paper. Index.

The archival holdings of 210 private businesses are described
in this directory.

6-26 _____. DIRECTORY OF COLLEGE AND UNIVERSITY ARCHIVES IN THE
UNITED STATES AND CANADA. Chicago: Society of American Archivists, 1980. 80 p. Paper. Index.

This listing of nearly one thousand college and university archives
includes name of institution, address, telephone, and staff members. It also indicates whether the holdings consist of institutional
archives or manuscript collections, but it does not provide any
further description of the holdings.

6-27 _____. A DIRECTORY OF STATE ARCHIVES IN THE UNITED STATES.
Compiled by Frank R. Levstik. Chicago: Society of American Archivists,
1980. ii, 65 p. Paper.

The chief archival and records management officials, the major
staff members, the agency's correct name, address, and telephone
are listed for each state archival repository. A brief summary
of each agency's holdings is also included.

6-28 _____. THE WPA HISTORICAL RECORDS SURVEY: A GUIDE TO THE
UNPUBLISHED INVENTORIES, INDEXES, AND TRANSCRIPTS. Chicago:
Society of American Archivists, 1980. 42 p. Paper.

During the 1930s, the Work Projects Administration's Historical
Records Survey produced inventories of many state, local, and

religious archives. Repositories which hold manuscript materials produced by these surveys are listed in this guide. A final listing of the published inventories issued between 1936 and 1943 is found in BIBLIOGRAPHY OF RESEARCH PROJECTS REPORTS: CHECKLIST OF HISTORICAL RECORDS SURVEY PUBLICATIONS, compiled by Sargent B. Child and Dorothy P. Holmes (Washington, D.C.: Work Projects Administration, 1943). Many of these publications, which had limited distribution, are available among the records of the Work Projects Administration (Record Group 69) in the Legislative and Natural Resources Branch of the National Archives. The survey is also described in Leonard Rapport, "Dumped from a Wharf into Casco Bay: The Historical Records Survey Revisited," AMERICAN ARCHIVIST 37 (April 1974): 201-10, and David L. Smiley, "A Slice of Life in Depression America: The Records of the Historical Records Survey," PROLOGUE 3 (Winter 1971): 153-59.

C. INDIVIDUAL INSTITUTIONAL GUIDES

6-29 American Antiquarian Society. CATALOGUE OF THE MANUSCRIPT COLLECTIONS OF THE AMERICAN ANTIQUARIAN SOCIETY. 4 vols. Boston: G.K. Hall, 1979. xiv, 2,622 p.

The American Antiquarian Society in Worcester, Massachusetts, collects both printed materials and historical manuscripts. The catalog for the manuscript collections is reproduced in this publication. A major component of these holdings is the private papers of various prominent New England families (especially religious, political, and military leaders). Also included are numerous diaries from the colonial and early national periods.

6-30 California, University of. Berkeley. Bancroft Library. A GUIDE TO THE MANUSCRIPT COLLECTIONS OF THE BANCROFT LIBRARY; Vol. 1: PACIFIC AND WESTERN MANUSCRIPTS (EXCEPT CALIFORNIA). Edited by Dale L. Morgan and George P. Hammond. Berkeley and Los Angeles: University of California Press, 1963. ix, 379 p. Index.

The Manuscript Division of the Bancroft Library holds manuscripts pertaining to the history of California, other western states, and Mexico. Included are personal papers of political leaders and literary figures; some national, state, and city records; and business and industrial records. Part of the collection is described in this volume. See also entry 9-2.

6-31 Henry E. Huntington Library and Art Galley. GUIDE TO AMERICAN HISTORICAL MANUSCRIPTS IN THE HUNTINGTON LIBRARY. San Marino, Calif.: Henry E. Huntington Library and Art Gallery, 1979. viii, 442 p. Index.

The Huntington Library's collection of historical manuscripts

pertaining to American society and culture is described in this
publication. The special concentration of these more than one
and a half million sixteenth through twentieth-century manuscripts
is the Revolution, Civil War, and Western history. The records
pertaining to several western railroad and mining companies are
included.

6-32 Historic American Building Survey. CATALOG OF THE MEASURED DRAW-
INGS AND PHOTOGRAPHS OF THE SURVEY IN THE LIBRARY OF CON-
GRESS MARCH 1, 1941. Washington, D.C.: Government Printing Office,
1941. viii, 470 p. Photos., illus., index.

The early records of the Historic American Building Survey
(HABS), a federal office whose primary mission is recording
graphically historic structure throughout the United States, are
listed in this catalog. HABS was organized in 1933 as a coop-
erative effort of the National Park Service, Library of Congress,
and American Institute of Architects; the records, which consist
of measured drawings and photographs, are housed in the Prints
and Photographs Division, Library of Congress. The variety of
recorded structures include dwellings (both vernacular and pro-
fessionally-designed), commercial and technical structures
(hotels, mills, stores, lighthouses, covered bridges, canals),
and public buildings (churches, schools, and government structures). Records created between 1941 and 1959 are listed in
CATALOG SUPPLEMENT (1959), while a general description
of the survey is found in John Poppeliers, et al., "Documenting
a Legacy: 40 Years of the Historic American Building Survey,"
QUARTERLY JOURNAL OF THE LIBRARY OF CONGRESS 30
(October 1973): 268-94. A similar project devoted to recording historic engineering and industrial structures is the Historic
American Engineering Record, which was founded in 1969. A
preliminary listing of these records is found in Donald E. Sack-
heim, comp., HISTORIC AMERICAN ENGINEERING RECORD
CATALOG, 1976 (Washington, D.C.: National Park Service,
1976). A mimeographed bibliography ("National Architectural
and Engineering Record Publications List") listing publications
by both offices is available from the Prints and Photographs
Division, Library of Congress.

6-33 Inter-University Consortium for Political and Social Research. GUIDE TO
RESOURCES AND SERVICES, 1978-79. Ann Arbor: University of Michigan,
Institute for Social Research, Center for Political Studies, n.d. 422 p.
Paper. Index.

The ICPSR, which is a partnership between the Center for Political Studies and over two hundred member universities, is a
central repository for machine readable social science data.
This guide describes the services and holdings, including election

data (county and state level variables from 1790 to 1970), roll-
call votes of U.S. Congresses (1790 to present), and French
census data (nineteenth century). This data will be useful for
studies involving urban topics, education, electoral behavior,
socialization, foreign policy, community studies, judicial behavior, race relations, and organizational behavior.

6-34 Melville, Annette, comp. SPECIAL COLLECTIONS IN THE LIBRARY OF
CONGRESS: A SELECTIVE GUIDE. Washington, D.C.: Library of Congress, 1980. xv, 464 p. Index. Maps, illus., photos., index.

Special collections that were selected for their rarity or potential interest to scholars are described in this guide. Entries
are included for 269 special collections of books and pamphlets,
drawings, films, manuscripts, maps, prints, photography, sound
recordings, and other nonbook materials from sixteen divisions
in the library. Personal papers described in NATIONAL UNION
CATALOG OF MANUSCRIPT COLLECTIONS (see entry 6-19)
are not included. Comments for individual collections pertain
to acquisition, contents, volume, organization, and relevant
finding aids. An overview of the library's holdings is found
in Charles A. Goodrum, TREASURES OF THE LIBRARY OF
CONGRESS (New York: Harry N. Abrams, 1980).

6-35 Michigan, University of. William L. Clements Library. GUIDE TO THE
MANUSCRIPT COLLECTIONS OF THE WILLIAM L. CLEMENTS LIBRARY.
3d ed. Edited by Arlene P. Shy. Boston: G.K. Hall, 1978. x, 435 p.
Index.

The manuscript collections of the William L. Clements Library
are described. British and American materials relating to the
colonial and revolutionary war periods provide the major emphasis of these collections; however, there are also materials
pertaining to the War of 1812, the antislavery movement,
and the Civil War.

6-36 National Archives and Records Service. GUIDE TO THE NATIONAL AR-
CHIVES OF THE UNITED STATES. Washington, D.C.: 1974. xxv, 884 p.
Index.

This comprehensive guide to the records accessioned by the National Archives as of June 30, 1970, includes entries for over
four hundred record groups (the designation for records of an
individual agency, bureau, or commission). These entries provide a brief administrative history; a general description of the
textual, cartographic, and audiovisual records; and a list of the
published finding aids. A select list of finding aids is also
found in Frank B. Evans, "The National Archives and Records
Service and Its Research Resources--A Select Bibliography,"

PROLOGUE 3 (Fall 1971): 88-112. Finding aids that are use-
ful for research in historical geography are described in entry
6-3. Agricultural records in the National Archives and the Re-
gional Archives Branches are described by Harold T. Pinckett in
"Federal Archives and Western Agriculture," and by Ann M.
Campbell in "Reaping the Records: Research Opportunities in
Regional Archives Branches," both printed in AGRICULTURAL
HISTORY 49 (January 1975): 95-104. Other articles describ-
ing the services, holdings, and published finding aids of the
Regional Archives Branches, which are located at Federal Records
Centers, include Norman D. Tutorow and Arthur R. Abel,
"Western and Territorial Research Opportunities in Trans-Mississippi
Federal Records Centers," PACIFIC HISTORICAL REVIEW 40
(February 1971): 501-18, and Gerald T. White, "Government
Archives Afield: The Federal Records Centers and the Historian,"
JOURNAL OF AMERICAN HISTORY 55 (March 1969): 833-42.

6-37 National Archives Conference on American Agriculture. FARMERS,
BUREAUCRATS, AND MIDDLEMEN: HISTORICAL PERSPECTIVES ON
AMERICAN AGRICULTURE. Edited by Trudy Huskamp Peterson.
Washington, D.C.: Howard University Press, 1980. xvii, 357 p. Maps,
illus., photos., diagrs., notes, index.

The papers presented at one of the National Archives conferences, which are designed to acquaint various academic groups
with the institution's holdings, are included in this volume. It
includes both scholarly articles on various topics of agricultural
history and resource articles describing sources in the National
Archives useful for the study of agricultural history. Other
volumes in this series follow a similar format, including both
scholarly and resource articles. Besides the conference for
historical geographers (see entries 6-3 and 12-6), other conference proceedings that will be of interest to historical geographers
include: AFRO-AMERICAN HISTORY: SOURCES FOR RESEARCH,
edited by Robert L. Clarke (Washington, D.C.: Howard University Press, 1981); INDIAN-WHITE RELATIONS: A PERSIS-
TENT PARADOX, edited by Jane F. Smith and Robert M.
Kvasnicka (Washington, D.C.: Howard University Press, 1976);
THE NATIONAL ARCHIVES AND URBAN RESEARCH, edited
by Jerome Finster (Athens: Ohio University Press, 1974); THE
AMERICAN TERRITORIAL SYSTEM, edited by John Porter Bloom
(Athens: Ohio University Press, 1973); THE NATIONAL ARCHIVES
AND STATISTICAL RESEARCH, edited by Meyer H. Fishbein
(Athens: Ohio University Press, 1973); and UNITED STATES
POLAR EXPLORATION, edited by Herman R. Friis and Shelby
G. Bale, Jr. (Athens: Ohio University Press, 1970).

6-38 Newberry Library. Chicago. A CATALOGUE OF THE EVERETT D. GRAFF COLLECTION OF WESTERN AMERICANA. Compiled by Colton Storm. Chicago: University of Chicago Press for the Newberry Library, 1968. xxv, 854 p. Index.

> Among the holdings of the Newberry Library are materials pertaining to western history, the American Indian (see entry 15-2), and the history of cartography. This publication describes the Everett D. Graff Collection, which includes over ten thousand books, pamphlets, maps, broadsides, and manuscripts relating to the exploration, settlement, and development of the country west of the Mississippi River. The Edward E. Ayer Collection, which specializes in the archaeology and ethnology of the American Indian, is described in A CHECK LIST OF MANUSCRIPTS IN THE EDWARD E. AYER COLLECTION, compiled by Ruth L. Butler (Chicago: Newberry Library, 1937). Two publications listing railroad archives are GUIDE TO THE ILLINOIS CENTRAL ARCHIVES IN THE NEWBERRY LIBRARY, 1851-1906, compiled by Carolyn Curtis Mohr (Chicago: Newberry Library, 1951), and GUIDE TO THE BURLINGTON ARCHIVES IN THE NEWBERRY LIBRARY, 1851-1901, compiled by Elisabeth C. Jackson and Carolyn Curtis (Chicago: Newberry Library, 1949).

6-39 PROLOGUE: JOURNAL OF THE NATIONAL ARCHIVES. Vols. 1-4, 1969-72. Three issues per year. Vol. 5-- . Washington, D.C.: National Archives and Records Service, 1973-- . Quarterly.

> Articles that utilize records in the National Archives as well as National Archives accessions, publications, and genealogical notes, are reported in this journal. Articles of interest to historical geographers, which have not been listed elsewhere, include: Jane F. Smith, "The Use of Federal Records in Writing Local History: A Case Study," 1 (Spring 1969): 29-51 (reconstruction of settlement patterns and pioneer history in one township in southwestern Wisconsin); Samuel P. Hays, "The Use of Archives for Historical Statistical Inquiry," 1 (Fall 1969): 7-15; Edward E. Hill, "The Tucson Agency: The Use of Federal Records in the National Archives," 4 (Summer 1972): 77-82 (Indian Agency records); Harry N. Scheiber, "Land Reform, Speculation, and Government Failure: The Administration of Ohio's State Canal Lands, 1836-60," 7 (Summer 1975): 85-98 (land disposal records and maps); Harold T. Pinkett, "Records of a Historic Thrust for Conservation," 8 (Summer 1976): 77-84 (conservation records of the 1930s); Kenneth R. Bowling, "'A Place to Which Tribute is Brought': The Contest for the Federal Capital in 1783," 8 (Fall 1976): 129-40; and Charles Stephenson, "The Methodology of Historical Census Record Linkage: A User's Guide to the Soundex," 12 (Fall 1980): 151-53.

6-40 Riggs, John B. A GUIDE TO THE MANUSCRIPTS IN THE ELEUTHERIAN MILLS HISTORICAL LIBRARY, ACCESSIONS THROUGH THE YEAR 1965.

Greenville, Del.: Eleutherian Mills Historical Library, 1970. xxii, 1,205 p. Index.

The Eleutherian Mills Historical Library, which is located near Wilmington, Delaware, collects historical manuscripts focusing on the economic, business, industrial, and technological history of the Middle Atlantic states. A major component of these collections is the Dupont family papers. Manuscripts accessioned through 1965 are described in this guide, while later accessions are covered in A GUIDE TO MANUSCRIPTS IN THE ELEUTHERIAN MILLS HISTORICAL LIBRARY, SUPPLEMENT CONTAINING ACCESSIONS FOR THE YEARS 1966 THROUGH 1975 (Greenville, Del.: Eleutherian Mills Historical Library, 1978). The library also supervised an inventory of the records of the seven railroad companies that merged into the Consolidated Rail Corporation (Conrail), April 1976. The results of this survey are recorded in Duane P. Swanson and Hugh R. Gibb, THE HISTORICAL RECORDS OF THE COMPONENTS OF CONRAIL: A SURVEY AND INVENTORY (Greenville, Del.: Eleutherian Mills Historical Library, 1978).

6-41 Wimmer, Larry T., and Pope, Clayne. "The Genealogical Society Library of Salt Lake City: A Source of Data for Economic and Social Historians." HISTORICAL METHODS NEWSLETTER 8 (March 1975): 51-58.

The Genealogical Society Library provides a major source of historical, economic, and social data, since it is the repository of one million reels of microfilm of vital records, probate records, land records, and census records derived from numerous county court houses, state archives, and foreign depositories. In addition, the library maintains related genealogical reference works and family genealogies. The library's holdings are also described in Larry R. Gerlach and Michael L. Nichols, "The Mormon Genealogical Society and Research Opportunities in Early American History," WILLIAM AND MARY QUARTERLY, 3d ser., 32 (October 1975): 625-29.

6-42 Yale University. Library. THE BEINECKE RARE BOOK AND MANUSCRIPT LIBRARY: A GUIDE TO ITS COLLECTIONS. New Haven: Yale University Library, 1974. xi, 111 p. Paper. Maps, photos., illus.

Yale University's rare book and manuscript collections are described briefly in this publication. The university's Collection of Western Americana, which includes some Lewis and Clark materials, is described more fully in A CATALOGUE OF THE FREDERICK W. AND CARRIE S. BEINECKE COLLECTION OF WESTERN AMERICANA, edited by Archibald Hanna (New Haven: Yale University Press, 1965), and A CATALOGUE OF MANUSCRIPTS IN THE COLLECTION OF WESTERN AMERICANA FOUNDED BY WILLIAM ROBERTSON COE, YALE UNIVERSITY LIBRARY, compiled by Mary C. Withington (New Haven: Yale University Press, 1952).

Chapter 7

NARRATIVE SOURCES

A variety of narrative or qualitative sources are mentioned in this chapter. Besides bibliographies and catalogs, these entries also refer to books and articles that describe the contents or analyze the geographic research potential and biases of these records. The entries are grouped into three sections: travel accounts and diaries, exploration accounts and government reports, and newspapers.

A. TRAVEL ACCOUNTS AND DIARIES

7-1   Adams, Percy G. TRAVELERS AND TRAVEL LIARS, 1660-1800. Berkeley and Los Angeles: University of California Press, 1962. xiv, 292 p. Maps, illus., notes, index.

> In surveying eighteenth-century travel literature, Adams considers the use of deception (untruths, pseudo voyages, plagiarism, and exaggeration) in travel accounts.

7-2   Bredeson, Robert C. "Landscape Description in Nineteenth-Century American Travel Literature." AMERICAN QUARTERLY 20 (Spring 1968): 864-94. Notes.

> Travel literature from the mid-nineteenth century is described in terms of three groupings: fashionable, informative, and utilitarian views of the landscape. Each type of travel literature is characterized by a special vocabulary and presupposes certain attitudes about man's expected response to a landscape.

7-3   Carson, Jane. TRAVELERS IN TIDEWATER VIRGINIA, 1700-1800: A BIBLIOGRAPHY. Williamsburg Research Studies. Charlottesville: University Press of Virginia for Colonial Williamsburg, 1965. xx, 121 p. Paper. Index.

> Travel accounts pertaining to eighteenth-century Tidewater Virginia are described in this bibliography. Annotations summarize the contents of the various accounts with particular emphasis on their coverage of Williamsburg and vicinity.

7-4   Clark, Thomas D., ed. TRAVELS IN THE OLD SOUTH: A BIBLIOGRAPHY.
       American Exploration and Travel Series, No. 19. 3 vols. Norman:
       University of Oklahoma Press, 1956-59.

       Pre-1860 travel accounts in the southern states are listed in three
       volumes: 1, THE FORMATIVE YEARS, 1527-1783 (xix, 330 p.);
       2, THE EXPANDING SOUTH, 1750-1825 (xv, 292 p.); and
       3, THE ANTEBELLUM SOUTH, 1825-1860 (xviii, 406 p.).
       Each volume consists of three to four chapters, each pertaining
       to a particular subregion and/or time period and each compiled
       by a different author. The entries, which are arranged alpha-
       betically by traveler within each chapter, include author, title,
       bibliographical data, and annotations summarizing the contents
       including geographic coverage in relation to the Old South.
       The chronological continuation of this bibliography of southern
       travel literature is found in E. Merton Coulter, TRAVELS IN
       THE CONFEDERATE STATES: A BIBLIOGRAPHY (Norman: Uni-
       versity of Oklahoma Press, 1948), which covers the period
       1860-65; and Thomas D. Clark, ed., TRAVELS IN THE NEW
       SOUTH: A BIBLIOGRAPHY, 2 vols. (Norman: University of
       Oklahoma Press, 1962). The first volume covers THE POSTWAR
       SOUTH, 1865-1900, while the second volume focuses on THE
       TWENTIETH CENTURY SOUTH, 1900-1955. All six volumes
       in this series include over 2,700 entries.

7-5   Coad, Oral S. NEW JERSEY IN TRAVELERS' ACCOUNTS, 1524-1971:
       A DESCRIPTIVE BIBLIOGRAPHY. Metuchen, N.J.: Scarecrow Press,
       1972. x, 211 p. Index.

       Travelers' accounts pertaining to New Jersey are listed in this
       bibliography. The entries, arranged chronologically, include
       descriptive comments that summarize the contents and geographi-
       cal coverage.

7-6   Hubach, Robert R. EARLY MIDWESTERN TRAVEL NARRATIVES: AN
       ANNOTATED BIBLIOGRAPHY, 1634-1850. Detroit: Wayne State Uni-
       versity, 1961. x, 149 p. Paper. Notes, index.

       Early midwestern travel literature is listed in this bibliography.
       Annotations summarize the contents and geographic coverage of
       the various entries, which are arranged essentially in chronologi-
       cal order.

7-7   Jakle, John A. IMAGES OF THE OHIO VALLEY: A HISTORICAL
       GEOGRAPHY OF TRAVEL, 1740 TO 1860. Andrew H. Clark Series
       in the Historical Geography of North America. New York: Oxford Uni-
       versity Press, 1977. xiii, 217 p. Maps, illus, notes, bibliog., index.

       This work reconstructs the various images of the Ohio River
       Valley as recorded by approximately four hundred travelers in
       the area between 1740 and 1860. After evaluating the biases

inherent in the travelers' accounts and in the various modes of transportation, the images are organized according to their observations of aboriginal and military life, and the physical, rural, and urban landscapes.

7-8   McDermott, John Francis, ed. TRAVELERS ON THE WESTERN FRONTIER. Urbana: University of Illinois Press, 1970. xii, 351 p. Maps, illus., notes, index.

Originally presented at the Conference on Travelers on the Western Frontier (held at the University of Southern Illinois, Edwardsville, February 1968), these thirteen essays by professionals trained in history, geography, English, and library science focus on the travel literature of the western frontier. Nine of these articles discuss sources of travel literature including Missouri River travelers' diaries; manuscript sources in the Yale University, Newberry, and Bancroft Libraries; documents and reports of the U.S. Congress (see entry 7-13); and travel articles in two periodicals (SPIRIT OF THE TIMES and the AMERICAN TURF REGISTER AND SPORTING MAGAZINE) and two newspapers (St. Louis REVEILLE and New Orleans PICAYUNE). Three articles illustrate the use of travel accounts in studying the myth of the Mississippi River keelboatmen, the travelers' perception of the Indian, and the documentation available on one traveler. The final article uses road maps found in county records to lay out the early roads used by travelers going west from St. Louis.

7-9   Matthews, William. AMERICAN DIARIES IN MANUSCRIPT, 1580-1954: A DESCRIPTIVE BIBLIOGRAPHY. Athens: University of Georgia Press, 1974. xvi, 176 p. Index.

Over five thousand manuscript diaries from 350 libraries are described. Entries are arranged chronologically, while annotations indicate subject, geographical coverage, and repository of the manuscript. Published diaries are listed in the following bibliography prepared by Matthews, AMERICAN DIARIES: AN ANNOTATED BIBLIOGRAPHY OF AMERICAN DIARIES WRITTEN PRIOR TO THE YEAR 1861 (Berkeley and Los Angeles: University of California Press, 1945).

7-10 Sibley, Marilyn M. TRAVELERS IN TEXAS, 1761-1860. Austin: University of Texas Press, 1967. 236 p. Maps, photos., notes, bibliog., index.

Although a critical essay and bibliography of Texas travel accounts are included, this book concentrates on the impressions of Texas found in the travel literature. Sibley distinguishes three types of accounts: reports of official or quasi-official government representatives, private letters and journals not intended for publication, and material written for publication.

B. EXPLORATION ACCOUNTS AND GOVERNMENT REPORTS

7-11 Cutright, Paul Russell. A HISTORY OF THE LEWIS AND CLARK JOUR-
NALS. Norman: University of Oklahoma Press, 1976. xxi, 311 p. Map,
illus., notes, bibliog., index.

> Cutright reviews the history of the records (journals, field notes,
> correspondence) associated with the Lewis and Clark expedition,
> emphasizing the individuals who collected, researched, edited,
> and published the records. One chapter reviews the nineteenth-
> and twentieth-century literature that has been written about
> Lewis and Clark while another chapter discusses the artists who
> illustrated the history of the expedition.

7-12 De Brahm, William G. DE BRAHM'S REPORT OF THE GENERAL SURVEY
IN THE SOUTHERN DISTRICT OF NORTH AMERICA. Edited by Louis De
Vorsey, Jr. Columbia: University of South Carolina Press, 1971. xvi,
325 p. Maps, notes, bibliog., index.

> Utilizing the manuscript copy in the British Museum, De Vorsey
> has edited and published De Brahm's complete report for the
> first time. This report represents conditions in the Southeast
> during the third quarter of the eighteenth century reflecting
> De Brahm's experience in that area dating from his arrival in
> Georgia in 1751. More specifically, the report was prepared
> to accompany his cartographic surveys of the southeastern
> coastal areas which were conducted as part of his official du-
> ties as Surveyor General of the Southern District, a post he
> assumed in 1764. This descriptive report provides a geographical
> reconnaissance of South Carolina, Georgia, and east Florida
> and includes comments on physical, cultural, social, economic,
> and political conditions. De Vorsey's fifty-nine page introduc-
> tion presents a detailed biography of De Brahm, emphasizing his
> professional activities as a military engineer, surveyor and
> cartographer. For other articles by De Vorsey about De Brahm,
> see entry 12-6 and "William Gerard De Brahm: Eccentric Ge-
> nius of Southeastern Geography," SOUTHEASTERN GEOGRAPHY
> 10 (April 1970): 21-29.

7-13 Friis, Herman R. "The Documents and Reports of the United States Congress:
A Primary Source of Information on Travel in the West, 1783-1861." In
TRAVELERS ON THE WESTERN FRONTIER, edited by John F. McDermott,
pp. 112-67. Urbana: University of Illinois Press, 1970. Maps, illus.,
notes.

> Friis demonstrates that the Congressional Serial Set (see entry
> 6-15), the official published documents of the U.S. Senate and
> House of Representatives, is a valuable source for nineteenth-
> century geographical and travel information because the annual

reports of several federal agencies that were forwarded to Congress included reports of various federally sponsored geographical expeditions. Friis's footnotes provide a guide to the published reports of numerous expeditions. Other articles by Friis which utilize the Congressional Serial Set are "The Image of the American West at Mid-Century (1840-60): A Product of Scientific Geographical Exploration by the United States Government," in THE FRONTIER RE-EXAMINED, edited by John F. McDermott, pp. 49-64 (Urbana: University of Illinois Press, 1967), and "Original and Published Sources in Research in Historical Geography: A Comparison," in PATTERN AND PROCESS, edited by Ralph E. Ehrenberg, pp. 139-59 (Washington, D.C.: Howard University Press, 1975).

7-14 Hasse, Adelaide R. REPORTS OF EXPLORATIONS PRINTED IN THE DOCUMENTS OF THE UNITED STATES GOVERNMENT: A CONTRIBUTION TOWARD A BIBLIOGRAPHY. Washington, D.C.: Government Printing Office, 1899. 90 p.

Exploration reports, most of which were published in the Congressional Serial Set, are listed in this bibliographical index.

7-15 Schmeckebier, Lawrence F. CATALOGUE AND INDEX OF THE PUBLICATIONS OF THE HAYDEN, KING, POWELL, AND WHEELER SURVEYS. Washington, D.C.: Government Printing Office, 1904. Reprint. New York: Da Capo Press, 1971. 208 p. Index.

The published annual reports, final reports, bulletins, miscellaneous publications, and maps that resulted from the Hayden, King, Powell, and Wheeler surveys (conducted between 1867 and 1879) are listed here. The publications contain a wealth of geographic, geologic, ethnologic, and archaeologic information about the western United States. An extensive index is also included.

7-16 Schubert, Frank N. "Legacy of the Topographical Engineers: Textual and Cartographic Records of Western Exploration, 1819-1860." GOVERNMENT PUBLICATIONS REVIEW 7A (1980): 111-16. Notes.

As historian for the Office of the Chief of Engineers, Schubert describes the major bibliographical guides to the textual and cartographic records produced by Army Topographical Engineers, most of which are now in the National Archives. The primary emphasis is the reports which were published in the Congressional Serial Set as House and Senate Executive Documents.

C. NEWSPAPERS

7-17 Brigham, Clarence S., comp. HISTORY AND BIBLIOGRAPHY OF AMERI-
CAN NEWSPAPERS, 1690-1820. 2 vols. Worcester, Mass.: American
Antiquarian Society, 1947. Reprint. Hamden, Conn.: Archon Books,
1962; Westport, Conn.: Greenwood Press, 1976. xvii, 1,558 p. Index.

> Bibliographic entries for 2,120 newspapers published between
> 1690 and 1820 are included in this publication. The entries,
> which are arranged by state and thereunder alphabetically by
> city and/or title, include publishing history and location of
> extant copies. The six largest collections of early newspapers
> are found at the American Antiquarian Society, Library of Con-
> gress, Harvard University, New York Historical Society, New
> York Public Library, and Wisconsin State Historical Society.
> These newspapers are useful not only for political news, but
> also for information about commerce, manufacturers, and agri-
> culture. The reprint edition includes a fifty-page supplement
> listing additions and corrections up to 1961. The eigtheenth-
> century holdings of the Library of Congress are also listed in
> A CHECK LIST OF AMERICAN EIGHTEENTH CENTURY NEWS-
> PAPERS IN THE LIBRARY OF CONGRESS, rev. ed. (Washing-
> ton, D.C.: Library of Congress, 1936).

7-18 Farrell, Richard T. "Advice to Farmers: the Content of Agricultural
Newspapers, 1860-1910." AGRICULTURAL HISTORY 51 (January 1977):
209-17. Table, notes.

> The contents of agricultural newspapers (1860-1910) are analyzed
> in terms of the types of advice given to farmers.

7-19 Gregory, Winifred. AMERICAN NEWSPAPERS, 1821-1936: A UNION
LIST OF FILES AVAILABLE IN THE UNITED STATES AND CANADA. New
York: H.W. Wilson Co., 1937. 791 p.

> Newspapers published between 1821 and 1936 are arranged by
> state or province and city and thereunder alphabetically by title
> of newspaper. Entries indicate date range and repository of ex-
> tant copies.

7-20 Hayward, Robert, and Osborne, Brian S. "The BRITISH COLONIST and
the Immigration to Toronto of 1847: A Content Analysis Approach to
Newspaper Research in Historical Geography." CANADIAN GEOGRAPHER
17 (Winter 1973): 391-402.

> Using a mid-nineteenth-century newspaper, the authors illustrate
> the use of newspapers through the application of content anal-
> ysis for immigration studies.

7-21 Library of Congress Catalogs. NEWSPAPERS IN MICROFORM: UNITED STATES, 1948-1972. Washington, D.C.: Library of Congress, 1973. xxiii, 1,056 p.

> A cumulation of all reports of microfilmed newspapers contained in the U.S. section of NEWSPAPERS ON MICROFILM (1948-67), along with all reports received through the summer of 1972, are included in this volume. The entries, which are arranged by state and city and thereunder by title of newspaper, include publishing data and location of microform copies. Cumulated reports up to 1977 are listed in NEWSPAPERS IN MICROFORM: UNITED STATES, 1973-1977 (1978).

7-22 Preston, Richard E. "Audit Bureau of Circulations Daily Newspaper Records as a Source in Studies of Post-1915 Settlement Patterns in the United States and Canada." HISTORICAL GEOGRAPHY NEWSLETTER 7 (1977): 1-12. Maps, tables, notes.

> Since 1915 the Audit Bureau of Circulations has kept circulation statistics for most daily newspapers in the United States and Canada primarily as a reference service for purchasers of advertising. Besides describing the availability and limitations of these records, Preston also demonstrates their utility in central place studies using Ontario as an example.

7-23 Wacker, Peter O. "Historical Geographers, Newspaper Advertisements, and the Bicentennial Celebration." PROFESSIONAL GEOGRAPHER 26 (February 1974): 12-18. Maps, table notes.

> Wacker evaluates newspaper advertisements of improved real property as a source for historical geographers in obtaining economic and cultural data. Examples from colonial New Jersey illustrate this critique.

Chapter 8
CENSUS RECORDS

The published statistics and manuscript census schedules produced by the federal government have been used by numerous historical geographers. Many of the entries in this chapter list the availability of the census records or describe their contents. Other entries by geographers discuss the research potential and limitations of these records. There are also several entries pertaining to population sources for the colonial period.

8-1 Andriot, John L. POPULATION ABSTRACT OF THE UNITED STATES. McLean, Va.: Andriot Associates, 1980. 925 p. Maps, index.

Population statistics from 1790 through 1970 have been abstracted for each state as a whole, each county in the state, and each city in the state with a population over 10,000. In addition, there are 1970 state maps showing the location of counties and abstracts of the 1970 population figures for all minor civil divisions. This volume is intended to be a companion to Andriot's TOWNSHIP ATLAS OF THE UNITED STATES (see entry 5-3).

8-2 Barrows, Robert G. "The Manuscript Federal Census: Source for 'New' Local History." INDIANA MAGAZINE OF HISTORY 69 (September 1973): 181-92. Illus., notes.

Barrows describes the content and limitations of the nineteenth-century manuscript census schedules and shows how they can be used in writing local histories. See also Barrows, "Instructions to Enumerators for Completing the 1900 Census Population Schedules," HISTORICAL METHODS NEWSLETTER 9 (September 1976): 201-12.

8-3 Conzen, Kathleen Neils. "Mapping Manuscript Census Data for Nineteenth Century Cities." HISTORICAL GEOGRAPHY NEWSLETTER 4 (Spring 1974): 1-7. Maps, notes.

Focusing on mid-nineteenth-century Milwaukee, Conzen discusses the problems of mapping manuscript census data at the micro level. She points out that city directories and fire insurance maps are useful aids for such a project.

8-4   Conzen, Michael P. "Spatial Data from Nineteenth Century Manuscript
       Censuses: A Technique for Rural Settlement and Land Use Analysis."
       PROFESSIONAL GEOGRAPHER 21 (September 1969): 337-43. Maps, notes.

       Conzen describes a technique for mapping spatial data from the
       nineteenth-century population and agricultural censuses for rural
       areas by correlating the information from the manuscript census
       schedules with township land ownership plats. He uses Blooming
       Grove Township in Dane County, Wisconsin, as his example.

8-5   Davidson, Katherine H., and Ashby, Charlotte M., comps. PRELIMINARY
       INVENTORY OF THE RECORDS OF THE BUREAU OF THE CENSUS. Pre-
       liminary Inventory, No. 161. Washington, D.C.: National Archives and
       Records Service, 1964. ix, 141 p. Paper.

       Over eight thousand cubic feet of census records dating from
       1790 to 1960 are described in this inventory. They consist of
       the administrative records of the Census Office and the Census
       Bureau and the census schedules collected in the field. Also
       included are an administrative history of the agency and a
       glossary of census terms.

8-6   Delle Donne, Carmen R. FEDERAL CENSUS SCHEDULES, 1850-80; PRI-
       MARY SOURCES FOR HISTORICAL RESEARCH. Reference Information
       Paper, No. 67. Washington, D.C.: National Archives and Records Ser-
       vice, 1973. v, 29 p. Paper.

       Originally prepared in 1971 for the Conference on the National
       Archives and Research in Historical Geography, this paper re-
       views the procedures for collecting census data and the content
       of the various schedules (population: free and slave; and non-
       population: industry, agriculture, social statistics, dependent
       classes, and mortality) completed between 1850 and 1880. An
       appendix lists the depositories of the nonpopulation schedules
       which were dispersed in 1918 to various state historical societies
       and universities.

8-7   Fishbein, Meyer H. THE CENSUS OF MANUFACTURERS, 1810-1890.
       Reference Information Paper, No. 50. Washington, D.C.: National Ar-
       chives and Records Service, 1973. vi, 31 p. Paper. Notes.

       Fishbein reviews the development of the censuses of manufac-
       turers from 1810 to 1890. In order for historians to evaluate
       these reports, he discusses the professional qualifications of the
       authors, the procedures used in compiling the schedules, and
       the contents of the reports. This article was originally published
       in NATIONAL ARCHIVES ACCESSIONS, no. 57 (June 1963),
       pp. 1-20.

8-8   Franklin, W. Neil, comp. FEDERAL POPULATION AND MORTALITY
       CENSUS SCHEDULES, 1790-1890, IN THE NATIONAL ARCHIVES AND
       THE STATES: OUTLINE OF A LECTURE ON THEIR AVAILABILITY, CON-

TENT, AND USE. Special List, No. 24. Washington, D.C.: National Archives and Records Service, 1971. vii, 89 p. Paper.

Although this publication was originally prepared as a lecture for genealogists, it will be useful to historical geographers because it provides a union list of microfilm and manuscript copies of the population and mortality censuses compiled by the U.S. Census Bureau. Also included is a discussion of the content of each census schedule, as well as a bibliography of published and manuscript finding aids for the census schedules.

8-9 Greene, Evarts B., and Harrington, Virginia B. AMERICAN POPULATION BEFORE THE FEDERAL CENSUS OF 1790. New York: Columbia University Press, 1932. xiii, 228 p. Tables, notes, index.

Population figures based on estimates derived from census, taxable, and militia enumerations are listed for the colonies as a whole, individual colonies, and counties and other localities within the colonies. There is no interpretation of the figures, but the manuscript sources are indicated for each estimate or tabulation. Although published in 1932, this book remains the standard reference for colonial population figures.

8-10 Hazel, Joseph A. "Semimicrostudies of Counties from the Manuscripts of the Census of 1860." PROFESSIONAL GEOGRAPHER 17 (July 1965): 15-19. Maps, notes.

Based on a study of slave-holding patterns in Alabama, Hazel discusses some of the inherent clues in the 1860 manuscript census schedules for mapping population statistics within a county.

8-11 Hollingsworth, Thomas H. HISTORICAL DEMOGRAPHY. Ithaca, N.Y.: Cornell University Press, 1969. 448 p. Tables, diagrs., notes, bibliog., index.

Although American sources are not emphasized, the major part of this book describes demographic techniques and historical sources of information on population, particularly censuses, taxation returns, vital registration data, inquests and wills, military data, and nonwritten sources (pictures and archaeological discoveries). The bibliography is also organized by type of record.

8-12 Kirkham, E. Kay. SURVEY OF AMERICAN CENSUS SCHEDULES. Salt Lake City: Deseret Book Company, 1959. 102 p. Paper.

Prepared primarily for genealogical research, this booklet summarizes the content of each census from 1790 to 1880.

8-13 Knights, Peter R. "A Method for Estimating Census Under-Enumeration." HISTORICAL METHODS NEWSLETTER 3 (December 1969): 5-8. Tables, notes.

Knights dicusses the accuracy of the nineteenth-century manuscript census schedules in this short note as well as in "Accuracy of Age Reporting in the Manuscript Federal Censuses of 1850 and 1860," HISTORICAL METHODS NEWSLETTER 4 (June 1971): 79-83.

8-14 Library of Congress. Census Library Project. CATALOG OF UNITED STATES CENSUS PUBLICATIONS, 1790-1945. Prepared by Henry J. Dubester. Washington, D.C.: Government Printing Office, 1950. x, 320 p. Index.

Dubester provides a comprehensive listing of the publications for each decennial census from 1790 to 1940, as well as of the publications resulting from special projects. Included are references to the 1870, 1890, 1900, 1910, and 1920 statistical atlases and minor civil division maps associated with the 1930 and 1940 censuses. This bibliography has been reprinted in U.S. Bureau of the Census, BUREAU OF THE CENSUS CATALOG OF PUBLICATIONS, 1790-1972 (Washington, D.C.: Government Printing Office, 1974), which also includes a listing of more than sixty thousand reports published since 1946.

8-15 _____. STATE CENSUSES: AN ANNOTATED BIBLIOGRAPHY OF CENSUSES OF POPULATION TAKEN AFTER THE YEAR 1790 BY THE STATES AND TERRITORIES OF THE UNITED STATES. Prepared by Henry J. Dubester. Washington, D.C.: Government Printing Office, 1948. v, 73 p. Paper. Notes.

The primary emphasis of this bibliography is the published tabulations of state and territorial censuses, although an appendix also lists the known manuscript schedules.

8-16 Muller, Edward K. "Town Populations in the Early United States Censuses: An Aid to Research." HISTORICAL METHODS NEWSLETTER 3 (March 1970): 2-8. Notes.

By utilizing occupation data recorded in the manuscript census schedules, Muller develops a method for estimating the population of small towns which were not recorded in the published versions of the U.S. censuses prior to 1870.

8-17 National Archives and Records Service. FEDERAL POPULATION CENSUSES, 1790-1890: A CATALOG OF MICROFILM OF THE SCHEDULES. Washington, D.C.: General Services Administration, 1975. viii, 90 p. Paper.

The geographical contents of the individual reels of the microfilm copies of the U.S. Census manuscript population schedules are listed in this catalog. The entries are arranged by census year, thereunder alphabetically by state and county. A list of the microfilm copies of the 1880 Soundex (personal name index) is also included. Ordering instructions are provided.

8-18 _____. 1900 FEDERAL POPULATION CENSUS: A CATALOG OF MI-
CROFILM COPIES OF THE SCHEDULES. Washington, D.C.: General
Services Administration, 1978. vii, 84 p. Paper.

The contents of the microfilm of the 1900 manuscript census
schedules are listed in this catalog. It also includes a list of
the microfilm copies of the 1900 Soundex (personal name index)
and the 1900 census enumeration district descriptions.

8-19 Rhoads, James B., and Ashby, Charlotte M. PRELIMINARY INVENTORY
OF THE CARTOGRAPHIC RECORDS OF THE BUREAU OF THE CENSUS.
Preliminary Inventory, No. 103. Washington, D.C.: National Archives
and Records Service, 1958. v, 108 p. Paper.

The cartographic records of the Bureau of the Census are described in this inventory. Included among these records are the
census enumeration district maps (1880-1940) and descriptions
(1850-1940). The maps and descriptions for the 1950 and 1960
censuses, which are now in the National Archives, are not
included in this listing.

8-20 Sobel, Joel. "Population Linkage and the Manuscript Census." HISTORI-
CAL GEOGRAPHY NEWSLETTER 4 (Spring 1974): 8-12. Tables, notes.

Sobel discusses the problems of data linkage using the 1870 and
1880 manuscript census schedules for Mankato, Minnesota. He
describes the results of a computer program which links individuals
on the basis of identical Soundex name codes (see entries 6-39
and 8-17).

8-21 U.S. Bureau of the Census. A CENTURY OF POPULATION GROWTH
FROM THE FIRST CENSUS OF THE UNITED STATES TO THE TWELFTH,
1790-1900. Washington, D.C.: Government Printing Office, 1909.
x, 303 p. Maps, diagrs., tables, notes, index.

This retrospective publication is primarily a tabulation and analysis of the 1790 census figures in comparison to later censuses,
particularly the one in 1900. It includes a series of state maps
showing 1790 county boundaries overlaid on 1900 county boundaries. One appendix lists population enumerations prior to 1790.

8-22 _____. HISTORICAL STATISTICS OF THE UNITED STATES, COLONIAL
TIMES TO 1970. 1949. 3d ed., rev. Bicentennial edition. 2 vols.
Washington, D.C.: Government Printing Office, 1975. xvi, 1,232 p.
Tables, notes, index.

This edition is a convenient reference tool which lists historical
statistics from a variety of sources. Most tabulations are presented for the nation as a whole, while a few are broken down
by region or state. The accompanying text and annotations refer to more detailed sources of data. The first twenty-three
chapters, which are arranged by subject (including population,
vital statistics, migration, labor, income and wealth, agricul-

ture, forestry and fisheries, minerals, land sales, manufactures, transportation, communications, and energy), pertain basically to the period from 1790 to the present. The final chapter is devoted to colonial and pre-federal statistics.

8-23 Walsh, Margaret. "The Census as an Accurate Source of Information: The Value of Mid-Nineteenth Century Manufacturing Returns." HISTORICAL METHODS NEWSLETTER 3 (September 1970): 3-13. Notes.

The value and accuracy of the mid-nineteenth-century census manufacturing returns are described in this article. Walsh also compares the value of printed and manuscript census records in "The Value of Mid-Nineteenth Century Manufacturing Returns: The Printed Census and Manuscript Census Compilations Compared," HISTORICAL METHODS NEWSLETTER 4 (March 1971): 43-51.

8-24 Wells, Robert V. THE POPULATION OF THE BRITISH COLONIES IN AMER-ICA BEFORE 1776: A SURVEY OF CENSUS DATA. Princeton: Princeton University Press, 1975. xii, 342 p. Tables, notes, index.

Although the major part of this study is devoted to a colony by colony description of various demographic topics (population size, growth and distribution, freeman and slaves or servants, age structure, sex ratios, and household size), its basis is 124 censuses covering twenty-one British colonies in North America. The introductory chapter lists these censuses, their content, and source, and discusses their creation, reliability, and utility. These censuses, which are actual enumerations rather than estimates, were found primarily among the colonial records in the Public Record Office and the British Museum. There is no bibliography, but the footnotes provide numerous references to recent studies pertaining to colonial demographic history.

8-25 Westfall, John E. "Estimating Minor Civil Division Boundaries Through the Manuscript Census Schedules: A Methodological Note." HISTORICAL GEOGRAPHY NEWSLETTER 3, no. 1 (Spring 1973): 3-6. Maps, notes.

Using the 1870 manuscript census schedules for Sierra County, California, Westfall describes a method for estimating the boundaries of minor civil divisions when adequate maps are not available. See also Westfall, "Historical Population Estimation Using Electoral Data," AAG PROCEEDINGS 5 (1973): 291-95.

8-26 Whitney, Herbert A. "Estimating Precensus Populations: A Method Suggested and Applied to the Towns of Rhode Island and Plymouth Colonies in 1689." AAG ANNALS 55 (March 1965): 179-89. Maps, tables, notes.

Whitney develops a method for estimating population size and densities for Rhode Island's minor civil divisions in 1689 based on similar ratios of family size to adult men (militia) that were recorded in nearby Bristol County, Plymouth Colony (Massachusetts).

Chapter 9

LAND RECORDS

References describing the contents, availability, and research potential of land
survey (plats and field notes) and landownership (patents, deeds, land entry papers,
and tract books) records for both public and nonpublic land states are included in
this chapter. Because county landownership maps and plat atlases are closely
related to landownership records, references to this cartographic product are
included in the second section of this chapter. Additional listings of county landownership atlases are found in entries 1-30 and 1-31.

A. SURVEY AND DISPOSAL RECORDS

9-1 Bouman, Lane J. "The Survey Records of the General Land Office and
Where They Can Be Found Today." American Congress on Surveying and
Mapping. PROCEEDINGS OF 36TH ANNUAL MEETING, Washington,
D.C., February 1976, pp. 263-72.

> Bouman briefly describes the survey records of the General Land
> Office (instructions, contracts, plats, field notes, manuals)
> and mentions the location of various copies in the National
> Archives, state archives, and the Eastern State Office, Bureau
> of Land Management.

9-2 Bowman, Jacob N. "Index of the Spanish-Mexican Private Land Grant
Records and Cases of California." Berkeley: University of California,
Bancroft Library, 1958. xxiii, 598 p. Typescript.

> Bowman describes and indexes the records (primarily expedientes,
> disenos, and court cases) relating to the confirmation of the
> Spanish-Mexican private land claims in California. The records
> are scattered in twelve repositories, including the Bancroft Li-
> brary and the National Archives. For examples of the disenos,
> see entry 3-8.

9-3 Bryant, Pat, and Hemperley, Marion R., comps. ENGLISH CROWN GRANTS
IN GEORGIA, 1755-1775. 9 vols. Atlanta: Surveyor-General Department,
1972. Paper.

> The royal land grants (1755-75) currently in the custody of the

Georgia Surveyor-General Department are abstracted in nine booklets. The first volume pertains to the Georgia coastal islands, while the others abstract the grants for St. Andrew; St. David, St. Patrick, St. Thomas, and St. Mary; St. John; St. Matthew; St. Philip; Christ Church; St. Paul; and St. George Parishes. Entries include the name of grantee, acreage, date, bounds, and references to grant and/or survey plat. Other Georgia land records are abstracted in Pat Bryant, ENTRY OF CLAIMS FOR GEORGIA LANDHOLDERS, 1733-55 (1978), and Alex M. Hitz, AUTHENTIC LIST OF ALL LAND LOTTERY GRANTS MADE TO VETERANS OF THE REVOLUTIONARY WAR BY THE STATE OF GEORGIA (2d ed., 1966).

9-4 Diaz, Albert James. A GUIDE TO THE MICROFILM OF PAPERS RELATING TO NEW MEXICO LAND GRANTS. University of New Mexico Publications, Library Series, No. 1. Albuquerque: University of New Mexico Press, 1960. vii, 102 p. Paper. Bibliog.

New Mexico private land claim records, which were in the custody of the Bureau of Land Management in Santa Fe, are included in this microfilm project. This publication serves as a guide and an index to both the sixty-three microfilm reels and the original records.

9-5 Gentry, Daphne, comp. VIRGINIA LAND OFFICE INVENTORY. Richmond: Virginia State Library, Archives Division, [1975]. xxxvi, 72 p. Paper. Index.

This inventory describes the records of the Virginia Land Office now in the Virginia State Library. These records include patents, survey plats, abstracts, and related materials from the colonial and Commonwealth periods, as well as from the Northern Neck Proprietary, (land between the Potomac and Rappahannock Rivers).

9-6 Heard, John P. "Resource for Historians: Records of the Bureau of Land Management in California and Nevada." FOREST HISTORY 12 (July 1968): 20-26.

The Bureau of Land Management records in the San Francisco Federal Records Center are described. These records include township surveys, land-entry papers, and tract books dating from 1861.

9-7 Kirkham, E. Kay. THE LAND RECORDS OF AMERICA AND THEIR GENEALOGICAL VALUE. Washington, D.C.: By the author, 1963. 70 p. Paper. Maps, illus.

Prepared as a guide for genealogical researchers, this booklet describes the content and availability of colonial, federal, state, and county land records. Examples of plats and various types of land-entry papers are included.

9-8 Maxwell, Richard S. PUBLIC LAND RECORDS OF THE FEDERAL GOVERN-
MENT, 1800-1950, AND THEIR STATISTICAL SIGNIFICANCE. Reference
Information Paper, No. 57. Washington, D.C.: National Archives and
Records Service, 1973. vi, 18 p. Paper. Notes.

> Maxwell, an archivist dealing primarily with the records of the
> General Land Office (Record Group 49) in the National Ar-
> chives, describes the procedure for obtaining land from the
> federal government and the resultant records: land-entry papers
> (including cash and credit sales, donation claims, military
> bounty land warrants, homestead entries, private land claims,
> and mineral entries), tract books, monthly abstracts, patents,
> and township plats. He also reviews recent literature that
> uses these records for statistical studies.

9-9 Pattison, William D. "Use of the U.S. Public Land Survey Plats and Notes
as Descriptive Sources." PROFESSIONAL GEOGRAPHER 8 (January 1956):
10-14.

> This short, but valuable, article reviews the availability of the
> U.S. Public Land Survey township plats and field notes at the
> county, state, and federal levels. In addition, Pattison demon-
> strates how these records can be used for historical geographical
> research by citing numerous secondary articles and dissertations
> produced primarily from the 1930s to the 1950s.

9-10 Smith, Clifford Neal. FEDERAL LAND SERIES. A CALENDAR OF AR-
CHIVAL MATERIALS ON THE LAND PATENTS ISSUED BY THE UNITED
STATES GOVERNMENT, WITH SUBJECT, TRACT, AND NAME INDEXES.
3 vols. Chicago: American Library Association, 1972-- . Maps, index.

> This ongoing publication is a useful guide to early federal land
> records. Volume 1 (1972, xxvii, 338 p.) and 3 (1980, xxxix,
> 341 p.) abstract archival materials dated from 1788 to 1814
> (mainly correspondence from the records of the General Land
> Office in the National Archives) relating to the transmittal
> of patents, the initial grant of land by the federal government
> to private individuals. The first volume pertains primarily to
> Ohio, while the third volume includes entries for Ohio, Indiana,
> Illinois, Alabama, Mississippi, and Louisiana. Volume 2 (1973,
> xxiii, 391 p.) includes only material relating to federal bounty-
> land warrants used for patenting land in the U.S. Military Dis-
> trict of Ohio, 1799-1835.

9-11 Smith, Jane F. "Settlement on the Public Domain as Reflected in Federal
Records: Suggested Research Approaches." In PATTERN AND PROCESS,
edited by Ralph E. Ehrenberg, pp. 290-304. Washington, D.C.: Howard
University Press, 1975. Map, notes.

> The public land records of the Bureau of Land Management are
> described in the context of four categories: survey records (plats

and field notes), status records (tract books and status plats), case records (land-entry papers), and legal records (control records, patents, proclamations, and orders). The research potential of these records is also discussed.

9-12 Yoshpe, Harry P., and Brower, Philip P., comps. PRELIMINARY INVENTORY OF THE LAND-ENTRY PAPERS OF THE GENERAL LAND OFFICE. Preliminary Inventory, No. 22. Washington, D.C.: National Archives, 1949. iii, 77 p. Paper.

Land-entry papers documenting the disposal of the public domain are listed in this inventory. The records pertain to cash entries, credit certificates, military bounty-land warrants, Indian scrip, private land claims, homestead entries, forest reserves, and mineral claims. The records are arranged by land office and type of transaction. Additional descriptions of these records and their research potential are found in Robert W. Harrison, "Public Land Records of the Federal Government," MISSISSIPPI VALLEY HISTORICAL REVIEW 41 (September 1954): 277–88; and Richard S. Lackey, "The Genealogist's First Look at Federal Land Records," PROLOGUE 9 (Spring 1977): 43–45.

B. LANDOWNERSHIP MAPS

9-13 Kingsbury, Robert C. "The County Atlas in Indiana, 1874–1926." Indiana Academy of the Social Sciences. PROCEEDINGS, 3d series, 11 (1976): 81–90. Maps, notes.

Kingsbury summarizes the geographical and temporal coverage of Indiana county atlases.

9-14 Ristow, Walter W. "From Maps to Riches, The Mapping Career of Jay Gould." MAP COLLECTOR, no. 7 (June 1979), pp. 2–10. Maps, notes.

Ristow examines the early career of the nineteenth-century financeer, Jay Gould, who began his financial aggrandizement as a surveyor and publisher of several New York county land ownership maps. The career of one of the major publishers from 1846 to 1864 is reviewed by Ristow in "The Map Publishing Career of Robert Pearsall Smith," QUARTERLY JOURNAL OF THE LIBRARY OF CONGRESS 26 (July 1969): 179–96. Ristow also discusses the career of Henry Francis Walling, another early publisher of landownership maps, in "Nineteenth Century Cadastral Maps in Ohio," Bibliographical Society of America, PAPERS 59 (3d quarter 1965): 306–15.

9-15 Sitwell, O.F.G. "County Maps of the Nineteenth Century as Historical Documents: A New Use." CANADIAN CARTOGRAPHER 7 (June 1970): 27-41. Maps, table notes.

> In assessing the accuracy of a 1879 county atlas for Pictou County, Nova Scotia, Sitwell shows that there was a close correlation with the number of farms recorded in the 1880 Canadian census.

9-16 Stephenson, Richard W., comp. LAND OWNERSHIP MAPS: A CHECK-LIST OF NINETEENTH CENTURY UNITED STATES COUNTY MAPS IN THE LIBRARY OF CONGRESS. Washington, D.C.: Library of Congress, 1967. xxv, 86 p. Paper. Maps, notes, index.

> The collection of 1,449 U.S. county landownership maps at the Library of Congress are recorded in this checklist. An introductory essay traces the historical development of this type of map.

9-17 Thrower, Norman J.W. "The County Atlas of the United States." SURVEYING AND MAPPING 21 (September 1961): 365-73. Maps, illus., notes.

> Thrower reviews the development, coverage, place of publication, and research potential of the county atlases or plat books published by private companies during the last half of the nineteenth and the early twentieth centuries. See also Thrower, "Cadastral Survey and County Atlases of the United States," CARTOGRAPHIC JOURNAL 9 (June 1972): 43-51.

9-18 Treude, Mai. WINDOWS TO THE PAST: A BIBLIOGRAPHY OF MINNESOTA COUNTY ATLASES. Minneapolis: University of Minnesota, Center for Urban and Regional Affairs, 1980. ix, 187 p. Paper. Maps, illus., photos., diagrs., tables, notes, bibliog., index.

> Over seven hundred county atlases in the Library of Congress and in seventy-five local Minnesota libraries and county historical societies are described in this union listing. The introduction, parts of which are reprinted in Special Libraries Association Geography and Map Division BULLETIN, no. 122, December 1980, pp. 9-12, provides a general analysis of county landownership atlases as well as a history of county atlas publishing with special reference to Minnesota.

Chapter 10

PICTORIAL SOURCES

Graphic sources other than maps are the subject of this chapter. Of particular interest are landscape paintings, prints (lithographs and engravings) and still photographs of landscape scenes and urban views, and aerial photographs. These entries include bibliographies, directories and guides to major repositories, general histories, selected picture collections or exhibit catalogs that emphasize these graphic records as historical sources, and articles illustrating the geographers' interpretation and use of these sources. References listed in the bibliographies by Keaveney (10-5), Sokol (10-8), Malan (10-24), and Shaw (10-34) are generally not repeated in this chapter.

A. LANDSCAPE PAINTING

10-1 Dawdy, Doris O. ARTISTS OF THE AMERICAN WEST: A BIOGRAPHICAL DICTIONARY. Chicago: Swallow Press, 1974. viii, 275 p. Bibliog.

> Brief biographies of over thirteen-hundred artists, all born before 1900, who painted in the West, are presented here. Dawdy discusses the work of one western artist in "The Wyant Diary: An Artist with the Wheeler Survey in Arizona, 1873," ARIZONA AND THE WEST 22 (Autumn 1980): 255-78.

10-2 Ewers, John C. ARTISTS OF THE OLD WEST. 1965. Enl. ed. Garden City, N.Y.: Doubleday, 1973. 240 p. Illus., bibliog.

> Ewers discusses the work of twenty-two western artists, putting them in the context of explorers and historians. Most of the paintings reproduced in this volume pertain to Indian scenes and activities, reflecting Ewers's interest in Indians. Other articles by Ewers pertaining to western art include "Gustavus Sohon's Portraits of Flathead and Pend d'Oreille Indians, 1854," SMITHSONIAN MISCELLANEOUS COLLECTIONS 100, no. 7 (1948); "Fact and Fiction in the Documentary Art of the American West," in THE FRONTIER RE-EXAMINED, edited by John Francis McDermott, pp. 79-95 (Urbana: University of Illinois Press, 1967); EARLY WHITE INFLUENCE UPON PLAINS INDIAN

PAINTING: GEORGE CATLIN AND CARL BODMER AMONG THE MANDAN INDIANS (Smithsonian Publication 4201, 1957. Reprint. Seattle: Shorey Book Store, 1971); "Folk Art in the Fur Trade of the Upper Missouri," PROLOGUE 4 (Summer 1972): 99-108; and "Artifacts and Pictures as Documents in the History of Indian-White Relations," in INDIAN-WHITE RELATIONS, edited by Jane F. Smith and Robert M. Kvasnicka (Washington, D.C.: Howard University Press, 1976, pp. 101-12).

10-3 Goetzman, William H. "The Grand Reconnaissance." AMERICAN HERITAGE 23 (October 1972), : 46-59. Maps, illus.

Accompanying this review of the Pacific Railroad Surveys of 1853 is a selection of original watercolors by John Mix Stanley and Gustavus Sohon, two artists who were members of Isaac Steven's survey expedition.

10-4 Johnson, Hildegard Binder. "The Framed Landscape." LANDSCAPE 23, no. 2 (1979): 26-32. Illus.

Johnson traces the development of landscape painting from its European origins and ends with the prominent landscape painters of the western United States during the last half of the nineteenth century.

10-5 Keaveney, Sydney Starr, ed. AMERICAN PAINTING: A GUIDE TO INFORMATION SOURCES. Art and Architecture Information Guide Series, vol. 1. Detroit: Gale Research Co., 1974. xiii, 260 p. Index.

Although there are no chapter headings pertaining specifically to landscape painting, the entries in this annotated bibliography pertain to general histories, period surveys (colonial, nineteenth and twentieth centuries), and individual artists. Additional chapters list research libraries that emphasize American painting and museums with important collections of American paintings. Since many of the publications mentioned in this bibliography include reproductions of various paintings, they can provide a guide to collections of American landscape paintings.

10-6 Novak, Barbara. NATURE AND CULTURE: AMERICAN LANDSCAPE AND PAINTING, 1825-1875. New York: Oxford University Press, 1980. xi, 323 p. Illus., photos., notes, bibliog., index.

The purpose of this recent history of American landscape painting is to examine this phase of painting in its own cultural context (philosophical, spiritual, and scientific). Novak examines the influence of new discoveries in geology, meteorology, and botany on the basic elements of the paintings: rocks, clouds, and plants. She views the artist as a recorder of explorations as well as a recorder of men's traces on the land (deforestation, railroads). She does not concentrate on biographies or works of individual artists. The book includes a useful but dated bibliography.

10-7 Rees, Ronald. "Historical Links between Cartography and Art." GEO-GRAPHICAL REVIEW 70 (January 1980): 60-76. Maps, illus., notes.

Although the context of this paper is the Middle Ages and the Renaissance, Rees establishes several relationships between cartography and landscape paintings which are still evident in the mid-nineteenth century. Other articles by Rees pertaining to landscape painting and geography include "Landscape in Art," in DIMENSIONS OF HUMAN GEOGRAPHY, edited by Karl W. Butzer, Department of Geography Research Paper, No. 186, pp. 48-68 (Chicago: University of Chicago, Department of Geography, 1978); "John Constable and the Art of Geography," GEOGRAPHICAL REVIEW 66 (January 1976): 59-72; and "Geography and Landscape Painting: An Introduction to a Neglected Field," SCOTTISH GEOGRAPHICAL MAGAZINE 89 (December 1973): 147-57.

10-8 Sokol, David M., ed. AMERICAN ARCHITECTURE AND ART: A GUIDE TO INFORMATION SOURCES. American Studies Information Guide Series, vol. 2. Detroit: Gale Research Co., 1976. xii, 341 p. Index.

Included in this annotated bibliography are three chapters pertaining to American painting: general histories, period surveys (colonial, and nineteenth and twentieth centuries), and individual painters. The latter chapter lists books and articles that are biographical or that analyze the style and technique of individual painters. Numerous works pertaining to nineteenth-century landscape painters are included and are not repeated in the present bibliography.

10-9 Stenzel, Franz. JAMES MADISON ALDEN: YANKEE ARTIST OF THE PACIFIC COAST, 1854-1860. Fort Worth: Amon Carter Museum, 1975. xiii, 209 p. Illus., notes, bibliog., index.

Stenzel presents a biography of Alden (1834-1922), an artist who accompanied the U.S. Coast Survey and the Canadian-U.S. Boundary Survey (from the Pacific to the Continental Divide). Included are ninety-eight illustrations pertaining primarily to landscape scenes in the Pacific Northwest (northern California to Vancouver Island).

10-10 Taft, Robert. ARTISTS AND ILLUSTRATORS OF THE OLD WEST: 1850-1900. New York: Charles Scribner's Sons, 1953. xvii, 400 p. Illus., notes, index.

Biographies of selected artists who depicted various aspects of the trans-Mississippi West (primarily the Plains and the Rockies) during the last half of the nineteenth century are included in this standard text. Their illustrations, which consisted of sketches, oil paintings, watercolors, and printed views in government reports, record mainly landscape scenes, town views, and Indian activities.

10-11 Taylor, Hugh A. "Documentary Art and the Role of the Archivist." AMERICAN ARCHIVIST 42 (October 1979): 417-28. Notes.

Using Canadian examples, Taylor discusses the role of documentary art (paintings, drawings, and prints) in archives and historical research.

10-12 Truettner, William H. NATIONAL PARKS AND THE AMERICAN LANDSCAPE. Washington, D.C.: Smithsonian Institution Press for the National Collection of Fine Arts, 1972. 141 p. Paper. Illus., photos., notes, bibliog., index.

In 1972 the National Collection of Fine Arts prepared an exhibit as part of the National Parks Centennial Year (commemorating the founding of Yellowstone Park). This accompanying exhibit catalog contains landscape paintings, sketches, and photographs depicting scenes in various western parks. Similar paintings were included in an earlier exhibit, commemorating the fiftieth anniversary of the National Park Service in 1966, which is cataloged in AMERICAN LANDSCAPE: A CHANGING FRONTIER (Washington, D.C.: Smithsonian Institution, National Collection of Fine Arts, 1966).

10-13 Wilmerding, John. AMERICAN LIGHT: THE LUMINIST MOVEMENT, 1850-1875. New York: Harper and Row for the National Galley of Art, Washington, D.C., 1980. 330 p. Illus., photos., notes, bibliog., index.

The landscape style known as luminism, which was practiced in America during the third quarter of the nineteenth century, was the subject of an exhibit at the National Galley of Art. This publication contains nine essays that examine various aspects of luminism and a selection of paintings and photographs that were included in the exhibit. The bibliography lists numerous works pertaining to nineteenth-century landscape paintings, as well as individual painters and photographers associated with this style.

B. PRINTS AND STILL PHOTOGRAPHS

10-14 AMERICAN PRINTMAKING BEFORE 1876: FACT, FICTION, AND FANTASY. Washington, D.C.: Library of Congress, 1975. v, 79 p. Paper. Illus., notes.

Nine papers presented at a symposium held at the Library of Congress, June 1972, are reproduced in this publication. The efforts of American artists to obtain highly accurate portraits and landscape scenes through the use of prephotographic devices such as the camera obscura, camera lucida, physiognotrace, and daguerreotype are reviewed in Josephine Cobb, "Prints, the Camera, and Historical Accuracy," pp. 1-10. The inaccuracy of some lithographs is demonstrated in Ronnie C. Tyler, "Prints of the Mexican War as Historical Sources," pp. 61-71. Other papers pertaining to prints as historical documents include Frank H. Sommer III, "Prints as Documents of Early American History," pp. 25-33, and Peter C. Marzio, "Illustrated News in Early American Prints," pp. 53-60.

10-15 Current, Karen. PHOTOGRAPHY AND THE OLD WEST. New York: Harry N. Abrams, Inc., for the Amon Carter Museum of Western Art, 1978. 272 p. Photos., notes, bibliog., index.

The purpose of this collection of photographs is to explain the role of the nineteenth-century photographer as a conscious historian of the West by recording events, people, and places. Brief biographies and selected works are presented for nineteen photographers. The photographs depict Indian activities and dwellings, white settlements, mining activities, railroads, and landscape scenes. Similar collections of nineteenth-century photographs are found in Ralph Warren Andrews, PHOTOGRAPHERS OF THE FRONTIER WEST: THEIR LIVES AND WORKS, 1875 TO 1915 (Seattle: Superior Publishing Co., 1965); Van Deren Coke, PHOTOGRAPHY IN NEW MEXICO FROM THE DAGUERREOTYPE TO THE PRESENT (Albuquerque: University of New Mexico Press, 1979); Weston J. Naef and James N. Wood, ERA OF EXPLORATION: THE RISE OF LANDSCAPE PHOTOGRAPHY IN THE AMERICAN WEST (Boston: New York Graphic Society, 1975); and David R. Phillips, ed., THE TAMING OF THE WEST: A PHOTOGRAPHIC PERSPECTIVE (Chicago: Regnery, 1974).

10-16 Da Capo Press. WALKER EVANS: PHOTOGRAPHS FOR THE FARM SECURITY ADMINISTRATION, 1935-1938. Introduction by Jerald C. Maddox. New York: Da Capo Press, 1973. xiv, 246 p. Photos.

Selected photographs taken by Walker Evans for the Farm Security Administration (FSA) are reproduced in this illustrated catalog. These photographs, which represent only a small portion of the 75,000 FSA photographs in the custody of the Prints and Photographs Division of the Library of Congress, depict rural and urban life in the southeastern United States and emphasize rehabilitation projects, ravages of soil erosion, plight of flood victims, and the daily lives of sharecroppers.

10-17 Evans, Hilary. THE ART OF PICTURE RESEARCH: A GUIDE TO CUR-
RENT PRACTICE, PROCEDURE, TECHNIQUES AND RESOURCES. Newton Abbot, Devon: David and Charles, 1979. 208 p. Illus., photos.,
index.

Although British sources are emphasized, this publication is a
basic guide to the growing profession of picture research. It
includes such topics as research procedure, reference books, and
types of collections. Another useful reference tool, which includes an international directory of picture sources, is Hilary
Evans, Mary Evans, and Andra Nelki, THE PICTURE RE-
SEARCHER'S HANDBOOK: AN INTERNATIONAL GUIDE TO
PICTURE SOURCES--AND HOW TO USE THEM (New York:
Charles Scribner's Sons, 1974).

10-18 Frassanito, William A. GETTYSBURG: A JOURNEY IN TIME. New
York: Charles Scribner's Sons, 1975. 248 p. Maps, photos., notes,
index.

Frassanito provides a systematic examination of the extant photographs associated with the Gettysburg Battle. By carefully
studying the content and context of the photographs and comparing them with the current landscape, he was able to judge
the accuracy of the photographs and the contemporary captions.
He found that some photographs were mislabeled, while others
were not taken at the time of the battle but were posed scenes
taken some time after the battle. Over one-hundred photographs
are reproduced, while maps show the location of the various
photographs. Using a similar format, Frassanito studies the photographs associated with another Civil War battle in ANTIETAM:
THE PHOTOGRAPHIC LEGACY OF AMERICA'S BLOODIEST
DAY (New York: Charles Scribner's Sons, 1978).

10-19 Green, Shirley L. PICTORIAL RESOURCES IN THE WASHINGTON, D.C.,
AREA. Washington, D.C.: Library of Congress, 1976. xv, 297 p.
Photos, index.

Picture collections (paintings, prints, and photographs) in the
Washington, D.C., area are described in this guide. The entries
are grouped in four categories: U.S. government agencies (including the Library of Congress and the National Archives),
District of Columbia government agencies, international organizations, and private organizations. Each entry summarizes
the subject coverage, regulations, and published finding aids.

10-20 Kouwenhoven, John. THE COLUMBIA HISTORICAL PORTRAIT OF NEW
YORK. Garden City, N.Y.: Doubleday, 1953. 550 p. Maps, illus.,
photos., index.

Kouwenhoven interprets the evolution of New York City in visual
terms, using approximately nine hundred pictures (maps, prints,
illustrations, paintings, and photographs). In addition to being

a picture history, it also emphasizes pictures as historical documents that are the source of factual information about topography, manners, and customs, and clues of attitudes, interests, and perceptions.

10-21 Krim, Arthur J. "Photographic Imagery of the American City, 1840-1860." PROFESSIONAL GEOGRAPHER 25 (May 1973): 136-39. Notes.

Krim discusses the introduction and development of photographic imagery in America from 1840 to 1860, stressing the coincidence with the shift from the mercantile-preindustrial to the commercial-industrial city. By surveying the urban photographic imagery that is presently available in published sources, he stresses its utility for historical urban studies.

10-22 Library of Congress. Prints and Photographs Division. A CENTURY OF PHOTOGRAPHS, 1846-1946: SELECTED FROM THE COLLECTIONS OF THE LIBRARY OF CONGRESS. Compiled by Reneta V. Shaw. Washington, D.C.: Library of Congress, 1980. viii, 211 p. Photos., notes.

Seventeen articles, which were previously published in the QUARTERLY JOURNAL OF THE LIBRARY OF CONGRESS, are reprinted in this volume. Since these articles describe selected collections of photographs, this book serves as a partial guide to the photographic holdings of the Library of Congress. For other publications describing the library's photographic holdings, see entries 10-16 and 10-23.

10-23 _____. VIEWPOINTS: A SELECTION FROM THE PICTORIAL COLLEC-TIONS OF THE LIBRARY OF CONGRESS. Washington, D.C.: Library of Congress, 1975. x, 223 p. Photos., illus., index.

Although not a comprehensive guide, this book of sample selections is intended to show the variety and scope of the print and photograph collections in the Library of Congress. Individual pictures as well as specific collections are discussed under seven headings: world history, transportation, U.S. history, American scene (landscape scenes, political and social problems, urban scenes, Indian life), architecture, lively arts, and artist prints. An earlier, but somewhat outdated, guide to the print and photograph collections is Paul Vanderbilt, comps., GUIDE TO THE SPECIAL COLLECTIONS OF PRINTS AND PHOTOGRAPHS IN THE LIBRARY OF CONGRESS (Washington, D.C.: Library of Congress, 1955).

10-24 Malan, Nancy E. "Selected Bibliography for Historical Photograph Collections." PICTURESCOPE 28 (Summer 1980): 6.

Although this bibliography is intended for the use of administrators of historical photograph collections, it does include a number of entries that pertain to the interpretation of historical photographs. Several of these works, especially those that view photographs as historical documents, are listed in the present bibliography.

10-25   Marzio, Peter C., and Kaplan, Milton. "Lithographs as Historical Documents." ANTIQUES 102 (October 1972): 669-74. Illus.

In evaluating the accuracy of historical prints, the circumstances under which the views were printed should be considered. A view prepared for an urban booster may show idealized settings and gross exaggerations while a view prepared for an official government survey has greater obligation to depict an accurate scene.

10-26   Mayer, Harold M., and Wade, Richard C. CHICAGO: GROWTH OF A METROPOLIS. Chicago: University of Chicago Press, 1969. vii, 510 p. Maps, illus., photos., bibliog., index.

Nearly eight hundred historical photographs, supplemented by a few maps, sketches, and prints, are used by a geographer and a historian to document the physical growth of Chicago from the middle of the nineteenth century until the present. The photographs are not used only as illustrations but also as documentary evidence in describing physical growth and internal spatial patterns. The biases of photographic documentation are discussed in the introductory essay.

10-27   National Archives and Records Service. Office of Educational Programs. THE AMERICAN IMAGE: PHOTOGRAPHS FROM THE NATIONAL ARCHIVES, 1860-1960. Introduction by Alan Trachtenberg. New York: Random House, 1979. xxxii, 191 p. Photos., notes, index.

Prepared as an exhibit catalog, this publication includes a selection of photographs from the approximately five million items in the custody of the Still Pictures Branch of the National Archives. Since there is no comprehensive published finding aid to these photographic holdings, this exhibit catalog provides the only overview of the photographic activities of the various agencies of the federal government. Other photograph collections in the National Archives holdings are described in Charlotte Palmer, "Conservation and the Camera," PROLOGUE 3 (Winter 1971): 183-96, and Joe D. Thomas, "Indians of the Southwest," PROLOGUE 4 (Summer 1972): 70-76.

10-28   Newhall, Beaumont. THE HISTORY OF PHOTOGRAPHY FROM 1839 TO THE PRESENT DAY. Rev. ed. London: Secker and Warburg, 1972. 216 p. Illus., photos., notes, bibliog., index.

In this definitive history, Newhall emphasizes the technological development of photography, including discussions on Civil War photography, the expeditionary photography of the late nineteenth century, and the documentary photography from the late nineteenth century until the 1930s.

10-29 Novotny, Ann, and Eakins, Rosemary. PICTURE SOURCES 3. New York: Special Libraries Association, Picture Division, 1975. xx, 387 p. Index.

This third edition of the Special Libraries Association directory of print and photograph collections describes over one thousand institutions in the United States and Canada. Entries are grouped by categories relating to the chief subject of the collections: general, geography and history (both U.S. and foreign), military history, fine arts, performing arts, natural history and anthropology, agriculture, science and technology, commerce and industry, and transportation. The introductory chapter discusses the tools and techniques of picture research.

10-30 Ohrn, Karin Becker. DOROTHEA LANGE AND THE DOCUMENTARY TRADITION. Baton Rouge: Louisiana State University Press, 1980. xvi, 277 p. Photos., notes, bibliog., index.

The life and work of photographer Dorothea Lange (1895-1965) are examined in this biography. Her reputation grew out of the documentary photography she produced for the Farm Security Administration (migrant camps during the 1930s) and the War Relocation Authority (relocation of Japanese-Americans to concentration camps during World War II). Besides a brief history of documentary photography (recording the contemporary social scene), Ohrn also compiled an extensive bibliography that includes numerous works on the history of photography.

10-31 Pattison, William D. "The Pacific Railroad Rediscovered." GEOGRAPHI-CAL REVIEW 52 (January 1962): 25-36. Map, photos., notes.

The American Geographical Society's collection of glass plate negatives (approximately four hundred stereoscopic and two hundred single views) pertaining to the construction and early operation of the Union Pacific and Central Pacific Railroads is described. These photographs, which comprise the largest known collection on this subject, represent the work of lecturer Stephen J. Sedgwick and the Union Pacific photographic corps under the direction of Andrew J. Russell. More than fifty of these photographs are reproduced in Barry B. Combs, WESTWARD TO PROMONTORY: BUILDING THE UNION PACIFIC ACROSS THE PLAINS AND MOUNTAINS (Palo Alto, Calif.: American West Publishing, Co., 1969).

10-32 Robertson, Peter. "More than Meets the Eye." ARCHIVARIA 1 (Summer 1976): 33-43. Photos., notes.

Although the "camera never lies," Robertson points out that historical photographs do not always provide a truthful image of the past. Nineteenth-century photographs were limited to motionless objects (portraits, buildings, landscapes), were strongly influenced by "boosterism," and were subject to manipulation (cropping, retouching, misleading captions, and limited selection). Another issue of this journal is devoted entirely to historical photographs; see "Photographs and Archives," ARCHIVARIA, no. 5, Winter 1977-78.

10-33 Rundell, Walter, Jr. "Photographs as Historical Evidence: Early Texas Oil." AMERICAN ARCHIVIST 41 (October 1978): 373-98. Photos., notes.

Based on his photographic study of Texas oil fields, Rundell demonstrates the potential contributions of photographs to historical research. Rundell's larger study was published as EARLY TEXAS OIL: A PHOTOGRAPHIC HISTORY, 1866-1936 (College Station: Texas A & M University Press, 1977).

10-34 Shaw, Renata V. PICTURE SEARCHING: TECHNIQUES AND TOOLS. Special Libraries Association Bibliography, No. 6. New York: Special Libraries Association, 1973. viii, 65 p. Paper. Illus.

Prepared as an aid for the general researcher, this bibliography includes materials published from 1960 to 1971. However, pictorial histories and works without proper pictorial credits are omitted. The entries are grouped under thirty headings including bibliographies, directories and guides, indexes, methodology, as well as various content categories (archaeology, architecture, artists, folk art, historic sites and buildings, natural history, photography, and social history). An introductory example shows that picture research involves not only finding the appropriate picture but also establishing the artist or photographer, time, place, and authenticity of the picture.

10-35 Taft, Robert. PHOTOGRAPHY AND THE AMERICAN SCENE: A SOCIAL HISTORY, 1839-1889. New York: MacMillan, 1938. Reprint. New York: Dover Publications, 1964. x, 546 p. Illus., photos., notes, index.

This work, an indispensable source for early American photography, concentrates on the first fifty years of photographic development in the United States. Particular attention is paid to the photography of the Civil War and the exploration of the American West.

10-36 Thomason, Michael. "The Magic Image Revisited: The Photograph as a Historical Source." ALABAMA REVIEW 16 (April 1978): 83-91. Notes.

Thomason discusses the problems of researching historical photographs as primary sources rather than illustrative material. In judging the biases of photographs, the original purpose of their creation should be considered. In his examples from Mobile, Alabama, he shows that the wealthy and whites tended to be photographed more than the poor and blacks.

C. AERIAL PHOTOGRAPHS

10-37 Bradford, John. ANCIENT LANDSCAPES: STUDIES IN FIELD ARCHAE-OLOGY. London: G. Bell and Sons, 1957. xvii, 297 p. Maps, photos., notes, index.

Using examples from Western Europe and the Middle East, Bradford demonstrates the use of aerial photographs in archaeological studies.

10-38 Lyons, Thomas R., and Hitchcock, Robert K., eds. AERIAL REMOTE SENSING TECHNIQUES IN ARCHAEOLOGY. Reports of the Chaco Center, No. 2. Albuquerque: Chaco Center, National Park Service, U.S. Department of Interior and University of New Mexico, 1977. xii, 201 p. Paper. Maps, photos., diagrs., tables, notes.

Ten papers presented at a symposium held May 1972 at the thirty-seventh annual meeting of the Society for American Archaeology illustrate the application of remote sensing to a variety of archaeological circumstances and environmental settings. See also Lyons and Thomas Eugene Avery, REMOTE SENSING: A HANDBOOK FOR ARCHEOLOGISTS AND CULTURAL RESOURCE MANAGERS, Contribution No. 4 of the Chaco Center, National Park Service and University of New Mexico (Washington, D.C.: Cultural Resource Management Division, National Park Service, 1977); and Lyons and Frances Joan Mathien, eds., CULTURAL RESOURCES REMOTE SENSING (Washington, D.C.: Cultural Resource Management Division, National Park Service, 1980).

10-39 Newcomb, Robert M. "An Example of the Applicability of Remote Sensing: Historical Geography." GEOFORUM, no. 2 (1970), pp. 89-92. Notes.

In this note, Newcomb explores the application and limitations of remote sensing imagery in future work in historical geography. His footnotes provide references to the use of aerial photographs and remote sensing imagery in the field of archaeology. See also Newcomb, "Two Keys for the Historical Interpretation of Aerial Photographs," CALIFORNIA GEOGRAPHER 7 (1966): 37-46.

10-40 St. Joseph, John K.S., ed. THE USES OF AIR PHOTOGRAPHY: NATURE AND MAN IN A NEW PERSPECTIVE. New York: John Day Co., 1966. 166 p. Photos., notes, index.

Although this collection of essays emphasizes the present varied

applications of air photography, it also includes two essays on the
use of air photographs in archaeology (J.K.S. St. Joseph) and
history (M.D. Knowles). The essays are based primarily on
British examples.

10-41 Taylor, Charles E., and Spurr, Richard E., comps. AERIAL PHOTOGRAPHS
IN THE NATIONAL ARCHIVES. Special List, No. 25. Rev. ed. Wash-
ington, D.C.: National Archives and Records Service, 1973. vii, 106 p.
Paper.

Aerial photographs from the records of five agencies in the Departments of Agriculture and the Interior are listed in this
publication. The approximately two million images cover over
85 percent of the contiguous land areas of the United States.

10-42 Tinney, Larry R.; Jensen, John R.; and Estes, John E. "Mapping Archaeological Sites from Historical Photography." PHOTOGRAMMETRIC EN-
GINEERING AND REMOTE SENSING 43 (January 1977): 35-44. Photos.,
diagrs., notes.

The application of image processing of historical photographs
is used as an aid to the archaeological excavations at two
California mission sites.

Part 3

SELECTED LITERATURE IN

HISTORICAL GEOGRAPHY

Chapter 11
GENERAL REFERENCE AIDS

General reference aids to the literature related to the historical geography of the United States by both geographers and historians are included in this chapter. The methodological articles listed in the first section include theoretical and philosophical statements as well as literature reviews by historical geographers. The second section concentrates on guides to geographical dissertations and theses, abstracts, guides to geographical periodicals, and general bibliographies of U.S. history.

A. METHODOLOGICAL STATEMENTS

11-1   Baker, Alan R.H., ed. PROGRESS IN HISTORICAL GEOGRAPHY. Newton Abbot, Devon: David and Charles; New York: Wiley-Interscience, 1972. 311 p. Maps, diagrs., notes, bibliog., index.

This anthology consists of ten essays on the progress of historical geography during the past twenty-five years in France, Germany, Austria and Switzerland, Scandinavia, Great Britain, Soviet Union, North America, Australia and New Zealand, Latin America, and Africa. In the introductory essay, "Rethinking Historical Geography," pp. 11-28, Baker urges an increasing use of quantitative, theoretical, and behavioral approaches in historical geography. The North American essay, "Historical Geography in North America," pp. 129-43, was contributed by Andrew H. Clark.

11-2   Clark, Andrew H. "Historical Geography." In AMERICAN GEOGRAPHY: INVENTORY AND PROSPECT, edited by Preston E. James and Clarence F. Jones, pp. 70-105. Syracuse: Syracuse University Press for the Association of American Geographers, 1954. Maps, notes.

In Clark's first methodological statement, he emphasizes the theme of geographic change through time. After defining the scope of historical geography, he explores the Old World traditions of historical geography and reviews the development of

historical-geographical research in North America. Clark also
stresses the concept of change in "Geographic Change: A Theme
for Economic History," JOURNAL OF ECONOMIC HISTORY
20 (December 1960): 607-13. Other methodological statements
by Clark are listed in entries 11-1, 12-6, and 17-4.

11-3   Conzen, Michael P. "Bibliographical Aid to Navel Contemplation for
Historical Geographers." HISTORICAL GEOGRAPHY NEWSLETTER 7
(1977): 13-19. Diagr., tables, notes, bibliog.

The primary utility of this short article is a bibliographical listing of approximately sixty entries that discuss the philosophy,
methodology, and substance of historical geography. Most works
included in Conzen's bibliography are not repeated in this listing.

11-4   Darby, H.C. "Historical Geography." In APPROACHES TO HISTORY,
edited by H.P.R. Finberg, pp. 127-56. London: Routledge and Kegan
Paul, 1962. Notes.

Darby defines four approaches to historical geography: geography of past periods (reconstructing geographical patterns for
past time periods or cross sections); changing landscapes (studying
the processes by which man changes the landscape); past in the
present (mapping and explaining the origins of elements of the
past visible in the present landscape); and geographical history
(investigating the influence of geographical conditions on the
course of history).

11-5   Harris, Richard Colebrook. "Theory and Synthesis in Historical Geography."
CANADIAN GEOGRAPHER 15 (Fall 1971): 157-72. Notes.

Harris advocates geographical synthesis as an approach for historical geography rather than the development of a theoretical
geography of spatial relations, which he sees as a current trend
in the field. He suggests that much of the best scholarship is
that which is characterized by a breadth of synthesis, studying
the interrelationships of a complex of phenomena that give
character to a place, region, or landscape. Another methodological statement by Harris is found in REFLECTIONS ON THE
FERTILITY OF THE HISTORICAL GEOGRAPHICAL MULE, Department of Geography Discussion Paper, No. 10 (Toronto: University of Toronto, Department of Geography, 1970).

11-6   Jakle, John A. "Time, Space, and the Geographic Past: A Prospectus
for Historical Geography." AMERICAN HISTORICAL REVIEW 76 (October
1971): 1084-103. Diagr., notes.

In addressing an audience of historians, Jakle reviews the development of the literature on the historical geography of North America.

After discussing historical geographers' various schemes for periodization and regionalization, he explains current trends in geographical research, particularly environmental perception and resource management, and the development of theoretical models of spatial relationships.

11-7   Meinig, Donald W. "The Continuous Shaping of America: A Prospectus for Geographers and Historians." AMERICAN HISTORICAL REVIEW 83 (December 1978): 1186-87. Notes.

This essay is a revised version of a paper presented at the 1976 annual meeting of the American Historical Association. It is not only a review of the recent literature in historical geography for historians, it is also an attempt to develop a coherent conceptual framework for the overall historical geography of the United States. This prospectus suggests that the United States should be viewed as a dynamic area that evolved from various points of initial colonization into nuclei of discrete colonization areas and eventually into recognizable regions. The task of historical geographers is to identify and describe the changing geography of these nuclei or regions in terms of spatial systems, cultural landscapes, and social geography. Following the basic article are comments and criticisms by an historical geographer, Carville V. Earle, and an historian, Edward M. Cook, Jr.

11-8   Merrens, Harry Roy. "Historical Geography and Early American History." WILLIAM AND MARY QUARTERLY, 3d ser., 22 (October 1965): 529-48. Notes.

Merrens reviews twentieth-century contributions to historical geography relating to early American history. The organization of his discussion follows three major traditions in geographical research: spatial, area studies, and man-land traditions. In noting the misinterpretations advanced by the environmental determinists during the first quarter of the twentieth century, he cites two examples: the Appalachian Mountains as a "barrier" to westward migration and the "fall line" as a determinant of urban settlement.

11-9   Smith, C.T. "Historical Geography: Current Trends and Prospects." In FRONTIERS IN GEOGRAPHICAL TEACHING, edited by R.J. Chorley and Peter Haggett, pp. 118-43. London: Methuen, 1965. Notes.

After dismissing several archaic definitions of historical geography (history of geography as a discipline, history of exploration and discovery, history of the mapping of the earth, and history of changing political boundaries), Smith concentrates on four other concepts of historical geography: the operation of geographical factors in history, the evolution of the cultural landscape, reconstruction of past geographies, and study of geographical change through time. He also reviews current trends and problems in historical geography.

11-10 Zelinsky, Wilbur. "In Pursuit of Historical Geography and Other Wild
       Geese." HISTORICAL GEOGRAPHY NEWSLETTER 3 (Fall 1973): 1-5.

       Although Zelinsky recognizes that there is a body of scholars
       who call themselves "historical geographers," he questions the
       use of this term to describe the field of study. He argues that
       all geography is temporal as well as spatial and that "historical
       geographers" deal with the same questions as those posed by other
       forms of geographical inquiry. Comments by John A. Jakle
       and Alan R. H. Baker are printed in HISTORICAL GEOGRAPHY
       NEWSLETTER 4 (Spring 1974): pp. 13-19, while a collective
       comment by D.W. Moodie, John C. Lehr, and John A. Alwin
       is printed in HISTORICAL GEOGRAPHY NEWSLETTER 4 (Fall
       1974): 18-21.

B. BIBLIOGRAPHIES

11-11 Browning, Clyde E. A BIBLIOGRAPHY OF DISSERTATIONS IN GEOG-
       RAPHY: 1901 TO 1969. Studies in Geography, No. 1. Chapel Hill:
       University of North Carolina, Department of Geography, 1970. ix,
       96 p. Paper. Index.

       Geography dissertations completed at American and Canadian
       universities between 1901 and 1969 are listed under twenty-three
       subject categories. The "Historical Geography" category in-
       cludes 101 entries, as well as cross references to 34 entries,
       listed under such categories as cultural, settlement, or urban
       geography. These entries were derived from lists of dissertations
       published in PROFESSIONAL GEOGRAPHER (see entry 12-25).

11-12 Cassara, Ernest, ed. HISTORY OF THE UNITED STATES: A GUIDE TO IN-
       FORMATION SOURCES. American Studies Information Guide Series,
       vol. 3. Detroit: Gale Research Co., 1977. xxi, 459 p. Index.

       The first chapter of this annotated bibliography is devoted to
       research aids (reference works, atlases, bibliographies, archives
       and libraries, microfilm and tape collections, and periodicals),
       while the remainder lists published monographs that follow the
       chronology of American history which are arranged chronologically
       and topically. Very few journal articles are included in this
       listing.

11-13 Council of Planning Libraries. "Exchange Bibliography." No. 1-1565.
       1958-78. Monticello, Ill. Mimeographed. Irregular but frequent.

       Bibliographies covering a wide range of topics are issued in
       this series. Several bibliographies of interest to historical geog-
       raphers include: No. 189, URBAN STUDIES IN GEOGRAPHY:
       A BIBLIOGRAPHY OF DISSERTATIONS AND THESES IN GE-

OGRAPHY, 1960-1970, by William W. Ray; No. 492, THE
GEOGRAPHICAL LITERATURE OF BLACK AMERICANS, 1949-
1972: A SELECTED BIBLIOGRAPHY OF JOURNAL ARTICLES,
SERIAL PUBLICATIONS, THESES, AND DISSERTATIONS, by
Robert T. Ernst; Nos. 583-84, A BIBLIOGRAPHY OF DISSERTA-
TIONS AND THESES IN GEOGRAPHY ON ANGLO-AMERICA,
1960-1972, by Dean R. Hodson; No. 651, PAST LANDSCAPES:
A BIBLIOGRAPHY FOR HISTORIC PRESERVATIONISTS SELECTED
FROM THE LITERATURE OF HISTORICAL GEOGRAPHY, by John
A. Jakle; No. 753, CALIFORNIA: A BIBLIOGRAPHY OF THESES
AND DISSERTATIONS IN GEOGRAPHY, by Sandra J. Lamprecht;
No. 796, THE AMERICAN CITY, 1800-1920: A PRIMER BIBLI-
OGRAPHY IN AMERICAN URBAN HISTORY, by Ian R. Stewart;
and No. 1288, A BIBLIOGRAPHY ON RAILROAD DEVELOP-
MENT AND URBANIZATION OF THE TRANS-MISSISSIPPI WEST,
CIRCA 1860-1890, by Thomas Nelson. Bibliographies of general
geographical interest are listed in Chauncy D. Harris, BIBLIOG-
RAPHY OF GEOGRAPHY (see entry 11-17), pp. 104-11. Indexes
for all bibliographies published before July 1978 were issued in
Nos. 716-17, 1194-95, and 1564-65.

11-14 CURRENT GEOGRAPHICAL PUBLICATIONS: ADDITIONS TO THE RE-
SEARCH CATALOGUE OF THE AMERICAN GEOGRAPHICAL SOCIETY
COLLECTION. Vols. 1-40. New York: American Geographical Society,
1938-77. Vol. 41-- . Milwaukee: University of Wisconsin, Milwaukee
Library, American Geographical Society Collection, 1978-- . Ten issues
per year.

Current additions to the American Geographical Society's library
are recorded in this serial bibliography. Each issue is divided
into four sections: topical listings, regional listings, selected
maps, and selected books and monographs. Periodically, the
topical section includes a historical geography category, but
most of the entries are articles of marginal interest from historical
journals. Entries of major interest to historical geographers must
be gleaned from other topical categories (travel and exploration,
history of cartography, rural settlements, and urban geography)
or regional categories (North America, United States, or individual states). Pre-1971 materials have been cumulated and
published in RESEARCH CATALOG OF THE AMERICAN GEO-
GRAPHICAL SOCIETY, 19 vols. (Boston: G.K. Hall, 1962-74).

11-15 Freidel, Frank, ed. HARVARD GUIDE TO AMERICAN HISTORY. Rev.
ed. 2 vols. Cambridge, Mass.: Belknap Press of Harvard Press, 1974.
1,346 p. Index.

As a basic bibliography of American history, this guide emphasizes secondary literature, both books and journal articles,
published before June 30, 1970. Included are sections on general
and topical bibliographies, periodicals, biographies, comprehensive histories, histories of special subjects (as well as a

brief section on historical geography), and more specialized studies arranged topically and chronologically by the main periods of American history.

11-16 GEO ABSTRACTS D: SOCIAL AND HISTORICAL GEOGRAPHY. Norwich, Engl.: University of East Anglia, Geo Abstracts Ltd., 1966-- . Bimonthly.

From 1966 until 1973 GEO ABSTRACTS D was subtitled SOCIAL GEOGRAPHY AND CARTOGRAPHY with one chapter of each issue devoted to historical topics. Beginning in 1974 the subtitle was changed to SOCIAL AND HISTORICAL GEOGRAPHY and each issue contained three chapters pertaining to historical geography: field evidence, documentary evidence, and regional. Other chapters that often contain entries of historical interest include culture, population change, urban, and rural. With abstracts of articles from a wide range of historical and geographical journals and publications, this serial can serve as a basic guide not only to literature that is in the mainstream of historical geography but also to literature that is somewhat peripheral. Although international in scope, British, Canadian, and U.S. publications predominate.

11-17 Harris, Chauncy D. BIBLIOGRAPHY OF GEOGRAPHY: PART 1, INTRODUCTION TO GENERAL AIDS. Department of Geography Research Paper No. 179. Chicago: University of Chicago, Department of Geography, 1976. ix, 276 p. Paper. Index.

As a basic guide to geographic reference aids published after 1946, this bibliography lists guides to bibliographies (bibliographies of bibliographies, comprehensive bibliographies of geography, and specialized bibliographies of geography), books (subject bibliographies and catalogs), serials (inventories and indexes), government documents, dissertations, photographs, maps and atlases, gazetteers, dictionaries, encyclopedias, statistics, and methodology in geography. Although this guide is international in scope, United States, British, and Canadian works are emphasized. Extensive annotations describe the contents and arrangement of each entry. Pre-1946 geographical reference aids are described in John K. Wright and Elizabeth T. Platt, AIDS TO GEOGRAPHICAL RESEARCH: BIBLIOGRAPHIES, PERIODICALS, ATLASES, GAZETTEERS, AND OTHER REFERENCE BOOKS (New York: Columbia University Press for American Geographical Society, 1947. Reprint. Westport, Conn.: Greenwood Press, 1971).

11-18 Harris, Chauncy D., and Fellman, Jerome D., comps. INTERNATIONAL LIST OF GEOGRAPHICAL SERIALS, THIRD EDITION, 1980. Department of Geography Research Paper, No. 193. Chicago: University of Chicago, Department of Geography, 1980. vi, 457 p. Paper. Index.

Over 3,400 geographical serials from 107 countries are listed in this comprehensive inventory of all known geographical serials both currently being published and those no longer active. Although there is no separate listing, this inventory does include several serials pertaining to historical geography. In a companion volume, 443 serials of greatest continuing geographic interest, usefulness, and accessibility are described: see Chauncy D. Harris, ANNOTATED WORLD LIST OF SELECTED CURRENT GEOGRAPHICAL SERIALS, FOURTH EDITION, 1980, Department of Geography Research Paper, No. 194 (Chicago: University of Chicago, Department of Geography, 1980).

11-19 Library of Congress. General Reference and Bibliography Division. A GUIDE TO THE STUDY OF THE UNITED STATES OF AMERICA: REPRESENTATIVE BOOKS REFLECTING THE DEVELOPMENT OF AMERICAN LIFE AND THOUGHT. Washington, D.C.: Government Printing Office, 1960. xv, 1,193 p. Index.

Selected books pertaining to the development of American life and thought are included in this annotated bibliography. The entries are organized topically into twenty-four chapters, including general history; American Indians; geography; diplomatic history; military history; local history; travel and travelers; population, immigration, and minorities; land and agriculture; and economic life. The geography category covers works relating primarily to physical geography, although a brief section on historical geography and atlases is included. This volume lists pre-1956 materials, while the SUPPLEMENT (Washington, D.C.: 1976) lists books published between 1956 and 1965.

11-20 McManis, Douglas R. HISTORICAL GEOGRAPHY OF THE UNITED STATES: A BIBLIOGRAPHY. Ypsilanti: Eastern Michigan University, Division of Field Services, 1965. vi, 249 p. Paper.

Over 3,550 entries representing books, monographs, and scholarly articles published through 1964 are included in this bibliography. Although a larger number of these works are by historians than by geographers, each entry was selected because it contained some historical geographical data pertaining to the United States (excluding Alaska and Hawaii) from pre-historic times to 1900. The entries are arranged geographically (United States, regions, states) and thereunder topically (exploration and settlement, population characteristics, agriculture, trade and commerce, manufacturing and industry, and urban development).

11-21 Snipe, Ronald H. A GUIDE TO GEOGRAPHICAL PERIODICALS. 2d ed. Manitou Springs, Colo.: R.H. Snipe Publications, 1972. iv, 380 p. Index.

Articles from all issues of the ANNALS OF THE ASSOCIATION OF AMERICAN GEOGRAPHERS, ECONOMIC GEOGRAPHY, and GEOGRAPHICAL REVIEW published through 1970 are listed regionally or topically in this guide. Although there is a historical geography category (pp. 38-40, 163-64, and 301-4), articles of historical interest can also be found under other topics (such as agriculture, settlement, transportation, or urban). Snipe has also indexed pre-1971 issues of several other geographical periodicals in A TRI-INDEX TO GEOGRAPHY PERIODICALS: CANADIAN GEOGRAPHER, PROFESSIONAL GEOGRAPHER, AND SOVIET GEOGRAPHY (Manitou Springs, Colo.: 1971); and SNIPE'S INDEX TO THE JOURNAL OF GEOGRAPHY (Manitou Springs, Colo.: 1971).

11-22 Stuart, Merrill M. A BIBLIOGRAPHY OF MASTER'S THESES IN GEOGRAPHY: AMERICAN AND CANADIAN UNIVERSITIES. Tualatin, Oreg.: Geographic and Area Study Publications, 1973. x, 275 p. Paper. Index.

Designed as a complement to Browning's BIBLIOGRAPHY OF DISSERTATIONS IN GEOGRAPHY (see entry 11-11), this work is based on listings of master's theses published in PROFESSIONAL GEOGRAPHER (after 1972, usually the first issue of each volume). Stuart lists over five thousand entries under twenty-seven categories, including one for historical geography. Cross-references indicate that other historical studies may be found under cultural, settlement, or land use geography.

Chapter 12

PERIODICALS AND COLLECTIONS OF ESSAYS

Most of the periodicals included in this chapter are geographical journals of general interest. In describing the contents of these publications those articles of historical interest that have not been mentioned elsewhere are listed. Only those volumes issued since 1965 were reviewed for pertinent literature. Also included in this chapter are general collections of essays that most often record the proceedings of a geographical, historical, or interdisciplinary conference. In the case of historical or interdisciplinary conferences, only the articles by geographers are mentioned. More specialized periodicals and collections of essays are included in the appropriate topical chapters.

12-1 ANNALS OF THE ASSOCIATION OF AMERICAN GEOGRAPHERS. Washington, D.C.: Association of American Geographers, 1911-- . Quarterly.

As the major scholarly journal of the association, this periodical contains articles on all geographic subjects. Since 1972 it has also included book reviews. Most articles of historical interest are listed separately, although there are a few others of interest: Stephen C. Jett, "The Origins of Navajo Settlement Patterns," 68 (September 1978): 351-62; John Leighly, "Town Names of Colonial New England in the West," 68 (June 1978): 233-48; W. Theodore Mealor, Jr., and Merle C. Prunty, "Open-Range Ranching in Southern Florida," 66 (September 1976): 360-76; Charles F. Gritzner, "Hispano Gristmills in New Mexico," 64 (December 1974): 515-24; Richard V. Francaviglia, "The Cemetery as an Evolving Cultural Landscape," 61 (September 1971): 501-9; Elliot G. McIntire, "Changing Patterns of Hopi Indian Settlement," 61 (September 1971): 510-21; Wilbur Zelinsky, "Cultural Variation in Personal Name Patterns in the Eastern United States," 60 (December 1970): 743-69; John Fraser Hart, "Loss and Abandonment of Cleared Farm Land in the Eastern United States," 58 (September 1968): 417-40; Duncan P. Randall, "Wilmington, North Carolina: The Historical Development of a Port City," 58 (September 1968): 441-51; and Robert H. Brown, "The Upsala, Minnesota, Community: A Case Study in Rural Dynamics," 57 (June 1967): 267-300.

12-2   Association of Pacific Coast Geographers. YEARBOOK. Corvallis: Oregon State University Press for Association of Pacific Coast Geographers, 1935-- .

The yearbook includes, but is not confined to, articles presented at the annual meeting of the association. Also included are abstracts or lists of other papers presented at the annual meetings. Several articles of interest to historical geographers include: Elizabeth K. Burns, "Subdivision Activity on the San Francisco Peninsula, 1860-1970," 39 (1977): 17-31; Howard J. Nelson, "Town Founding and the American Frontier," 36 (1974): 7-23; Larry R. Ford, "The Diffusion of the Skyscraper as an Urban Symbol," 35 (1973): 49-60; Donald G. Holtgrieve, "The Effects of the Railroads on Small Town Population Changes: Linn County, Oregon," 35 (1973): 87-102; and Robert M. Newcomb, "Twelve Working Approaches to Historical Geography," 31 (1969): 27-50.

12-3   Blouet, Brian W., and Lawson, Merlin P., eds. IMAGES OF THE PLAINS: THE ROLE OF HUMAN NATURE IN SETTLEMENT. Lincoln: University of Nebraska Press, 1975. xiv, 214 p. Maps, diagrs., tables, notes.

Papers presented at the conference, "Images of the Plains," which was held April 30-May 1, 1973 at the University of Nebraska, Lincoln, are included in this volume. The conference also honored the career of Leslie Hewes, whose research interests are associated with the Great Plains. In addition to a foreword by Andrew H. Clark, the papers are organized in six sections: "Exploratory Images of the Plains," papers by John L. Allen (subjectivity in the exploratory evaluations of the Plains) and Waldo R. Wedel (changing interpretation of the Plains as an Indian habitat); "Resource Evaluation in the Prefrontier West," papers by G. Malcolm Lewis (recognition and delimitation of the grasslands) and David J. Wishart (fur trade); "Government Appraisers on the Western Frontier," papers by Herman R. Friis (U.S. Topographical Engineers) and John L. Tyman (Canadian land surveyors); "Real and Imagined Climatic Hazards," papers by Merlin P. Lawson (reconstruction of 1849 climate along Oregon trail) and C.J. Tracie (climatic evaluations in Peace River country, Canada); "The Desert and the Garden," papers by David M. Emmons (positive images of the Plains reflected in six gazetteers), Richard H. Jackson (Mormon perceptions and settlements), John Warkentin (concept of Great American Desert in Canada), Irene M. Spry (early visitors to the Canadian Plains), and John F. Davis (British view of the Great Plains); and "Adaptations to Reality," papers by Martyn J. Bowden (changing images and land use patterns in Jefferson County, Nebraska) and Leslie Hewes (the Great Plains one hundred years after John Wesley Powell).

12-4 Blouet, Brian W., and Luebke, Frederick C., eds. THE GREAT PLAINS: ENVIRONMENT AND CULTURE. Lincoln: University of Nebraska Press for the Center for Great Plains Studies, 1979. xxviii, 246 p.

Papers presented at the Cultural Heritage of the Plains Symposium, April 13-15, 1977, at the University of Nebraska, Lincoln, are reprinted in this volume. These essays, which were prepared by anthropologists, historians, and geographers, illustrate the two changing and contrasting interpretations of the interaction of environment and culture on the Great Plains (environmentalists versus culturalists). The articles by geographers include: G. Malcolm Lewis, "The Cognition and Communication of Former Ideas about the Great Plains," pp. 27-42; Bradley H. Baltensperger, "Agricultural Adjustments to Great Plains Drought: The Republican Valley, 1870-1900," pp. 43-62; Timothy J. Rickard, "The Great Plains as Part of an Irrigated Western Empire, 1890-1914," pp. 81-99; John C. Hudson, "The Plains Country Town," pp. 99-118; and Leslie Hewes, "Agricultural Risk in the Great Plains," pp. 157-86.

12-5 ECONOMIC GEOGRAPHY. Worchester, Mass.: Clark University, 1925-- . Quarterly.

Although the primary focus of this journal is economic geography on an international basis, there are occasional articles pertaining to the historical geography of the United States, particularly urban topics. Those historical articles that are not listed elsewhere include David R. Meyer, "A Dynamic Model of the Integration of Frontier Urban Places into the United States System of Cities," 56 (April 1980): 120-40; Irwin Feller, "Determinants of the Composition of Urban Inventions," 49 (January 1973): 47-58 (relation between urbanization and inventive activity using 1910 Patent Office data); James E. Vance, Jr., "Land Assignment in the Precapitalist, Capitalist, and Postcapitalist City," 47 (April 1971): 101-20; Vance, "Housing the Worker: Determinative and Contingent Ties in Nineteenth Century Birmingham," 43 (April 1967): 95-127; and Vance, "Housing the Worker: The Employment Linkage as a Force in Urban Structure," 42 (October 1966): 294-325. There are also occasional book reviews of historical interest including two special sections, "Reviews in Historical Geography," 48 (April 1972): 214-19 and 46 (April 1970): 199-206.

12-6 Ehrenberg, Ralph E., ed. PATTERN AND PROCESS: RESEARCH IN HISTORICAL GEOGRAPHY. Washington, D.C.: Howard University Press, 1975. xv, 360 p. Maps, illus., diagrs., tables, notes, index.

The papers and proceedings of the Conference on the National Archives and Research in Historical Geography, which was held November 8-9, 1971, in Washington, D.C., are published in this volume. The conference provided a forum for historical geographers to present their current research, as well as an opportunity for the archivists to introduce the geographers to pertinent archival materials. The published proceedings include keynote addresses by James B. Rhodes (then Archivist of the United States) and Andrew H. Clark (the nature of research interests of historical geographers) as well as the papers and commentaries from four thematic sessions: "Afro-American Population," papers by Peter O. Wacker (patterns of Afro-American population in New Jersey from early eighteenth to mid-nineteenth century) and Robert L. Clarke (archival sources for the study of Afro-American population); "Exploration, Surveying, and Mapping," papers by Louis De Vorsey, Jr. (the De Brahm survey of British East Florida, 1765-1771), John L. Allen (Thomas Jefferson's pre-exploratory image of the Missouri River), Hildegard Binder Johnson and William D. Pattison (reflections on the U.S. rectangular survey system), and Herman R. Friis (comparison of original and published sources relative to the exploration and mapping of the American West); "Transportation, Commerce, and Industry," papers by Martyn J. Bowden (persistence, failure, and mobility of business establishments in the central district of San Francisco, 1846-1936), John A. Jakle and Robert L. Janiskee (the application of historical geography in the management of a historic landscape, i.e., covered bridges in Parke County, Indiana), Sam B. Hilliard (the role of the Mississippi River in the antebellum interregional trade), Franklin W. Burch (the role of archives in transportation research), and Meyer H. Fishbein (archival materials relating to commerce and industry); "Rural and Urban Settlement," papers by H. Roy Merrens (archival sources and the study of settlement patterns in colonial America), Terry G. Jordan (vegetation patterns and the selection of settlement sites in frontier Texas), David Ward (ethnic division of labor in mid-nineteenth-century New York City), John W. Reps (urban planning on the western mining frontier), and Jane F. Smith (the use of the records of the former General Land Office in studying the settlement of the public domain). This publication is concluded with an appendix which is an annotated bibliography prepared by Ehrenberg of resources on historical geography in the National Archives (see entry 6-3).

12-7   GEOGRAPHICAL ANALYSIS. Columbus: Ohio State University Press, 1969-- . Quarterly.

Primarily a journal of theoretical geography, this contains several articles of historical interest: Allan Pred, "The Impact of Technological and Institutional Innovations on Life Content: Some Time-Geographic Observations," 10 (October 1978): 345-72; M.J. Webber, "Population Growth and Town Location in an Agricultural Community: Iowa, 1840-1960," 4 (April 1972): 134-55; Pred, "Large City Interdependence and the Preelectronic Diffusion of Innovations in the U.S.," 3 (April 1971): 165-81; and G.F. Pyle, "The Diffusion of Cholera in the United States in the Nineteenth Century," 1 (January 1968): 59-75. An article by David Ward is listed in entry 18-43.

12-8 GEOGRAPHICAL REVIEW. New York: American Geographical Society, 1916-- . Quarterly.

Although the articles and book reviews in this journal pertain to all aspects of modern geography, there are occasional articles relating to the historical geography of the United States. Articles of interest that are not listed elsewhere include Karl B. Raitz, "Ethnic Maps of North America," 68 (July 1978): 335-50 (review of literature pertaining to mapping of ethnic groups); Judith W. Meyer, "Ethnicity, Theology, and Immigrant Church Expansion," 65 (April 1975): 180-97 (correlation of Lutheran Church-Missouri Synod to immigration of German Lutherans); Robin W. Doughty, "San Francisco's Nineteenth Century Egg Basket: The Farallons," 61 (October 1971): 554-72; James O. Wheeler and Stanley D. Brunn, "An Agricultural Ghetto: Negroes in Cass County, Michigan, 1845-1968," 59 (July 1969): 317-29; Edward T. Price, "The Central Courthouse Square in the American County Seat," 58 (January 1968): 29-60 (diffusion throughout eastern United States); and Wilbur Zelinsky, "Classical Town Names in the United States: The Historical Geography of an American Idea," 57 (October 1967): 463-95.

12-9 GEOGRAPHICAL SURVEY. Vols. 1-4, 1972-75. Mankato, Minn.: Mankato State College for the Blue Earth County Geographical Society. Vol. 5-- . 1976- . Muncie, Ind.: Ball State University, Department of Geography and Geology, 1976-- . Quarterly.

Originally published as a county geographical society journal, this publication now serves a wider audience, especially emphasizing conceptual or policy-oriented articles. The first four volumes contained several historical articles including David Hornbeck, "Processes of Change and the Concept of Acculturation in Historical Geography," 1 (April 1972): 24-33; Jane Pyle, "Perception and Change in a Minnesota Landscape," 2 (January 1973): 27-40; Branko Colakovic, "A Hypothetical Model of the European Emigration to the United States," 2 (July 1973): 135-54; and Bernard C. Peters, "The Remaking of an Image: The Propaganda Campaign to Attract Settlers to Michigan, 1815-1840," 3 (January 1974): 25-52.

12-10 Gibson, James R., ed. EUROPEAN SETTLEMENT AND DEVELOPMENT IN NORTH AMERICA: ESSAYS ON GEOGRAPHIC CHANGE IN HONOUR AND MEMORY OF ANDREW HILL CLARK. Toronto: University of Toronto Press, 1978. viii, 231 p. Maps, diagrs., tables, notes.

This festschriften was compiled in memory of Andrew H. Clark, the dominant figure in historical geography for twenty years from the mid-fifties until the mid-seventies. The major component is a collection of eight essays by former doctoral students:

Richard Colebrook Harris, "The Extension of France into Rural
Canada"; James R. Gibson, "Old Russia in the New World:
Adversaries and Adversities in Russian America"; Robert D.
Mitchell, "The Formation of Early American Cultural Regions:
An Interpretation"; Sam B. Hilliard, "Antebellum Tidewater
Rice Culture in South Carolina and Georgia"; Arthur J. Ray,
"The Hudson's Bay Company Fur Trade in the Eighteenth Century:
A Comparative Economic Study"; D. Aidan McQuillan, "Terri-
tory and Ethnic Identity: Some New Measures of an Old Theme
in the Cultural Geography of the United States" (concentrating
on Swedish, Mennonite, and French Canadian settlements in
central Kansas); David Ward, "The Early Victorian City in England and America: On the Parallel Development of an Urban
Image"; and James T. Lemon, "The Weakness of Place and
Community in Early Pennsylvania." It also includes essays by
two colleagues: Donald W. Meinig's Prologue is a critical
appreciation of Clark's work as a historical geographer while
John Warkentin's Epilogue reviews the eight essays putting
them in the perspective of Clark's work as well as the broader
field of historical geography. Also included are a list of Clark's
publications and a list of his doctoral students and their dissertation titles. A short biography, an unpublished speech, and a
list of dissertations supervised by Clark are printed in HISTORI-
CAL GEOGRAPHY NEWSLETTER 6 (Spring 1976): 12-20, 58-
68, and 80-81.

12-11   GREAT PLAINS-ROCKY MOUNTAIN GEOGRAPHICAL JOURNAL. Lara-
mie: University of Wyoming, Department of Geography for the Great
Plains-Rocky Mountain Division of the Association of American Geographers, 1972-- . Annual.

Composed mainly of the papers (or abstracts) presented at the
annual meeting of the division, this publication includes several
articles pertaining to the historical geography of this region:
Marshall Bowen, "Perception and Mormon Pioneering in the Big
Horn Basin: Cowley Flat, Wyoming," 1 (1972): 14-18; James
Hamburg, "Railroads and the Settlement of South Dakota During
the Great Dakota Boom, 1878-1887," 1 (1972): 40-45; Richard
H. Jackson, "The American Indian: A Neglected Area of Geographical Study?" 1 (1972): 46-52; Merlin P. Lawson, "A Be-
havioristic Interpretation of Pike's Geographical Knowledge of
the Interior of Louisiana," 1 (1972): 58-64; and Lynn A. Rosenvall, "Mormon Settlement Plats: Their Design and Origin," 1
(1972): 88-93.

12-12   Hilliard, Sam B., ed. MAN AND ENVIRONMENT IN THE LOWER
MISSISSIPPI VALLEY. Geoscience and Man, vol. 19. Baton Rouge:
Louisiana State University, School of Geoscience, 1978. viii, 165 p.
Paper. Maps, illus., photos., diagrs., tables, notes.

The papers presented at the second R.J. Russell symposium,
November 1978, are contained in this volume. A wide variety

of papers, which were presented by geomorphologists, climatologists, hydrologists, historians, archaeologists, and geographers, pertain to the physical and cultural geography of the lower Mississippi River Valley. Papers of historical interest include Paul F. Paskoff, "The Areal Spread of a Systematic Innovation: The Case of the Telephone in Louisiana, 1898-1913," pp. 101-9; Carolyn French, "Land Survey and Land Acquisition in the Florida Parishes of Louisiana," pp. 111-21; John B. Rehder, "Diagnostic Landscape Traits of Sugar Plantations in Southern Louisiana," pp. 135-50; and Charles S. Aiken, "The Decline of Sharecropping in the Lower Mississippi River Valley," pp. 151-65.

12-13 HISTORICAL GEOGRAPHY NEWSLETTER. Northridge: California State University, Department of Geography, 1971-- . Biannual.

This newsletter serves as a means of communication among the historical geographers in the United States and Canada. It contains short articles, review essays, book reviews, dissertation and thesis abstracts, conference reports, and other relevant news. Most articles pertaining to methodology or describing archival and cartographic sources are listed separately. Other articles of interest include Edward K. Muller, "Sharpening the Focus on Mid-Nineteenth Century Urban Life: A Review Essay," 8 (Fall 1978): 1-16; Tertius Chandler, "The Forty Largest Cities: A Statistical Note," 7 (1977): 21-24; Charles S. Sargent, "Towns of the Salt River Valley, 1870-1930," 5 (Fall 1975): 1-9 (Arizona); Douglas R. McManis, "In Search of a Rational World: The Encyclopedists' Image of Northern and Western North America," 5 (Fall 1975): 18-29; and Donald G. Holtgrieve, "Frederick Jackson Turner Map Collection, An Annotated Bibliography," 5 (Spring 1975): 25-28.

12-14 "The Historical Geography of New Jersey." In PROCEEDINGS OF THE SECOND ANNUAL SYMPOSIUM OF THE NEW JERSEY HISTORICAL COMMISSION, pp. 35-80. Newark: New Jersey Historical Society, 1971. Paper. Maps, photos., notes.

The second annual symposium of the New Jersey Historical Commission, which was held in Trenton, December 5, 1970, included a session on New Jersey's early historical geography. The two papers in this session were presented by Peter O. Wacker, "New Jersey's Cultural Landscape Before 1800," and Theodore W. Kury, "Iron as a Factor in New Jersey Settlement"; A. Philip Muntz was commentator. Papers presented at the Fifth Annual New Jersey History Symposium (December 1973) are printed in ECONOMIC AND SOCIAL HISTORY OF COLONIAL NEW JERSEY, edited by William D. Wright (Trenton: New Jersey Historical Commission, 1974). Several papers of interest include Edward S. Rutsch, "The Colonial Plantation Settlement Pattern in New Jersey: Iron and Agricultural Examples," pp. 10-23; Gary S. Horowitz, "New Jersey Land Riots, 1745-1755," pp. 24-33; and Peter O. Wacker, "Comments," pp. 34-40.

12-15 HISTORICAL METHODS. Vols. 1-10, 1967-77. Pittsburgh: University of Pittsburgh, University Center for International Studies and the Department of History. Vol 11-- . Washington, D.C.: Heldref Publications, 1978-- . Quarterly.

The articles and newsnotes in this interdisciplinary newsletter are devoted to descriptions of new research methodology, advanced statistical techniques, computer applications to history, newly available source material, and review essays. Articles describing new source materials are listed separately in part 2 of this guide to information sources. Methodological articles pertaining to historical geography include Edward M. Cook, Jr., "Geography and History: Spatial Approaches to Early American History," 13 (Winter 1980): 19-28; and David Ward, "The Debate on Alternative Approaches in Historical Geography," 8 (March 1975): 82-87. Review essays covering works in historical geography include Robert P. Swierenga, "Towards the 'New Rural History': A Review Essay," 6 (June 1973): 111-22; and Allan Kulikoff, "Historical Geographers and Social History: A Review Essay," 6 (June 1973): 122-28.

12-16 International Geographical Congress. INTERNATIONAL GEOGRAPHY, 1972. Edited by W. Peter Adams and Frederick M. Helleiner. 2 vols. Toronto: University of Toronto Press for the 22d International Geographical Congress, 1972. xxiv, 1354 p. Index.

Short versions (twelve hundred words and selected references) of papers submitted to the Twenty-second International Geographical Congress in Montreal are published in this work. Papers included in the section, "Historical Geography," pp. 393-472, which pertain to the United States, include: John L. Allen, "Pyramidal Height-of-Land: A Persistent Myth in the Exploration of Western Anglo-America," pp. 395-96; Robert W. Bastian, "Technological Evolution and Resource Revaluation: Lake Superior Iron Ores," pp. 391-98; Louis De Vorsey, "La Florida Revealed: The De Brahm Surveys of the British East Florida,"' pp. 411-12; Paul A. Groves, "Alley Population: An Element in the Social and Physical Structure of Late Nineteenth Century Washington," 422-24; Leslie Hewes, "Transformation of an Agrarian Landscape: The Suitcase-Farming Frontier of the Central Great Plains," pp. 432-34; H.B. Johnson, "Man, Rectangularity, and Landscape," pp. 436-38; James E. Landing, "The Pioneer Urbanist: A Microstudy in Entrepreneurial Historical Geography," pp. 438-39 (Michigan City); and Stanley W. Trimble, "Man-Induced Soil Erosion on the Southern Piedmont of the USA: A Perspective," pp. 454-57.

12-17 _____ . INTERNATIONAL GEOGRAPHY '76. Vol. 9: HISTORICAL GEOGRAPHY. Edited by I.P. Gerasimov et al. Oxford: Pergamon Press for Organizing Committee of the 23d International Geographical Congress, 1978. 100 p.

Short papers on historical geography that were presented at the

Twenty-third International Geographical Congress, which was held in Moscow in 1976, are printed in this volume. Papers pertaining to U.S. topics include Donald G. Janelle, "Temporal and Spatial Co-ordinates of Stagecoach Service in Maine, 1826-1829," pp. 56-58; Charles F. Kovacik, "Land Use Change on the South Carolina Rice Plantation Lands," pp. 64-67; and Donald W. Meinig, "Spatial Models of a Sequence of Trans-Atlantic Interactions," pp. 30-35. The historical geography sessions are reviewed in Robert Gohstand, "Historical Geography at the 23rd International Geographical Congress, Moscow, U.S.S.R., 1976," HISTORICAL GEOGRAPHY NEWSLETTER 7, nos. 1 and 2 (1977): 25-38.

12-18 _____. SELECTED PAPERS. Vol. 3: POPULATION AND SETTLEMENT GEOGRAPHY, POLITICAL AND HISTORICAL GEOGRAPHY. Edited by S.P. Chatterjee and S.P. Das Gupta. Calcutta: National Committee for Geography, 1971. xvi, 507 p. Maps, photos., tables, diagrs., notes.

Papers presented at the Twenty-first International Geographical Congress in New Delhi in December 1968 are printed here. Although many of the papers in the settlement and historical geography sessions pertained to India, several covered Canadian topics and one discussed a U.S. topic: Sherwin H. Cooper, "The Survey Grid as a Control of Settlement and Circulation," pp. 71-78 (Ohio).

12-19 Jackson, Richard H., ed. THE MORMON ROLE IN THE SETTLEMENT OF THE WEST. Charles Redd Monographs in Western History, No. 9. Provo, Utah: Brigham Young University Press, 1978. 169 p. Paper. Maps, diagrs., tables, notes.

The Mormon role in the occupation of the land provides the general theme of these seven original essays. Jackson examines the overland journey to the Salt Lake Valley based on an analysis of diaries; Melvin T. Smith describes Mormon exploration of the lower Colorado River area; Lynn A. Rosenvall determines which Mormon settlements failed, 1830-1930, and explores the reasons for these failures; Alan H. Grey puts Mormon settlement in a global context by comparing it with the settlement of Christchurch, New Zealand; Charles S. Peterson analyzes the development of Mormon agricultural systems and their imprint on the landscape; Wayne L. Wahlquist examines population growth in the Mormon core area, 1847-1890; and Dean Louder and Lowell Bennion map the diffusion of Mormons across the western United States.

12-20 JOURNAL OF GEOGRAPHY. Houston: University of Houston for the National Council for Geographic Education, 1902-- . Seven issues per year.

Although the short articles in this serial are intended primarily for teachers of elementary, secondary, and college geography,

there are several articles of interest to historical geographers:
Donald G. Holtgrieve, "Land Speculation and Other Processes
in American Historical Geography," 75 (January 1976): 53-64;
Russel L. Gerlach, "Our Cultural Roots: A Classroom Exercise
in Historical Geography," 75 (February 1976): 82-89; Allen G.
Noble, "Evolution and Classification of Nineteenth Century
Housing in Ohio," 74 (May 1975): 285-302; Charles E. Tatum
and Lawrence M. Sommers, "The Spread of the Black Christian
Methodist Episcopal Church in the United States, 1870 to 1970,"
74 (September 1975): 343-57; Larry R. Ford, "The Urban House-
type as an Illustration of the Concentric Zone Model: The Perception of Architectural Continuity," 73 (February 1974): 29-
39; Andrew F. Burghardt; "The Economic Impact of War: The
Case of the U.S. Civil War," 72 (September 1973); 7-10;
Richard L. Nostrand, "The Colonial New England Town," 72
(October 1973): 45-53; Paul M. Koroscil, "Historical Geography: A Resurrection," 70 (October 1971): 415-20; and Eugene
J. Wilhelm, "Animal Drives--A Case Study in Historical Geography," 66 (September 1967): 327-34.

12-21 JOURNAL OF HISTORICAL GEOGRAPHY. London: Academic Press,
1975-- . Quarterly.

As the only English-language journal devoted entirely to historical geography, the articles, book reviews, and newsnotes are
international in scope. There are usually one or two articles
per issue that pertain to the United States and/or Canada. Articles of interest that have not been listed elsewhere include John
T. Cumbler, "Transatlantic Working Class Institutions," 6 (July
1980): 275-90 (migration of textile workers from Lancashire,
England, to Fall River, Massachusetts); Gretchen A. Condran
and Eileen Crimmins, "Mortality Differentials between Rural
and Urban Areas of States in the Northeastern United States,
1890-1900," 6 (April 1980): 179-202; Jon Gjerde, "The Effect
of Community on Migration: Three Minnesota Townships, 1885-
1905," (October 1979): 403-22; and John B. Sharpless, "The
Economic Structure of Port Cities in the Mid-Nineteenth Century:
Boston and Liverpool, 1840-1860," 2 (April 1976): 131-44.

12-22 Mitchell, Robert D., and Muller, Edward K., eds. GEOGRAPHICAL
PERSPECTIVES ON MARYLAND'S PAST. Occasional Papers in Geography,
No. 4. College Park: University of Maryland, Department of Geography,
1979. x, 187 p. Paper. Maps, illus., photos., diagrs., tables, notes.

Selected elements of Maryland's historical geography are portrayed
in this collection of papers that are based on research by University
of Maryland graduate students. The topics that are covered include: the perception of the eastern shore landscape through the
rise of seventeenth-century toponyms (Janet H. Gritzner); the
tobacco marketing system in the Patuxent River basin (Basel H.
Brune) ; frontier settlement of western Maryland, 1722-32 (Frank

W. Porter III); migration from St. Mary's County to Kentucky
(Bayly Ellen Marks); the formation of a black community in Annapolis, 1870–85 (Sallie M. Ives); immigrant home ownership in
Baltimore, 1865–1914 (Martha J. Vill); and residential stability
among urban workers in Baltimore, 1880–1930 (D. Randall Beirne).
The editors' introductory chapter reviews the literature on Maryland's historical geography.

12-23 New England-St. Lawrence Valley Geographical Society. PROCEEDINGS.
New Britain: Central Connecticut State College, Geography Department,
1971-- . Annual.

The proceedings of the annual meetings of this regional division
of the Association of American Geographers are recorded here.
The 1976 and 1977 meetings included two sessions devoted pri-
marily to the historical geography of New England: "Historical-
Cultural Geography of New England," 6 (1976): 7–41; and
"Settlement and Landscape," 7 (1977): 16–61. Short papers
from other meetings include Judith Meyer, "Continuity in the
Evolution of an Industrial Community, Chicopee, Massachusetts," 2 (1972): 64–69; Thomas R. Lewis, Jr., "Looms, Life
and Landscape: A Glimpse of the Growth of a New England
Industrial Village," 3 (1973): 32–38 (Manchester, Conn.); and
Stanford E. Demars, "Nineteenth Century Shore Resorts on Nar-
rangansett Bay," 5 (1975): 51–55. Historical geography sessions
from the 1968–70 meetings are reported in HISTORICAL GEOG-
RAPHY NEWSLETTER 1 (1971): 3–6.

12-24 PROCEEDINGS OF THE ASSOCIATION OF AMERICAN GEOGRAPHERS.
Vols. 1–8. Washington, D.C.: Association of American Geographers,
1969–76. Annual.

Selected short papers and abstracts from the annual meeting of the
association were printed in these PROCEEDINGS. Articles of
historical interest that are not listed elsewhere include William
A. Bowen, "American Ethnic Regions, 1880," 8 (1976): 44–46;
Robert J. Meyer, "Modelling the Dynamics of Urban and Rural
Migration: An Application to the Alabama Black Belt," 8 (1976):
47–49; Robert H. Fuson and Walter H. Treftz, "A Theoretical Re-
construction of the First Atlantic Crossing of Christopher Columbus,"
8 (1976): 154–57; Gordon R. Lewthwaite, "Cows in the Corn:
The Emergence of the Tri-State Butter Region," 7 (1975): 113–17;
Dean R. Louder, "A Simulation Approach to the Diffusion of the
Mormon Church," 7 (1975): 126–30; Robert W. Bastian, "Mesabi
Mine Locations: An Example of Population Reconstruction," 5
(1973): 10–13; Robert LeBlanc, "The Differential Perception of
Salt Marshes by the Folk and Elite in the 19th Century," 5 (1973):
138–43; Conrad T. Moore, "Communication: A Major Reason for
Indian Grass Fires in the American West, 1535–1890," 5 (1973):
181–85; Gerald Walker, "The Town Oriented Rural Neighborhood:
A Nineteenth Century Example," 5 (1973): 276–79 (Sonora
County, Calif.); I.E. Quastler, "The Core Area of Images Con-

cept and American Perceptions of California Agriculture, 1800-1890," 4 (1972): 91-95; Martyn J. Bowden, Bruce L. LaRose, and Brian Mishara, "The Development of Competition Between Central Places on the Frontier: Vermont, 1790-1830," 3 (1971): 32-38; William O. Koelsch, "Monitoring Historical Geography: The Book Reviewer as Remote Sensor, 1960-1969," 3 (1971): 100-105; Philip L. Wagner, "A Sense of History," 3 (1971): 178-81; and John E. Westfall, "The Demographic Inflection: Iowa and Nebraska," 2 (1970): 149-52 (definition of frontier settlement).

12-25 PROFESSIONAL GEOGRAPHER. Vols. 1-22, 1949-70. Bimonthly. Vol. 23-- . Washington, D.C.: Association of American Geographers, 1971-- . Quarterly.

Short scholarly articles, association news, and book reviews provide the main contents of this journal. The first issue of each volume usually contains a list of completed dissertations and theses. Selected articles of historical interest include Robert W. Bastian, "Southeastern Pennsylvania and Central Wisconsin Barns: Examples of Independent or Parrallel Development?" 27 (May 1975): 200-204; Louis De Vorsey, Jr., "Florida's Seaward Boundary: A Problem in Applied Historical Geography," 25 (August 1973): 214-20; Alan R.H. Baker, "A Cliometric Note on the Citation Structure of Historical Geography," 25 (November 1973): 347-49; Ralph D. Vicero, "French-Canadian Settlement in Vermont Prior to the Civil War," 23 (October 1971): 290-94; David D. Brodeur, "Evolution of the New England Town Common, 1630-1966," 19 (November 1967): 313-18; and Robert D. Mitchell, "The Presbyterian Church as an Indicator of Westward Expansion in 18th-Century America," 18 (September 1966): 293-99.

12-26 Sauer, Carl O. LAND AND LIFE: A SELECTION FROM THE WRITINGS OF CARL ORTWIN SAUER. Ed. by John Leighly. Berkeley and Los Angeles: University of California Press, 1963. vi, 435 p. Maps, photos., diagrs., notes, index.

A selection of articles, which represents Sauer's wide range of interests in cultural and historical geography, are reproduced here. The articles are grouped under five headings: "The Midland Frontier" (Kentucky and Illinois); "The Southwest and Mexico"; "Human Uses of the Organic World" (agricultural origins and domestication); "The Farther Reaches of Human Time" (origin of man); and "The Pursuit of Learning," which includes two major methodological statements, "The Morphology of Landscape" (1925) and "Forward to Historical Geography" (1941). A list of Sauer's pre-1963 publications is also included. A short biography, several unpublished articles and remarks, and a list of dissertations supervised by Sauer are printed in HISTORICAL GEOGRAPHY NEWSLETTER 6 (Spring 1976): 3-11, 21-57, and 69-80.

12-27 SOUTHEASTERN GEOGRAPHER. Knoxville: University of Tennessee for the Southeastern Division of the Association of American Geographers. Vols. 1-8, 1961-68. Annual. Vol. 9-- , 1969-- . Biannual.

Articles pertaining to the historical geography of the southeastern United States include: Kevin J. Laws, "The Origin of the Street Grid in Atlanta's Urban Core," 19 (November 1979): 69-79; John J. Winberry, "Indigo in South Carolina: A Historical Geography," 19 (November 1979): 91-102; John Morgan, "The Ordering Pit, A Relict Feature of the Flue-Cured Tobacco Landscape," 18 (November 1978): 102-14; Robert A. Sauder, "Architecture and Urban Growth in Nineteenth Century New Orleans," 17 (November 1977): 93-107; John J. Winberry, "Formation of the West Virginia-Virginia Boundary," 17 (November 1977): 108-24; Judith J. Schulz, "The Hinterland of Revolutionary Camden, South Carolina," 16 (November 1976): 91-97; Steven W. Engerrand, "The Evolution of Landholding Patterns on the Georgia Piedmont, 1805-1830," 15 (November 1975): 73-80; Douglas C. Wilms, "Cherokee Settlement-Patterns in Nineteenth Century Georgia," 14 (May 1974): 43-53; Robert Dolan and Robert Glassen, "Oregon Inlet, North Carolina--A History of Coastal Change," 13 (May 1973): 41-53; and Douglas C. Wilms, "The Development of Rice Culture in Eighteenth Century Georgia," 12 (May 1972): 45-57.

12-28 "Special Issue: CUKANZUS '79." HISTORICAL GEOGRAPHY NEWSLETTER 9 (1979): 1-64. Photos.

The contents of this special issue of the newsletter are devoted to the proceedings of an international conference of historical geographers from Canada, the United Kingdom, Australia, New Zealand, and the United States (CUKANZUS) which was held August 26-September 2, 1979 at the University of California, Northridge. While the overall theme of the conference was "Rural, Urban, and Physical Environments in Frontier Transition," the individual sessions focused on a variety of topics: "Perspectives on the Southern California Frontier" (Anthony R. Orme, David Hornbeck, William Bowen, and J. Nicholas Entrikin); "Perspectives on Frontier Studies: General Concepts" (Michael Williams and Charles F.J. Whebell), "European Overseas Expansion" (Leonard Guelke and Robert D. Mitchell), and "Urban Perspectives" (Denis J.B. Shaw and Edward K. Muller); "Native Americans on the Frontier" (D. Wayne Moodie, Victor A. Konrad, and Aidan McQuillan); "Rural Frontier Studies" (Charles F. Heller, John T. Houdek, James Richtik, O.F.G. Sitwell, Marshall E. Bowen, Brian P. Birch, Roger Kain, Gerald Walker, and Audrey Kobayuski); "Urban Frontier Studies" (R. Louis Gentilcore, David R. Meyer, Paul Laxton, and Y. Ben-Arieh); "Mapping the Frontier" (J.B. Harley, Michael P. Conzen, and

Robert H. Block); "Demographic Dimensions of the Frontier" (Edward T. Price, Joseph S. Wood, Alan G. Macpherson, Linda A. Newson, Richard L. Nostrand, Darrell A. Norris, and Douglas K. Meyer); "Staples and Regional Development" (Carville V. Earle); "The Frontier: Concept, Ethic, and Geosophy" (Gerald Kearns, Stanley W. Trimble, Frank Norris, and John A. Jakle); "Perspectives on International Frontiers" (Eric G. Grant, F.H. Bauer, Gordon R. Lewthwaite, June B. Bauer, Frank C. Innes, A.J. Christopher, James R. Gibson, and Ronald G. Knapp); and "Historic Preservation" (Hugh Prince). Abstracts of the individual papers as well as the summary remarks by H.C. Darby and Hugh Prince are included.

12-29 Syracuse University. Department of Geography. DISCUSSION PAPER SERIES. 1975-- . Irregular, but approximately ten issues per year.

The following papers in this series pertain to various aspects of the historical geography of the United States: Michael O. Roark, "Nineteenth Century Population Distributions of the Five Civilized Tribes in Indian Territory, Oklahoma," no. 15 (1976); Doris O'Keefe, "Marriage and Migration in Colonial New England: A Study in Historical Population Geography," no. 16 (1976); Robert P. Donnell, "Location Response to Catastrophe: The Shoe and Leather Industry of Salem, Massachusetts, after the Conflagration of June 25, 1914," no. 20 (1976); Cathy Kelly, "Marriage Migration in Massachusetts, 1765-1790," no. 30 (1977); Jonathan S. Mesinger, "Peddlers and Merchants: The Geography of Work in a Nineteenth Century Jewish Community," no. 38 (1977); Patricia Lambert, "Ho for Kansas! The Origins and Spread of 'Kansas Fever,' 1870-1880," no. 44 (1978); Carolyn G. McGovern, "Comparing Population Pyramids: Two Techniques and a Test on Alta California Data from 1790 and the 1830s," no. 53 (1978); William K. Wyckoff, "On the Louisiana School of Historical Geography and the Case of the Upland South," no. 54 (1979); Robert C. Spillman, "Hispanic Population Patterns in Southern Texas, 1850-1970," no. 57 (1979); and David J. Robinson, ed., "A Preliminary Guide to Primary Documentary Sources for the Historical Geography of pre-1900 Syracuse," no. 61 (1979). Most of these papers are abstracted in GEO-ABSTRACT D (see entry 11-16).

12-30 Upchurch, John C., and Weaver, David C., eds. GEOGRAPHIC PERSPECTIVES ON SOUTHERN DEVELOPMENT. West Georgia College, Studies in the Social Sciences, Vol. 12. Carrollton: West Georgia College, 1973. vi, 93 p. Paper. Maps, diagrs., tables, notes.

Published in conjunction with the sixty-ninth annual meeting of the Association of American Geographers held in Atlanta, Georgia, April 15-18, 1973, this volume contains seven essays on the historical geography of the Southeast. Included are essays by

Sam B. Hilliard (land survey systems in the Southeast), Joseph A. Ernst and Harry Roy Merrens (mid-eighteenth-century South Carolina economy viewed from Philadelphia), W. Frank Ainsley and John W. Florin (religious diversity on the North Carolina piedmont), Howard G. Adkins (urban retardation in Mississippi, 1800-1840), Leonard W. Brinkham (home manufacturers as an indication of an emerging Appalachian subculture, 1840-1870), Burke G. Vanderhill (historic spas in Florida), and John B. Rehder (origin and dispersal of sugar plantations in Louisiana). Volume 16 (1977) of the West Georgia College, Studies in the Social Sciences also includes several articles pertaining to the historical geography of the southeastern states: Douglas C. Wilms (agricultural changes in the Cherokee nation prior to removal); James B. Gouger (grain farming in Virginia's Northern Neck, 1760-1860), and John P. Radford (race and residential patterns in Charleston, South Carolina, 1860-80).

12-31 Vaughan, Thomas, ed. THE WESTERN SHORE: OREGON COUNTY ESSAYS HONORING THE AMERICAN REVOLUTION. Portland: Oregon Historical Society and American Revolution Bicentennial Commission of Oregon, 1975. xii, 374 p. Paper. Maps, illus., photos., tables, notes, index.

Three articles by geographers are included in this collection of essays on Oregon's history which was prepared in conjunction with the bicentennial celebration of the American Revolution. The articles by geographers are Samuel N. Dicken, "Oregon Geography before White Settlement, 1770-1840"; James R. Gibson, "Bostonians and Muscovites on the Northwest Coast, 1788-1841"; and William Bowen, "The Oregon Frontiersman: A Demographic View." Topics of other articles, mainly by historians, include Spanish and British exploration of the Oregon Coast, the Chinnook Indians, wheat farming, and environmental perception. The book is well illustrated with contemporary maps, photographs, and landscape scenes.

12-32 Vining, James W. "State Geographical Societies Today." JOURNAL OF GEOGRAPHY 74 (March 1975): 167-79. Maps, tables.

Twenty-five state geographical societies are discussed in terms of their affiliation (National Council for Geographic Education, National Education Association, or unaffiliated), age, membership, and publications. Some of these publications, such as CALIFORNIA GEOGRAPHER, FLORIDA GEOGRAPHER, BULLE-TIN OF THE ILLINOIS GEOGRAPHICAL SOCIETY, MISSISSIPPI GEOGRAPHER, PENNSYLVANIA GEOGRAPHER, and VIRGINIA GEOGRAPHER, contain articles of historical interest. Articles from the more recent issues are abstracted in GEO-ABSTRACTS D (see entry 11-16).

12-33 Ward, David, ed. GEOGRAPHIC PERSPECTIVES ON AMERICA'S PAST: READINGS ON THE HISTORICAL GEOGRAPHY OF THE UNITED STATES. New York: Oxford University Press, 1979. xi, 364 p. Maps, photos., diagrs., tables, notes, bibliog.

A selection of previously published articles by both geographers and historians provides the basis for this anthology of readings on the historical geography of the United States. The articles are grouped in three sections, each with two subsections: "The Land and Its People" includes articles discussing the diversity of landscapes ("Landscape and Identity") and people ("Migrants in a Plural Society"); "The Regional Mosaic" includes articles that describe the uneven distribution of distinctive traits and divergent experiences of different regions ("The Colonial Inheritance" and "Westward Expansion"); and "Urbanization" includes articles pertaining to the relations among cities ("Regional Urban Systems") and the internal structure of cities ("The City from Within"). Each section includes a list of additional readings. Most of these articles are abstracted separately in the present bibliography.

Chapter 13

REGIONAL SYNTHESIS

All the studies in this chapter are characterized by their comprehensive or synthetic interpretations of a particular region, state, colony, or parish. Each study addresses a number of geographical topics such as frontier settlement, agriculture, population origins and immigration, economic activity, or rural and urban settlement.

A. UNITED STATES

13-1 AAG ANNALS 62 (June 1972): 155-373. Maps, illus., photos., diagrs., tables, notes.

> This special issue of the ANNALS, which was prepared for distribution at the Twenty-second International Geographic Congress in Montreal, consists of ten essays pertaining to the regional geography of the United States. Although the emphasis in general is current geographic patterns and recent geographic changes, most of the articles refer to the specific region's settlement history and development. Besides Meinig's essay on interpreting the regional development of the American West (see entry 13-7), the other contributions include: John B. Jackson, "Metamorphosis," pp. 155-58; James E. Vance, Jr., "California and the Search for the Ideal," pp. 185-210; Robert Darrenberger, "The Colorado Plateau," pp. 211-36; E. Cotton Mather, "The American Great Plains," pp. 237-57; John Fraser Hart, "The Middle West," pp. 258-82; Merle C. Prunty and Charles S. Aiken, "The Demise of the Piedmont Cotton Region," pp. 283-306; George K. Lewis, "Population Change in Northern New England," pp. 307-22; Peirce F. Lewis, "Small Town in Pennsylvania," pp. 323-51 (development of Bellefonte, Centre County, as example of the role of small towns in American life); and John R. Borchert, "America's Changing Metropolitan Regions," pp. 352-73.

13-2 Brown, Ralph H. HISTORICAL GEOGRAPHY OF THE UNITED STATES. New York: Harcourt, Brace and World, 1948. viii, 596 p. Maps, illus., photos., diagrs., tables, notes, bibliog., index.

> Although published in 1948, this remains the most comprehensive

survey of the historical geography of the United States. The organization of the text is regional and chronological rather than thematic. For the colonial period, Brown covers not only the English settlement of the original thirteen colonies but also the French settlements in Canada and the Spanish settlements in Florida and the far west. After describing the geographical patterns of the nineteenth century, he moves westward discussing the initial occupancy and formative development of several broad regions: the Ohio River and lower Great Lakes region; the new Northwest (upper Great Lakes, Michigan, Wisconsin, and Minnesota); the Great Plains and bordering regions; and the Rocky Mountains to the Pacific Coast. For the last three areas, he terminates the study around 1870. Each chapter is accompanied by a list of bibliographical references.

13-3 _____ . MIRROR FOR AMERICANS: LIKENESS OF THE EASTERN SEABOARD (1810). Special Publication, No. 27. New York: American Geographical Society, 1943. Reprint. New York: Da Capo Press, 1968. xxxii, 312 p. Maps, illus., tables, notes, bibliog., index.

Employing the cross-sectional approach, Brown recreates the historical geography of the eastern seaboard at the beginning of the nineteenth century. The narrative is presented as if it were written in 1810 by an imaginary Philadelphian, Thomas Pownall Keystone. Topics covered in this reconstructed geography include population, transportation, economic activities, commerce, and descriptions of several regions: northern border regions (Canada), southern New England, interior New York, eastern Pennsylvania, the Chesapeake country, and the Carolina low county. Brown's research is based on books, periodicals, newspapers, and maps that were contemporary with the period.

13-4 Conzen, Michael P., ed. "Fashioning the American Landscape." GEOGRAPHICAL MAGAZINE 52 (1979-80): passim. Maps, illus., photos.,

This series of twelve essays, which emphasize the regional settlement and development of North America, include George H. Dury, "Vast Continent with a Simple Layout," 52 (October 1979): 37-46; Karl W. Butzer, "This is Indian Country," 52 (November 1979): 140-48; Richard L. Nostrand, "Spanish Roots in the Borderlands," 52 (December 1979): 203-9; Richard Colebrook Harris, "Brief Interlude with New France," 52 (January 1980): 274-80; Peirce Lewis, "When America Was English," 52 (February 1980): 342-48; Sam Hilliard, "Plantations Created the South," 52 (March 1980): 409-16; Michael P. Conzen, "The Woodland Clearances," 52 (April 1980): 483-91; James E. Vance, "Utopia on the American Earth," 52 (May 1980): 555-60; David R. Meyer, "Industrious Entrepreneurs Make Their Mark," 52 (June 1980): 647-54; Martyn J. Bowden, "Creating Cowboy Country," 52 (July 1980): 693-701; Edward K. Muller, "Distinctive Downtown," 52 (August 1980): 747-55; and Wilbur Zelinsky, "Lasting Impact of the Prestigious Gentry," 52 (September 1980): 817-24.

13-5   Harris, Richard Colebrook. "The Historical Geography of North American
Regions." AMERICAN BEHAVIORAL SCIENTIST 22 (September–October
1978): 115–30. Notes.

> Harris provides an overview of European settlement of North
> America based on a review of the scattered literature produced
> by historical geographers during the 1960s and 1970s. He stresses
> three themes: the common influence of environmental opportunity
> (cheap land); regional cultural differentiation, and regional con-
> sciousness (circulation of information and development of urban
> systems).

13-6   Meinig, Donald W. "The American Colonial Era: A Geographic Commentary." PROCEEDINGS OF THE ROYAL GEOGRAPHICAL SOCIETY OF
AUSTRALIA, SOUTH AUSTRALIAN BRANCH 59 (1957–58): 1–22. Maps,
notes.

> In this summary interpretation of the historical geography of the
> Atlantic seaboard during the colonial period, Meinig stresses the
> growth of population; the development of settlement, agricultural,
> and industrial patterns; and the formation of broad regional divi-
> sions.

13-7   _____. "American Wests: Preface to a Geographical Interpretation."
AAG ANNALS 62 (June 1972): 159–84. Maps, diagrs., notes.

> Meinig provides a framework for interpreting the historical de-
> velopment of the American West as a set of dynamic regions.
> He identifies six major nuclei of European settlement (Hispano
> New Mexico, the Mormon region, Colorado, the Oregon Coun-
> try, northern California, and southern California), each of which
> can be examined as a complex changing through four stages (nu-
> clear, regional, regional-national, and metropolitan national).
> This regional development focuses on four categories of regional
> features (population, circulation, political areas, and culture).
> This article is reprinted in entry 12-33.

B. STATES AND REGIONS

13-8   Bowen, William A. THE WILLAMETTE VALLEY: MIGRATION AND SET-
TLEMENT ON THE OREGON FRONTIER. Seattle: University of Washington Press, 1978. xxii, 120 p. Maps, illus., diagrs., tables, notes,
bibliog., index.

> The primary component of this study is a series of forty-five de-
> tailed, accurate maps that portray the settlement of Oregon's
> frontier during the 1840s. These maps and the accompanying
> narrative emphasize population distribution, source of immigrants
> by state, and agricultural statistics. In an appendix Bowen dis-
> cusses the use of the 1850 manuscript census schedules, General

Land Office township survey plats, and Donation Land certificates in the cartographic reconstruction of the 1850 frontier landscape. For other articles by Bowen, see entry 12-31 and "Mapping an American Frontier: Oregon in 1850," AAG ANNALS 65 (March 1975), map supplement no. 18.

13-9   Earle, Carville V. THE EVOLUTION OF A TIDEWATER SETTLEMENT SYSTEM: ALL HALLOW'S PARISH, MARYLAND, 1650-1783. Department of Geography Research Paper, No. 170. Chicago: University of Chicago, Department of Geography, 1975. x, 239 p. Paper. Maps, diagrs., tables, bibliog.

Earle examines the evolution of the settlement system in one Tide-water parish (All Hallow's Parish near Annapolis in Anne Arundel County, Maryland), an area that was characterized during the colonial period by the production of a staple crop (tobacco), dispersed plantations, decentralized trade, and slavery. Specific topics that are investigated include the changing population (growth, composition, density, and distribution), urban settle-ments (specialized occupations and decentralized sites), rural settlements (plantations), landownership (the cadastre, land holding and tenancy), and commerce (transportation and trade). His reconstruction is based on travel journals and diaries, local census and tax assessment lists, and county probate records.

13-10   Gibson, James R. IMPERIAL RUSSIA IN FRONTIER AMERICA: THE CHANGING GEOGRAPHY OF SUPPLY OF RUSSIAN AMERICA, 1784-1867. Andrew H. Clark Series in the Historical Geography of North America. New York: Oxford University Press, 1976. xiii, 257 p. Maps, illus., tables, notes, bibliog., index.

After reviewing the settlement and economic history of the Rus-sian colonies in Alaska, which were based primarily on the fur trade, Gibson analyzes the problems of providing food and other provisions for these peripheral colonies. Supplies were obtained by several methods: by transport from Russia (either overland through Siberia or overseas via Cape Horn or Cape of Good Hope); by local agriculture (either in Alaska or in Russian colo-nies in northern California or Hawaii); and by foreign trade (with Yankee traders from Boston, Spaniards or Mexicans in California, the Hudson's Bay Company, or Hawaiians). This study is based on numerous archival documents from Russian, U.S., and Canadian institutions. In an earlier work, Gibson explores Russia's expansion into far eastern Siberia. The problems of pro-viding provisions for this area are described in FEEDING THE RUSSIAN FUR TRADE: PROVISIONMENT OF THE OKHOTSK SEABOARD AND THE KAMCHATKA PENINSULA, 1639-1856 (Madison: University of Wisconsin Press, 1969). More recently Gibson has compared Russia's expansion into Siberia which was based on the sable fur trade with the colonial expansion into

Alaska which was based on the sea otter fur trade; see "Russian Expansion in Siberia and America," GEOGRAPHICAL REVIEW 70 (April 1980): 127-36. Numerous other articles by Gibson pertaining to Russia's colonization of the northern Pacific are mentioned in the footnotes in these three publications. Other articles by Gibson are listed in entries 12-10 and 12-31.

13-11 Gottmann, Jean. VIRGINIA IN OUR CENTURY. 2d ed. Charlottesville: University Press of Virginia, 1969. xii, 656 p. Maps, photos., diagrs., notes, bibliog., index.

Originally published in 1955 as VIRGINIA AT MID-CENTURY (New York: Henry Holt), this new printing includes a supplementary chapter describing changes in the intervening fifteen years. Although the study is primarily concerned with current geographic patterns within the state, it does include a lengthy chapter, "Three and a Half Centuries of Change," pp. 54-141, which discusses the history of settlement and socioeconomic organization. This historical account is based on the political and social interpretations of historians, particularly Thomas Jefferson Wertenbaker.

13-12 Kulikoff, Allan. "The Colonial Chesapeake: Seedbed of Antebellum Southern Culture?" JOURNAL OF SOUTHERN HISTORY 45 (November 1979): 513-40. Notes.

Through the synthesis of recent works in the social and economic history of the colonial Chesapeake, Kulikoff developed an overview of Chesapeake society from 1607 to 1800 which emphasizes various economic (land acquistion and staple production) and demographic (population growth and labor supply) variables. He suggests that patterns developed in this region provided the basis for similar developments in other southern frontier areas.

13-13 Lemon, James T. THE BEST POOR MAN'S COUNTRY: A GEOGRAPHICAL STUDY OF EARLY SOUTHEASTERN PENNSYLVANIA. Baltimore: Johns Hopkins Press, 1972. xviii, 295 p. Maps, diagrs., tables, notes, index.

Recipient of the American Historical Association's Beveridge Award, this study traces the settlement and transformation of the landscape in southeastern Pennsylvania from 1680 to 1800. Major themes include the physical environment; the economic, ethnic, and religious background of the early settlers; population distribution, diffusion, and mobility; land tenure; rural settlement patterns; urban development; and regional variations in agricultural practices and land use patterns. Most studies of this area emphasize the different contributions of the various ethnic and religious groups; however, Lemon contends that a major motivating force in the settlement of this region was a

liberal philosophy, which resulted in fulfillment of personal and
family needs rather than the formation of strong community relationships. Generalizations are based on statistical data that were
reconstructed for Chester and Lancaster Counties, using wills,
deeds, and inventories from the respective county court houses
as well as tax assessment lists, diaries, and personal papers from
the respective county historical societies. Parts of this study
were previously published as "The Agricultural Practices of National Groups in Eighteenth-Century Southeastern Pennsylvania,"
GEOGRAPHICAL REVIEW 56 (October 1969): 467-96 (reprinted
in entry 12-33); "Urbanization and the Development of Eighteenth-
Century Southeastern Pennsylvania and Adjacent Delaware,"
WILLIAM AND MARY QUARTERLY, 3d ser. 24 (October 1967):
501-42; Lemon and Gary B. Nash, "The Distribution of Wealth
in Eighteenth Century America: A Century of Change in Chester
County, Pennsylvania, 1693-1802," JOURNAL OF SOCIAL
HISTORY 2 (Fall 1968): 1-24; and "Household Consumption in
Eighteenth-Century America and Its Relationship to Production
and Trade: The Situation among Farmers in Southwestern Penn-
sylvania," AGRICULTURAL HISTORY 41 (January 1967): 59-70.
For more recent revisions of the general theme of liberalism and
a lack of the sense of community, see entry 12-10 and "Early
Americans and Their Social Environment," JOURNAL OF HIS-
TORICAL GEOGRAPHY 6 (April 1980): 115-32.

13-14 McManis, Douglas R. COLONIAL NEW ENGLAND: A HISTORICAL
GEOGRAPHY. Andrew H. Clark Series in the Historical Geography of
North America. New York: Oxford University Press, 1975. xiv, 159 p.
Maps, illus., photos., diagrs., tables, bibliog., index.

This overview of selected topics of colonial New England's historical geography deals primarily with pre-European settlement
contact, beginning English settlement, settlement and demographic patterns, and various economic activities, including agriculture, fishing, commerce, forestry, shipbuilding, manufacturing,
and communications. Since footnotes are not included nor does the
bibliography include any unpublished primary sources, it appears
that this is a synthesis in a geographic framework of secondary works
which were developed primarily by historians.

13-15 Meinig, Donald W. THE GREAT COLUMBIA PLAIN: A HISTORICAL
GEOGRAPHY, 1805-1910. Seattle: University of Washington Press,
1968. xxi, 576 p. Maps, illus., photos., diagrs., tables, notes, bibliog.,
index.

Meinig presents a detailed reconstruction of the nineteenth-
century historical geography of the Great Columbia Plain (eastern Washington and northeastern Oregon), emphasizing man's
relation with the physical environment and his organization of

the area. His approach is chronological, focusing on the physical and Indian landscape, early nineteenth-century exploration,
the fur trade and mission era, mid-century military campaigns
and exploration, late nineteenth-century colonization and settlement (mining, ranching, and wheat farming), and the development
of railroads and towns. His concluding chapter places the study
area in a broader geographical perspective by discussing interregional relationships and the flows of people, economic activities,
and ideas into and through the region.

13-16 _____. IMPERIAL TEXAS: AN INTERPRETIVE ESSAY IN CULTURAL
GEOGRAPHY. Austin: University of Texas Press, 1969. 145 p. Maps,
photos., diagrs., bibliog., index.

Relying on secondary works (articles, monographs, and dissertations), Meinig provides an interpretive essay on the historical
development of Texas' cultural geography. He discusses population origins, settlement patterns, and trade and circulation
networks in the context of four time periods: the Spanish and
Mexican era, the Republic and early statehood years, the post-
Civil War period, and the twentieth century. This historical
framework provides the basis for identifying nine major culture
regions within the state.

13-17 _____. SOUTHWEST: THREE PEOPLES IN GEOGRAPHICAL CHANGE,
1600-1970. Andrew H. Clark Series in the Historical Geography of
North America. New York: Oxford University Press, 1971. xii, 151 p.
Maps, table, bibliog., index.

Although the temporal coverage of this monograph spans four
centuries (1600-1970), Meinig concentrates on the historical
social geography of the Southwest (primarily New Mexico and
Arizona) for two periods, 1820 to 1900 and 1900 to 1970. He
examines the contributions of three peoples (Indians, Hispanos,
and Anglos) to this regional development emphasizing socio-
cultural, demographic, political, and economic patterns. Based
almost entirely on secondary sources the book sketches the broad
outlines of regional structure and interaction, aerial relationships
of the three groups, and circulation patterns into and through
the region.

13-18 Merrens, Harry Roy. COLONIAL NORTH CAROLINA IN THE EIGHTEENTH
CENTURY: A STUDY IN HISTORICAL GEOGRAPHY. Chapel Hill: University of North Carolina Press, 1964. xv, 293 p. Maps, tables, notes,
bibliog., index.

The changing geography of pre-revolutionary North Carolina
provides the focus of this study. Concentrating on the third
quarter of the eighteenth century, Merrens describes the colony's
administrative and political organization; the colonists' perception

of the physical environment; population growth, distribution, and composition; and economic activities including forest utilization, commercial agricultural crops, plantations, urban development, and decentralized trade. In an appendix he discusses techniques and sources for compiling population and export data.

13-19 Mitchell, Robert D. COMMERCIALISM AND FRONTIER: PERSPECTIVES ON THE EARLY SHENANDOAH VALLEY. Charlottesville: University Press of Virginia, 1977. xiv, 251 p. Maps, diagrs., tables, notes, index.

Although Mitchell emphasizes the influence of economic processes on land utilization and social stratification in his study of Virginia's eighteenth-century Shenandoah Valley, he also mentions the role of environmental, political, and cultural factors on these emerging patterns. Various geographical themes are discussed, including the location and timing of settlement, the origin of settlers from southeastern Pennsylvania and Tidewater Virginia, land acquisition and speculation, population change and social stratification, pioneer economy, agricultural specialization particularly in hemp and wheat, and developing transportation, trade, and urban networks. His research is based primarily on county records (deed books, order books, rent rolls, tithtables, will books, and inventories). Other articles by Mitchell pertaining to Virginia and the Shenandoah Valley include "The Commercial Nature of Frontier Settlement in the Shenandoah Valley of Virginia," AAG PROCEEDINGS 1 (1969): 109-13; "The Shenandoah Valley Frontier," AAG ANNALS 62 (September 1972): 461-86; "Agricultural Change and the American Revolution: A Virginia Case Study," AGRICULTURAL HISTORY 47 (April 1973): 119-32; and "Content and Context: Tidewater Characteristics in the Early Shenandoah Valley," MARYLAND HISTORIAN 5 (Fall 1974): 79-92.

13-20 Thompson, John H., ed. GEOGRAPHY OF NEW YORK STATE. Syracuse: Syracuse University Press, 1966. xvi, 543 p. Maps, illus., photos., diagrs., tables, bibliog., index.

Primarily concerned with current geographical patterns in New York state, this textbook includes a historical section, "Part Two: Three and A Half Centuries of Change," pp. 111-96. It consists of four chapters, one by Robert J. Rayback, "The Indian," and three by Donald W. Meinig, "The Colonial Period, 1609-1775," "Geography of Expansion, 1785-1855," and "Elaboration and Change, 1850s-1960s." Several themes that are repeated in these chapters include spread of population and differential population growth, development of transportation networks, and patterns of agricultural and industrial activity. Each author lists a selected bibliography.

13-21   Webb, Walter Prescott.   THE GREAT PLAINS.   Boston: Ginn and Co.,
        1931.   xv, 525 p.   Maps, illus., tables, notes, bibliog., index.

        Because of its environmentalist interpretation, Webb's controver-
        sial history of the Great Plains still stands as the point of de-
        parture for most studies of the region.   Gregory M. Tubin traces
        Webb's intellectual and educational development, as well as the
        preparation and writing of the book in THE MAKING OF A
        HISTORY: WALTER PRESCOTT WEBB AND 'THE GREAT PLAINS'
        (Austin;   University of Texas Press, 1976).   A collection of essays
        on Webb appears in Kenneth R. Philip and Elliott West, eds.,
        ESSAYS ON WALTER PRESCOTT WEBB, Walter Prescott Webb
        Memorial Lectures, vol. 10 (Austin: University of Texas Press,
        1976).   Terry G. Jordan presents a perceptive review of both
        books and Webb in HISTORICAL GEOGRAPHY NEWSLETTER 8
        (Spring 1978): 29-32.

Chapter 14

EXPLORATION AND FRONTIER SETTLEMENT

The two earliest phases (exploration and frontier settlement) in the European occupation of the American landscape are treated in this chapter. The section on discovery and exploration covers both the European exploration of littoral North America and the nineteenth-century exploration of the interior portions of the continent. The second section deals with the westward movement of the frontier and the early settlement of the frontier areas. Both sections include a number of works by historians reflecting the strong relationships between historians and geographers in these two research areas.

A. DISCOVERY AND EXPLORATION

14-1   Allen, John L. PASSAGE THROUGH THE GARDEN: LEWIS AND CLARK AND THE IMAGE OF THE AMERICAN NORTHWEST. Urbana: University of Illinois Press, 1975. xxvi, 412 p. Maps, notes, bibliog., index.

In examining the Lewis and Clark expedition of 1804-06 through the American Northwest, Allen studies the relationship between the exploration process and the creation of geographic images. Using geographical journals, travel accounts, private correspondence, and contemporary maps, Allen determines what geographical information was available to Lewis and Clark and Thomas Jefferson, the expedition's sponsor, prior to the expedition. From this information two images, which influenced the planning of the expedition, were derived: a short passage or water connection was believed to exist between the Missouri and Columbia Rivers while the Northwest was thought to be a garden or an area rich in agricultural and natural resources. Other articles by Allen dealing with exploration and geographic images include: "An Analysis of the Exploratory Process: The Lewis and Clark Expedition of 1804-1806," GEOGRAPHICAL REVIEW 62 (January 1972), 13-39; "Geographical Knowledge and American Images of the Louisiana Territory," WESTERN HISTORICAL QUARTERLY 2 (April 1971): 151-70 (reprinted in entry 12-33); and "Lewis and Clark on the Upper Missouri: Decision at the Marias," MONTANA, THE MAGAZINE OF WESTERN HISTORY 21 (Summer 1971): 2-17. Other articles by Allen are found in 12-3, 12-6, and 12-16.

14-2   Bartlett, Richard A. GREAT SURVEYS OF THE AMERICAN WEST. Nor-
        man: University of Oklahoma Press, 1962. xxiii, 408 p. Maps, illus.,
        photos., notes, bibliog.,index.

> Bartlett presents a detailed account of the Great Surveys, four
> geographical and geological surveys of the western United States
> (1867-79) from which the U.S. Geological Survey was founded.
> Two of these surveys were sponsored by the War Department (the
> U.S. Geological Exploration of the Fortieth Parallel headed
> by Clarence King and the U.S. Geographical Surveys West of
> the One Hundredth Meridian led by Lt. George M. Wheeler),
> while the other two were associated with the Department of the
> Interior (U.S. Geological and Geographical Surveys of the
> Territories directed by Ferdinand Hayden and the U.S. Geo-
> graphical and Geological Survey of the Rocky Mountain Region
> led by John Wesley Powell). The research for this study was
> based primarily on the published reports of the surveys and manu-
> script materials in the National Archives. The published reports
> are listed in entry 7-15.

14-3   Cook, Warren L. FLOOD TIDE OF EMPIRE: SPAIN AND THE PACIFIC
        NORTHWEST, 1543-1819. New Haven: Yale University Press, 1973.
        xiv, 620 p. Maps, illus., photos., notes, biblog., index.

> Cook provides a detailed history of the Spanish role in the explor-
> ation and exploitation of the Pacific Coast from Cape Mendocino
> to Alaska. He focuses on Spanish interaction with Indians, British,
> Russians, and Americans in competing for hegemony over this region.
> The research is based on archival sources in Spain and Mexico.

14-4   Cumming, William P., et al. THE DISCOVERY OF NORTH AMERICA.
        New York: American Heritage Press, 1972. 304 p. Maps, illus.,
        photos., notes, bibliog., index.

> The discovery and exploration of North America before 1630
> is summarized in six chapters written by Cumming, R.A.Skelton,
> and D.B. Quinn. Each chapter deals with a broad theme: the
> discovery of the Atlantic in the Middle Ages; the discovery and
> exploration of the West Coast; colonization attempts before 1600;
> the search for the northern passage; and the first settlements of
> the early seventeenth century. The summary statements in each
> chapter are complemented by selections from the explorers' orig-
> inal narrative, as well as by contemporary illustrations. In
> fact, the book is highlighted by 362 illustrations including maps,
> landscape scenes, portraits, drawings of plant and animal life,
> and scenes depicting native Americans and their activities.

14-5   Cumming, William P., et al. THE EXPLORATION OF NORTH AMERICA,
        1630-1776. New York: G.P. Putnam's Sons, 1974. 272 p. Maps,
        illus., notes, bibliog., index.

> Following the format established in the preceeding volume, this
> summarizes the exploration of North America between 1630 and

the American Revolution. Each of the six chapters deals with
a broad region: Great Lakes and Mississippi, northeast seaboard,
southern coastal colonies, the southeast, Louisiana and the
southwest, and the fur trading areas from the Rockies to the
Arctic. Authors of other chapters are S.E. Hillier, D.B. Quinn,
and G. Williams. This volume includes four hundred illustrations.

14-6   Friis, Herman R., ed. THE PACIFIC BASIN: A HISTORY OF ITS GEO-
        GRAPHICAL EXPLORATION. New York: American Geographical Society,
        1967. xiii, 457 p.

This collection of essays on the history of the exploration of the
Pacific Basin is an expansion of papers presented at a symposium,
"Highlights of the History of Scientific Exploration in Relation to
the Development of the Pacific Map," held as part of the Tenth
Pacific Science Congress meeting in Honolulu, Hawaii, August
21 to September 6, 1961. Papers which include references to
the western coast of North America were presented by Donald D.
Brand (Spanish exploration), Dimitri M. Lebedev and Vadim I.
Grekov (Russian exploration), Robert J. Garry, (French exploration), Richard I. Ruggles (English exploration), and Kenneth J.
Bertrand (U.S. exploration). The copious footnotes are a good
guide to the manuscript and published reports of the various expeditions as well as the pertinent secondary literature. Illustrations include both reproductions of contemporary maps and reconstructed maps showing the routes of various exploring parties.
Friis also prepared an exhibit consisting primarily of maps from
the National Archives for this conference which is documented
in the exhibit catalog, THE UNITED STATES SCIENTIFIC GEO-
GRAPHICAL EXPLORATION OF THE PACIFIC BASIN, 1783-1899
(Washington, D.C.: National Archives, 1961), pp. 1-26.

14-7   Goetzman, William H. EXPLORATION AND EMPIRE: THE EXPLORER
        AND THE SCIENTIST IN THE WINNING OF THE AMERICAN WEST.
        New York: Alfred A. Knopf, 1966. xliv, 656 p. Maps, illus., photos.,
        notes, bibliog., index.

Goetzman provides a comprehensive history of nineteenth-century
western exploration emphasizing three periods, which he entitles,
"Exploration and Imperialism, 1805-1845" (Lewis and Clark,
mountain men, and fur traders); "The Great Reconnaissance and
Manifest Destiny, 1845-1860" (Pacific Railroad Surveys); and
"Exploration and the Great Surveys, 1860-1900" (California
Geological Survey and the Wheeler, King, Hayden, and Powell
surveys). The role of the federal government is evident in many
of these surveys. Twenty-two reconstructed maps show the routes
of the various exploring expeditions. A bibliographical essay dis-
cusses the historical materials that are available in the National
Archives and other manuscript collections. An earlier work by
Goetzman describes the role of the Army Topographical Engineers
in exploring the West; see ARMY EXPLORATION IN THE AMERI-
CAN WEST, 1803-1863 (New Haven: Yale University Press, 1959).

14-8   Johnson, Adrian. AMERICA EXPLORED: A CARTOGRAPHICAL HISTORY
        OF THE EXPLORATION OF NORTH AMERICA. New York: Viking Press,
        1974. 264 p. Maps, illus., index.

    Over 350 illustrations consisting of early maps, several in full
    color, as well as numerous pictorial views including portraits and
    landscape views, are the most salient feature of this summary
    account of the discovery and exploration of North America. Al-
    though the coastal explorations of the fifteenth through seven-
    teenth centuries receive the greatest attention, the penetrations
    into the interior parts of the United States and Canada during
    the eighteenth through mid-nineteenth centuries are also covered.

14-9   McManis, Douglas R. EUROPEAN IMPRESSIONS OF THE NEW ENGLAND
        COAST, 1497-1620. Department of Geography Research Paper, No.
        139. Chicago: University of Chicago, Department of Geography, 1972.
        vii, 147 p. Paper. Maps, notes, bibliog.

    Based on contemporary records of explorers, maps, official re-
    ports, and promotional literature, McManis recreates the Euro-
    pean image of the New England coast (Cape Cod to Maine).
    The first chapter is devoted to cartographic images created during
    the first half of the sixteenth century, while the remaining chapters
    focus primarily on English impressions and secondly on French
    observations during the last half of the century. This accumula-
    tion of geographic knowledge led to the permanent settlement
    of this area in the early seventeenth century. Other articles by
    McManis pertaining to this general topic include "English Evalu-
    ation of North American Iron during the Late Sixteenth and
    Early Seventeenth Centuries," PROFESSIONAL GEOGRAPHER
    21 (March 1969): 93-96; and "The Traditions of Vinland,"
    AAG ANNALS 59 (December 1969): 797-814.

14-10   Morison, Samuel Eliot. THE EUROPEAN DISCOVERY OF AMERICA:
        THE NORTHERN VOYAGES, A.D. 500-1600. New York: Oxford
        University Press, 1971. xviii, 712 p. Maps, illus., photos., notes,
        bibliog., index.

    Morison presents a comprehensive account of the mythical,
    semimythical, and actual voyages across the North Atlantic
    to North America prior to 1600. His narrative emphasizes
    the Irish (St. Brendan), the Norsemen (Leif Ericson, Greenland
    and Vinland), the Portuguese and British sailors of the fifteenth
    century, and the sixteenth century explorers (Verrazzano, Car-
    tier, Frobisher, Davis, and Raleigh). Much of his research is
    based on contemporary maps that have been redrawn to depict
    specific voyages and to compare the recorded features with
    current place names and coast lines. He also uses oblique
    aerial photographs to help identify some of the places visited
    by the early explorers. His experience as a navigator is evi-
    dent in the discussions of early fishing techniques and sailing

ships. Each chapter is followed by a bibliographical essay that discusses the literary, cartographic, and legendary evidence that is available for the various voyages. In a companion volume, Morison describes the voyages to South and Central America (emphasizing Columbus, Magellan, and Drake); see THE EUROPEAN DISCOVERY OF AMERICA: THE SOUTHERN VOYAGES, A.D. 1492-1616 (New York: Oxford University Press, 1974).

14-11 National Geographic Society. Special Publications Division. INTO THE WILDERNESS. Washington, D.C.: 1978. 208 p. Maps, illus., photos., index.

Seven semischolarly essays, each by a different author, recount and trace the explorations of selected adventurers in the late eighteenth- and early nineteenth-century American wilderness. These explorers include friars Francisco Atanasio Dominguez and Silvestre Vélez de Escalante in the southwest; botanist William Bartram in the southeast; Daniel Boone in Kentucky; Alexander MacKenzie and David Thompson in western Canada; Meriwether Lewis and William Clark in northwestern U.S.; the mountain men in the Rockies; and John C. Fremont in California. Although the book is richly illustrated with over one hundred twentieth-century photographs of the various landscapes these men explored, twenty-four specially commissioned paintings of the explorers' activities, and eight reconstructed maps of the explorers' routes, it also includes selected eighteenth- and nineteenth-century paintings, illustrations, and maps.

14-12 Quinn, David Beers. ENGLAND AND THE DISCOVERY OF AMERICA, 1481-1620. New York: Alfred A. Knopf, 1974. xxxii, 497 p. Maps, illus., notes, bibliog., index.

Quinn examines the role of the English in the discovery and eventual exploitation and settlement of North America. Starting with the voyages of the British sailors during the late fifteenth century, he views the succeeding events (the explorations of Sebastian Cabot through the trial and error colonization attempts of the late sixteenth century) as a continuous process ending in permanent settlements at Jamestown and Plymouth.

14-13 _____, ed. THE HAKLUYT HANDBOOK. 2 vols. Works Issued by the Hakluyt Society, 2d ser., nos. 144-45. London: British Library, Hakluyt Society, 1974. xxvii, 706 p. Maps, illus., notes, index.

This handbook provides a detailed guide to the writing of and about the greatest English editor of travel narratives, Richard Hakluyt the younger, 1552-1616. The first volume consists of a series of essays on the significance of Hakluyt's work, various studies of the extent to which Hakluyt used the materials available to him (including the chapter, "North America," by D.B. Quinn, pp. 244-53), and a guide to the events in Hakluyt's life. The second volume includes a bibliography of books for which Hakluyt was responsible (books that he compiled, translated, or published and works he was influential in having published), secondary works about Hakluyt, and works published by the Hakluyt Society, 1846-1973.

14-14   Sauer, Carl O. NORTHERN MISTS. Berkeley and Los Angeles: University of California Press, 1968. 204 p. Maps, notes, index.

Sauer examines the European explorations of the Northern Atlantic prior to Columbus's voyages, starting with the fifteenth century and moving backward to the sixth century. Combining information from documentary sources, legendary sagas, and archaeological investigations, he reconstructs the maritime activities of the Portuguese navigators and fishermen, the British sailors, the Vikings, and the Irish monks in the exploration of Iceland, Greenland, and possibly Newfoundland and New England.

14-15   _____. SIXTEENTH CENTURY NORTH AMERICA: THE LAND AND THE PEOPLE AS SEEN BY THE EUROPEANS. Berkeley and Los Angeles: University of California Press, 1971. xii, 319 p. Maps, illus., notes, bibliog., index.

Emphasizing the land (flora and fauna) and the people (Indian cultures), Sauer reconstructs the presettlement geography of North America (United States and Canada) based on the accounts of sixteenth-century explorers. In order to place the explorers' accounts in the proper physical context, he maps the routes of various expeditions including Cartier, Cabeza de Vaca, Coronado, and De Soto. The narrative focuses on the Atlantic coast before mid-century, the Spanish entries into the interior and far West, the strategic importance of Florida, and the English settlements at the end of the century. Similar techniques and interpretations were initiated by Sauer in his study of the Spanish explorations of the Caribbean islands and rimland from 1492 to 1519 in THE EARLY SPANISH MAIN (Berkeley and Los Angeles: University of California Press, 1966).

14-16   Schubert, Frank N. VANGUARD OF EXPANSION: ARMY ENGINEERS IN THE TRANS-MISSISSIPPI WEST, 1819-1879. Washington, D.C.: Office of the Chief of Engineers, 1980. xii, 160 p. Paper. Maps, illus., photos., notes, index.

An overview of the Corps of Engineers' nineteenth-century activities is presented in this compact narrative. Numerous maps and sketches reflect the Corps' exploration of the West and related cartographic activities. The footnotes provide a guide to the published and manuscript exploration reports of the Engineers.

14-17 TERRAE INCOGNITAE: THE ANNALS OF THE SOCIETY FOR THE HIS-
TORY OF DISCOVERIES. Vols. 1-10, 1969-78. Amsterdam: Nico Israel.
Vol. 11-- . Detroit: Wayne State University Press, 1979-- . Annual.

Primarily devoted to the history of geographic discoveries on an
international basis, this journal does contain several articles and
book reviews on the history of discoveries in North America.
Some articles of interest are: Barbara B. McCorkle, "Recent
Literature in Discovery History," 11 (1979): 71-82, and 12
(1980): 85-94; Albert E. Doerr, revised by Oliver Dunn, "Drake's
California Harbor: Another Look at William Caldeira's Story,"
9 (1977): 49-59; John T. Juricek, "English Territorial Claims in
North America under Elizabeth and the Early Stuarts," 7 (1976):
7-22; John Parker, "Willard Glazier and the Mississippi Headwaters Controversy," 7 (1976): 53-63; Warren Heckrotte, "The
Discovery of Humbolt Bay: A New Look at an Old Story,"
5 (1973); 27-41; Peter J. Piveronus, Jr., "John Rustell's Proposed Voyage to North America from Ireland, 1517-19," 3 (1971)
59-65; Mutti Enn Kaups, "Shifting Vinland--Tradition and Myth,"
2 (1978): 29-60; and Vsevolod Slessarev and Pirie Sublett, "The
Vinland Caption Re-examined," 1 (1969): 58-67.

14-18 Tyler, David B. THE WILKES EXPEDITION: THE FIRST UNITED STATES
EXPLORING EXPEDITION (1838-1842). Philadelphia: American Philosophical Society, 1968. xvi, 435 p. Maps, illus., notes, bibliog., index.

The history of the U.S. Navy's first expedition in the Pacific
Basin is recounted in this volume. This expedition, which was
led by Charles Wilkes, is noted for its exploration of Antarctica
and the South Pacific Islands, but its itinerary also included the
northwest coast of the United States (Oregon and California).

B. THE FRONTIER AND EARLY SETTLEMENT

14-19 Alwin, John A. "Post Office Locations and the Historical Geographer:
A Montana Example." PROFESSIONAL GEOGRAPHER 26 (May 1974):
183-86. Maps, notes.

Alwin uses and evaluates post office locations as a tool for mapping the spread of settlement in Montana from 1865 to 1900.

14-20 Bartlett, Richard A. THE NEW COUNTRY: A SOCIAL HISTORY OF THE
AMERICAN FRONTIER, 1776-1890. New York: Oxford University Press,
1974. viii, 487 p. Maps, illus., photos., notes, bibliog., index.

In this synthetic history of the frontier process, Bartlett discusses
traditional topics (frontier myths, land legislation, and the sweep
across the continent) as well as several neglected themes (the
despoilment of the land, social conditions, and urban aspects of
the frontier). His bibliographical essay, which is organized
topically, evaluates the best secondary sources on these particular
topics.

14-21 Billington, Ray Allen. AMERICA'S FRONTIER HERITAGE. Histories of the American Frontier. New York: Holt, Rinehart and Winston, 1966. x, 310 p. Paper. Notes, bibliog., index.

Billington, the chief student and interpreter of Frederick Jackson Turner's frontier hypothesis, not only reviews the development of the thesis by Turner and the subsequent attacks by his critics, but also summarizes the new interpretations that have resulted from modern research in history and the social sciences. Specific topics that Billington explores are the migration process and particularly the pioneers' motivations for moving west, the role of the physical and societal environments of the frontier in shaping regional and national characters, the structure of frontier society, political and social aspects of frontier democracy, and the economic impact of the frontier. Other volumes in this series (Histories of the American Frontier), which is edited by Billington, pertain to specific time periods, regions or topics (such as the northern colonial frontier, 1607-1763; the farmers' frontier, 1865-1900; and mining frontiers, 1848-1880). Recent publications by Billington that pertain to the evolution and/or interpretation of the frontier hypothesis include THE GENESIS OF THE FRONTIER THESIS: A STUDY IN HISTORICAL CREATIVITY (San Marino, Calif.: Huntington Library, 1971), and AMERICA'S FRONTIER CULTURE: THREE ESSAYS (College Station: Texas A & M University Press, 1977). Billington's most recent history of the American frontier, which utilizes a chronological and regional approach, is WESTWARD EXPANSION: A HISTORY OF THE AMERICAN FRONTIER, 4th ed. (New York: Macmillan, 1974). The bibliographical notes in this publication, as well as in the others, list a wide range of secondary sources pertaining to frontier history.

14-22 Davis, James E. FRONTIER AMERICA, 1800-1840: A COMPARATIVE DEMOGRAPHIC ANALYSIS OF THE SETTLEMENT PROCESS. Glendale, Calif.: Arthur H. Clark Co., 1977. 220 p. Maps, illus., tables, notes, bibliog., index.

Davis explores the effect of the frontier experience on selected demographic characteristics (household size and composition, age and sex, racial characteristics, and occupations) for people moving to the frontier from 1800 to 1840. Using federal census data, he develops a frontier classification for counties based on density and locational criteria. His findings are analyzed both temporally (the five censuses are compared with each other) and spatially (northern and southern frontiers are compared with each other and with settled areas).

14-23 Florin, John W. THE ADVANCE OF FRONTIER SETTLEMENT IN PENN-
SYLVANIA, 1638-1850: A GEOGRAPHICAL INTERPRETATION. Papers
in Geography, No. 14. University Park: Pennsylvania State University,
Department of Geography, 1977. iv, 108 p. Maps, notes, bibliog.

The location and movement of the frontier in Pennsylvania is
portrayed on seventeen maps (one for each decade between 1680
and 1830). The basis for this reconstruction is the date of earliest permanent settlement (the beginnings of agricultural and
urban settlement) by township. Florin also reviews the secondary literature, primarily by geographers, pertaining to the spread
of settlement in the United States as a whole and in individual
states or colonies.

14-24 Harris, Richard Colebrook. "The Simplification of Europe Overseas."
AAG ANNALS 67 (December 1977): 469-83. Notes.

By comparing seventeenth- and eighteenth-century northwestern
Europe settlements in French Canada, Dutch South Africa, and
English New England, Harris develops a model for explaining
the structure of frontier societies. When introduced to a situation that was characterized by easy access to land but with limited
access to markets, these Europeans, who had a common heritage
of strong nuclear families with a desire for private ownership
of land, produced a homogeneous rural society of subsistence
farmers. This response represented the simplification of European
society rather than a fragmentation based on the removal and
separation of specific groups. Comments by Robert D. Mitchell
and Adrian Pollock are printed in AAG ANNALS 69 (September
1979): 474-80. An earlier version of this thesis was presented
by Harris and Leonard Guelke in "Land and Society in Early
Canada and South Africa," JOURNAL OF HISTORICAL GEOG-
RAPHY 3 (April 1977): 134-53.

14-25 Ironside, Robert G., et al., eds. FRONTIER SETTLEMENT. Edmonton:
University of Alberta, Department of Geography, 1974. xii, 283 p.
Paper. Maps, diagrs., tables, notes, index.

Fourteen papers from the Symposium on Frontier Settlement on
the Forest-Grassland Fringe, held in Edmonton and Saskatoon
in 1972 as one of the events of the Twenty-second International
Geographical Congress, are reprinted in this volume. The
papers, which are international in coverage, pertain to both
historical and contemporary themes. Five papers emphasize
the historical development of frontier settlement with three
pertaining to the United States: John H. Paterson, "Unit Size
as a Factor in Land Disposal Policy," pp. 151-63 (land disposal
practices in the United States); J.F. Davis, "The Role of the
Railroad in the Settling of Nebraska, 1860-1900," pp. 164-77;
and B.P. Birch, "Initial Perception of Prairie--An English Settlement in Illinois," pp. 178-94.

14-26   Jakle, John A. "Salt on the Ohio Valley Frontier, 1770-1820." AAG
        ANNALS 59 (December 1969): 687-709. Maps, tables, notes.

    Jakle suggests that the natural salt licks and associated bison
    trails were an important factor in the frontier settlement and
    economic development of the Ohio Valley (Ohio, Kentucky,
    West Virginia, and western Pennsylvania). The salt not only
    provided a resource for preserving meats, but also was instru-
    mental in sustaining early urban activity.

14-27   Klose, Nelson. A CONCISE STUDY GUIDE TO THE AMERICAN FRON-
        TIER. Lincoln: University of Nebraska Press, 1964. xi, 269 p. Maps,
        bibliog., index.

    This reference guide provides a synopsis of the major topics re-
    lating to the American frontier and westward expansion. It
    compares the content of the major textbooks on the subject and
    presents an extensive bibliography that is arranged topically.
    These topics include Turner and the frontier hypothesis, the
    successive regional frontiers, problems and features of the fron-
    tier (Indians, public domain, transportation, religion, culture,
    and politics), and types of frontiers (agriculture, fur trade, min-
    ing, cattle raising, and urbanization).

14-28   McDermott, John Francis, ed. THE FRONTIER RE-EXAMINED. Urbana:
        University of Illinois Press, 1967. x, 192 p. Maps, illus., notes, index.

    Thirteen essays presented at a conference on the frontier held
    at Southern Illinois University, November 1965, are printed in
    this volume. Although the conference was not intended to be
    either pro or anti Turnerian, several authors used Turner's thesis
    as a starting point. A variety of topics were covered, including
    the early development of urban centers and the role of Missouri
    River towns in the westward movement, the Spanish reaction to
    the American entrada into the Southwest, transportation in fron-
    tier development, the cartographic image of the West based on
    reports of U.S. government explorations (see entry 7-13), the
    Great Revival and religion on the frontier, the documentary art
    of the Indian (see entry 10-2), the significance of territorial
    records, and the fur trade as a business in St. Louis and its effect
    of Indian life. In addition, three articles deal with the literary
    treatment of the frontier.

14-29   Merk, Frederick. HISTORY OF THE WESTWARD MOVEMENT. New York:
        Alfred A. Knopf, 1978. xvii, 665 p. Maps, photos., diagrs., tables,
        bibliog., index.

    Merk, who was a student of the frontier historian, Frederick Jack-
    son Turner, presents his interpretation of the westward progression
    of settlement in the United States from the seventeenth to twen-
    tieth centuries, with an emphasis on land acquisition, the de-
    velopment of agriculture and natural resources, and man's
    control over the environment. The narrative, which is an out-

growth of a course at Harvard on the westward movement, is
developed in sixty-four short, unfootnoted chapters accompanied
by 116 illustrations, most of which are maps from secondary sources.

14-30 Miller, David H., and Steffen, Jerome O., eds. THE FRONTIER: COM-
PARATIVE STUDIES. Norman: University of Oklahoma Press, 1977. viii,
327 p. Maps, illus., diagrs., tables, notes, index.

As the first publication in an ongoing program in comparative
and interdisciplinary frontier studies sponsored by the University
of Oklahoma, this volume consists of papers presented at symposiums in 1975 and 1976 by anthropologists, geographers, and
historians. Those articles by geographers include John C. Hudson,
"Theory and Methodology in Comparative Frontier Studies," pp.
11-32; David J. Wishart, "The Fur Trade of the West, 1807-
1940; A Geographical Synthesis," pp. 161-200; Brian S. Osborne, "Frontier Settlement in Eastern Ontario in the Nineteenth
Century: A Study in Changing Perceptions of Land and Opportunity," pp. 201-26; and Geoffrey Wall, "Nineteenth-Century
Land Use and Settlement on the Canadian Shield Frontier," pp.
227-42. The second volume in this program (edited by William
W. Savage, Jr., and Stephen I. Thompson and published by the
University of Oklahoma Press in 1979) consists of invited papers
as well as papers presented at symposiums in 1976 and 1977.
Articles by geographers include Brian P. Birch, "British Evalua-
tions of the Forest Openings and Prairie Edges of the North-
Central States, 1800-1850," pp. 167-92 (Edwards Co., Illinois);
Jeanne Kay, "Indian Responses to a Mining Frontier," pp. 193-
204 (Wisconsin); and Carolyn B. Lewis, "Agricultural Evolution
on Secondary Frontiers: A Florida Model," pp. 205-34.

14-31 Paul, Rodman W., and Etulain, Richard W. THE FRONTIER AND THE
AMERICAN WEST. Goldentree Bibliographies in American History. Ar-
lington Heights, Ill.: AHM Publishing Corp., 1977. xviii, 169 p. Index.

Books, articles, and doctoral dissertations pertaining to the lands
west of the 98th meridian from the 1840s to the present provide
the focus of this unannotated bibliography. There are 2,973 entries
arranged in thirty-six topical chapters, including bibliographical
guides and selected reference works, the frontier hypothesis and
Frederick Jackson Turner, frontiers east of the Missouri, Indians,
fur trade, nineteenth-century explorers and scientists, mining,
cattle and sheep, agriculture, land policy, transportation, and
western cities and towns. Other volumes in the Goldentree
Bibliographies are listed in entry 11-12, pp. 14-15.

14-32 Powell, Joseph M. MIRRORS OF THE NEW WORLD: IMAGES AND IMAGE-
MAKERS IN THE SETTLEMENT PROCESS. Studies in Historical Geography.
Folkestone, Kent: William Dawson and Sons; Hamden, Conn.: Archon
Books, 1977. 207 p. Maps, diagrs., notes, bibliog., index.

Powell examines the process of image-making as a complementary interpretation in understanding the evolution of settlement in Australia, New Zealand, and North America. After reviewing the social and intellectual climate of eighteenth- and nineteenth-century Europe, he describes selected images or ideologies that influenced settlement: the yeoman farmer and the intensive development of relatively small farms, the quest for a healthy environment, and the search for a home by religious and utopian groups. This presentation does not represent original research but is intended to be a guide to a particular viewpoint for students in human geography.

14-33 Rohrbough, Malcolm J. THE TRANS-APPALACHIAN FRONTIER: PEOPLE, SOCIETIES, AND INSTITUTIONS, 1775-1850. New York: Oxford University Press, 1978. xv, 444 p. Maps, tables, notes, bibliog., index.

This historian traces the occupation and settlement of the middle third of the United States from the Appalachian Mountains to the Mississippi River (the Old Northwest and the Old Southwest), 1775 to 1850, with an emphasis on the development of a variety of societies and institutions. With the westward movement of the frontier through this fourteen-state area, he analyzes the settlers' initial concern for security (food, shelter, and physical security) and their eventual concern for stability (more complex economic life; the organization of county, territorial and state governments; law; and social institutions). Also included are thirteen maps which show the early towns, county and territorial boundaries, and Indian land cessions for the various frontier areas that are discussed. This study is based on a wide variety of manuscript records from numerous historical societies and state archives that are enumerated in the bibliography.

14-34 Unruh, John D., Jr. THE PLAINS ACROSS: THE OVERLAND EMIGRANTS AND THE TRANS-MISSISSIPPI WEST, 1840-60. Urbana: University of Illinois Press, 1979. xviii, 565 p. Maps, illus., photos., notes bibliog., index.

Unruh provides a thorough analysis, with revised interpretations, of the trans-Mississippi migration from 1840 to 1860. In discussing the interaction of the emigrants to other groups in the West (Indians, U.S. Army, Mormons, and traders) and with the flora and fauna, he emphasizes that the trails, the country, and the emigrants were continually changing. His sources included emigrant diaries, journals, letters, and contemporary newspapers.

14-35 Wishart, David J. "The Changing Position of the Frontier of Settlement on the Eastern Margins of the Central and Northern Great Plains, 1854-1890." PROFESSIONAL GEOGRAPHERS 21 (May 1969): 153-57. Maps, notes.

Using population density and percentage of improved land as determinants, Wishart maps the westward movement of the settlement frontier in Kansas, Nebraska, and the Dakotas.

Chapter 15

NATIVE AMERICANS

In recording the literature on the historical geography of native Americans, this section reflects Indian-white relations after initial contact, rather than precontact conditions. This literature is divided into four sections: bibliographies; Indian land cessions and tenure; Indians and the fur trade; and Indian population, settlement patterns and acculturation. Geographical discussions of the fur trade are included in this chapter (rather than in chapter 17, "Economic Activities") because these studies emphasize the role of the Indians in this trading network. The section on fur trade also includes several studies of the Canadian fur trade in the Great Plains and around the Great Lakes because these studies illustrate the Indian's role in an economic activity that was not limited by an international boundary. The final section represents a miscellaneous grouping of publications which are highlighted by discussions of Indian population, settlement patterns, and acculturation.

A. BIBLIOGRAPHIES

15-1   Carlson, Alvar W. "A Bibliography of the Geographical Literature on the American Indian, 1920-1971." PROFESSIONAL GEOGRAPHER 24 (August 1972): 258-63. Map, tables, notes.

> Entries for ninety-five articles, monographs, dissertations, and theses are listed in this bibliography. Although the emphasis is on current geographical problems, some articles of a historical or retrospective orientation are included.

15-2   Jennings, Francis, ed. THE NEWBERRY LIBRARY CENTER FOR THE HISTORY OF THE AMERICAN INDIAN BIBLIOGRAPHICAL SERIES. 18 vols. Bloomington: Indiana University Press for the Newberry Library, 1976-79.

> The purpose of this bibliographical series is to provide a guide to reliable sources and studies pertaining to the history of the American Indian. Each volume consists of a critical bibliographical essay and an alphabetical author list of works cited. Although works by historians and anthropologists are emphasized, there are

occasional items by geographers. The topics covered by the in-
dividual bibliographies pertain either to culture areas (Robert
S. Grumet, NATIVE AMERICANS OF THE NORTHWEST COAST
[1979]; Robert F. Heizer, INDIANS OF CALIFORNIA [1976];
June Helm, INDIANS OF THE SUBARCTIC [1976]; E. Adamson
Hoebel, PLAINS INDIANS (1977); Frank W. Porter, III, INDIANS
IN MARYLAND AND DELAWARE [1979]; Elisabeth Tooker, IN-
DIANS OF THE NORTHEAST [1978]; and William E. Unrau,
EMIGRANT INDIANS OF KANSAS [1979]), individual tribes
(Raymond D. Fogelson, CHEROKEES [1978]; Michael D. Green,
CREEKS [1979]; Herbert T. Hoover, SIOUX [1979]; Peter Iver-
son, NAVAJOS [1976]; Michael E. Melody, APACHES [1977];
Helen Hornbeck Tanner, OJIBWAS [1976]; and C.A. Weslager,
DELAWARES [1978]), or other significant historical issues (Henry
F. Dobyns, NATIVE AMERICAN HISTORICAL DEMOGRAPHY
[1976]; Francis Paul Prucha, UNITED STATES INDIAN POLICY
[1977]; James P. Ronda and James Axtell, INDIAN MISSIONS
[1978]; and Dean K. Snow, NATIVE AMERICAN PREHISTORY
[1979]).

15-3   Prucha, Francis Paul. A BIBLIOGRAPHICAL GUIDE TO THE HISTORY
OF INDIAN-WHITE RELATIONS IN THE UNITED STATES. Chicago:
University of Chicago Press for the Center for the History of the American
Indian of the Newberry Library, 1977. x, 454 p. Index.

Over 9,700 entries published before 1974 are included in this
bibliography on Indian-white relations. The first part lists
guides and reference works to government archives and publications, manuscript collections, newspapers, and periodicals. The
second section lists books and articles arranged topically, including treaties, land, military relations, trade, missions, social and
economic development, and Indian groups.

15-4   Smith, Dwight L., ed. INDIANS OF THE UNITED STATES AND CANADA:
A BIBLIOGRAPHY. Intro. by John C. Ewers. Santa Barbara, Calif.:
American Bibliographical Center, Clio Press, 1974. xvii, 453 p. Index.

Annotated citations derived from the data bank of the abstract
publication, AMERICA: HISTORY AND LIFE, are included
for 1,687 entries, representing the great bulk of scholarship on
Indians in the historical and social science periodical literature
from 1954 to 1972. Most entries are arranged by geographic-
culture area and thereunder by tribe.

15-5   Smithsonian Institution. LIST OF PUBLICATIONS OF THE BUREAU OF
AMERICAN ENTHNOLOGY. Bureau of American Ethnology Bulletin
200. Washington, D.C.: Government Printing Office, 1971. 134 p.
Paper. Index.

As the final BAE BULLETIN, this bibliography lists the various
BAE publications by series: Annual Reports, Bulletins, Contribu-

tions to North American Ethnology, Introductions, Miscellaneous Publications, and Publications of the Institute of Social Anthropology. This listing represents nearly one hundred years of publications on the ethnology, linguistics, archaeology, and physical anthropology of the American Indian. An author and title index is included.

15-6 Sturtevant, William C., ed. HANDBOOK OF NORTH AMERICAN IN-DIANS. 20 vols. projected. Washington, D.C.: Smithsonian Institution, 1978-- . Maps, illus., photos., tables, notes, bibliog., index.

An encyclopedic summary of what is known about the prehistory, history, and cultures of the aboriginal peoples of North America will form the basis of this proposed twenty-volume work (as of 1980 only three volumes were completed). Eleven volumes will deal with broad culture regions (Arctic, Subarctic, Northwest Coast, California, Southwest, Great Britain, Plateau, Plains, Southeast, and Northeast) while the remaining volumes will cover such topics as Indians in contemporary society; environment, origins, and population; history of Indian-white relations; technology and visual arts; and languages. Each volume is a collection of summary articles (well illustrated with maps, historical photographs, and photographs and drawings of artifacts) on individual tribes and/or themes contributed by qualified specialists.

B. INDIAN LAND CESSIONS AND TENURE

15-7 Hilliard, Sam B. "Map Supplement Number Sixteen: Indian Land Cessions." AAG ANNALS 62 (June 1972): 374.

This map supplement consists of a chronological series of maps showing Indian land cessions in the United States based on negotiations between the tribes and the federal government. A further discussion of this topic is found in Hilliard, "Indian Land Cessions West of the Mississippi," JOURNAL OF THE WEST 10 (July 1971): 493-510.

15-8 Royce, Charles C., comp. INDIAN LAND CESSIONS IN THE UNITED STATES. Eighteenth Annual Report of the Bureau of American Ethnology, 1896-97, part 2. Washington, D.C.: Government Printing Office, 1899. Reprint. New York: Arno Press, 1971. 277 p., 67 map plates. Index.

Included in this classic report is a chronological schedule of land cessions, which provides references to the appropriate statutes and abstracts of the land cession boundaries. There are also maps of the individual territories and states showing the boundaries of the various land cessions.

15-9   Sutton, Imre. INDIAN LAND TENURE: BIBLIOGRAPHICAL ESSAYS
        AND A GUIDE TO THE LITERATURE. The Library of American Indian
        Affairs. New York: Clearwater Publishing Co., 1975. xvii, 290 p.
        Maps, notes, bibliog., index.

   Seven essays provide critical discusssions of relevant literature
   from the fields of history, geography, and anthropology pertaining to Indian land tenure. Also included are a bibliography
   listing works alphabetically by author and subject, tribal, and
   geographical indexes. Major themes include aboriginal occupancy and territoriality, land cessions and the establishment of
   reservations, and land administration and utilization. Sutton
   examines the changing political-geographical definition of
   Indian reservation in "Sovereign States and the Changing Definition of the Indian Reservation," GEOGRAPHICAL REVIEW 66
   (July 1976): 281-95.

15-10   Washburn, Wilcomb E. RED MAN'S LAND/WHITE MAN'S LAW: A
        STUDY OF THE PAST AND PRESENT STATUS OF THE AMERICAN
        INDIAN. New York: Charles Scribner's Sons, 1971. viii, 280 p.
        Notes, index.

   The legal status of the American Indian, in terms of his person
   and his land, is discussed in this book. The Indian concept of
   sovereignty is examined as well as the changes that were effected
   by the white man's concept of land ownership. Several specific
   examples (Oklahoma, Alaska, and New Mexico) of the unique
   treatment of Indians and their legal rights after resettlement are
   examined. Finally, present efforts to preserve the special legal
   status of the Indians are discussed. An overview of Indian-
   white relations is presented by Washburn in THE INDIAN IN
   AMERICA (New York: Harper and Row, 1975). In this work
   he discusses Indian-white interactions in the context of three
   time periods: the initial stage of relative equality when the
   white man obtained his land from the Indian and the Indian ac-
   quired trade goods, the second period of Indian resettlement on
   reservations when the Indian had been successfully dominated,
   and the third present stage when a new and more successful working arrangement has emerged between the two groups. His bibliography is particularly useful for works by historians and anthropologists.

15-11   Webber, Joe D. "Indian Cessions within the Northwest Territory". ILLI-
        NOIS LIBRARIES 61 (June 1979): 507-64. Maps.

   Webber reviews the provisions of the various Indian treaties
   ceding land within the Old Northwest Territory (Illinois, Indiana, Michigan, Minnesota, Ohio, and Wisconsin). These Indian land cessions are depicted graphically on fifteen maps.

C. INDIANS AND THE FUR TRADE

15-12 Heidenreich, Conrad E. HURONIA: A HISTORY AND GEOGRAPHY
OF THE HURON INDIANS, 1600-1650. Toronto: McClelland and
Stewart, Ltd., 1971. 337 p. Maps, illus., tables, notes, bibliog.

Heidenreich reconstructs the historical geography of the Huron
Indians (Simcoe County, Ontario) during the first third of the
seventeenth century, representing the earliest period of direct
French-Huron contact. After delimiting the Huron culture area,
he reconstructs the natural setting, population size and density,
settlement patterns, subsistence economy, and external relations
and trade. Heidenreich contends that trading was not a major
activity for the Hurons until the 1640s when they became the
middlemen in the French fur trade. An appendix discusses the
primary sources, which included seventeenth-century maps and
ethnohistorical accounts and archaeological evidence. Heidenreich and Arthur J. Ray combined their research interests to
provide a general account of the British and French fur trading
systems in pre-nineteenth century Canada in THE EARLY FUR
TRADES: A STUDY IN CULTURAL INTERACTION (Toronto:
McClelland and Stewart, 1976). Other publications by Ray
pertaining to the fur trade are listed in entry 15-15.

15-13 Kay, Jeanne. "Wisconsin Indian Hunting Patterns, 1634-1836." AAG
ANNALS 69 (September 1979): 402-18. Maps, tables, notes.

Based on her dissertation research, Kay discusses Indian hunting
patterns both for subsistence and fur trade in Wisconsin prior
to systematic European settlement. Hunting grounds were mapped
using contemporary narrative accounts recorded by fur traders,
travelers, and missionaries, while wildlife habitat elements
(vegetation and water) were derived from the records of the
original township surveys. Another article by Kay is listed in
entry 14-30.

15-14 Martin, Calvin. KEEPERS OF THE GAME: INDIAN-ANIMAL RELATION-
SHIPS AND THE FUR TRADE. Berkeley and Los Angeles: University of
California Press, 1978. xi, 226 p. Notes, index.

In studying the Ojibwa, Cree, Montagnais-Naskapi, and Mic-
mac Indians of eastern Canada, Martin presents a novel interpretation of the Indians' role in the fur trade. In the pre-contact
era, the Indians conserved their use of game, because they feared
the spiritual consequences of indiscriminate hunting. During the
post-contact era, the European diseases, which decimated the
Indian population were associated with offended animal spirits
rather than the Europeans. When the Indians perceived that
their compact with nature was broken, they willingly participated in the fur trade, not only because it brought them profit,
but also because it gave them an opportunity to attack their
new enemy, the animal.

15-15 Ray, Arthur J. INDIANS IN THE FUR TRADE: THEIR ROLE AS HUNTERS, TRAPPERS, AND MIDDLEMEN IN THE LANDS SOUTHWEST OF HUDSON BAY, 1660-1870. Toronto: University of Toronto Press, 1974. xxi, 249 p. Maps, illus., diagrs., tables, notes, bibliog., index.

Ray has used the records of the Hudson's Bay Company as the basis for several studies concerning the role of the Indians in the fur trade of the southern Prairie provinces. This volume, which is the published version of his 1971 dissertation completed under the direction of Andrew H. Clark, examines the role of the Assinibone, Cree, and Ojibwa Indians in northern Ontario, Manitoba, and Saskatchewan, in the trading system dominated by the Hudson's Bay Company. Concentrating on three time periods (pre-1763, 1763 to 1821, and 1821 to 1870), he examines the changing population and tribal distributions, the Indian utilization of various physical environments (woodland, parkland, and grassland), the changing strategies of the fur trade, and the cultural adaptations made by the Indians. In the latter period when the customary resources were depleted, the Indians began to focus their attention on the bison of the northern Great Plains and the trading networks of the upper Missouri River. A detailed economic analysis of the trading patterns between the Indians and the Hudson's Bay Company is found in Arthur J. Ray and Donald B. Freeman, 'GIVE US GOOD MEASURE': AN ECONOMIC ANALYSIS OF RELATIONS BETWEEN THE INDIANS AND THE HUDSON'S BAY COMPANY BEFORE 1763 (Toronto: University of Toronto Press, 1978). Other articles by Ray include "Indian Adaptations to the Forest-Grassland Boundary of Manitoba and Saskatchewan, 1650-1821: Some Implications for Inter-regional Migration," CANADIAN GEOGRAPHER 16 (Summer 1972): 103-18; and "Some Conservation Schemes of the Hudson's Bay Company, 1821-50; An Examination of the Problems of Resource Management in the Fur Trade," JOURNAL OF HISTORICAL GEOGRAPHY 1 (January 1975): 49-68. See also entries 12-10 and 15-12.

15-16 Wishart, David J. THE FUR TRADE OF THE AMERICAN WEST, 1807-1840: A GEOGRAPHICAL SYNTHESIS. Lincoln: University of Nebraska Press, 1979. 237 p. Maps, illus., diagrs., tables, notes, bibliog., index.

Wishart provides a geographical interpretation of the western fur trade by describing the geographical setting and the spatial organization of the fur trade. By the 1820s two production systems emerged: the "Upper Missouri Fur Trade" was based on bison robes obtained by Indians, exchanged at trading posts for manufactured goods, and transported to St. Louis by water, while the "Rocky Mountain Trapping System" was based on beaver pelts, the Euro-American trapper, the rendezvous trade nexus, and the Platte overland supply route. Both systems merged in St. Louis. Primary sources included newspapers as well as manuscripts and journals pertaining to the fur trade and western exploration.

Other articles by Wishart pertaining to the fur trade of the Great Plains include "Agriculture at the Trading Posts on the Upper Mississippi Prior to 1843," AGRICULTURAL HISTORY 47 (January 1973): 57-62; and "Cultures in Co-operation and Conflict: Indians in the Fur Trade in the Northern Great Plains, 1807-1840," JOURNAL OF HISTORICAL GEOGRAPHY 2 (October 1976): 311-28. See also entries 12-3 and 14-30.

D. POPULATION, SETTLEMENTS, AND ACCULTURATION

15-17 Burrill, Robert M. "The Establishment of Ranching on the Osage Indian Reservation." GEOGRAPHICAL REVIEW 62 (October 1972): 524-43. Maps, tables, notes.

Using Bureau of Indian Affairs records and Osage Agency Archives, Burrill traces the development of cattle ranching on the Osage Indian Reservation during the last quarter of the nineteenth century. Key factors in the establishment of ranching on the reservation were the geographic location of the reservation and the interplay of the Indians, cattlemen, and the federal government.

15-18 Cook, Sherburne F. THE POPULATION OF THE CALIFORNIA INDIANS, 1767-1970. Berkeley and Los Angeles: University of California Press, 1976. xvii, 222 p. Diagrs., tables, bibliog., index.

Six essays which analyze native California demography from the discovery era to the present decade are presented in this posthumous publication. The major themes covered include the size of the aboriginal population, population change from 1860 to 1970, age distribution, vital statistics, interbreeding with other races, and spatial distribution. Although Cook was a long-time student of native populations in Mexico and California, his study of New England's native population is presented in THE INDIAN POPULATION OF NEW ENGLAND IN THE SEVENTEENTH CENTURY, University of California Publications in Anthropology, vol. 12 (Berkeley and Los Angeles: University of California Press, 1976).

15-19 Denevan, William M., ed. THE NATIVE POPULATION OF THE AMERICAS IN 1492. Madison: University of Wisconsin Press, 1976. xxii, 353 p. Maps, diagrs., tables, notes, bibliog., index.

Pre-Columbian population estimates for various parts of the Americas provide the focus for this collection of essays by geographers, historians, archaeologists, and anthropologists. Although the primary emphasis is Central and South America, one essay concerns North America: Douglas H. Ubelaker, "The Sources and Methodology for Mooney's Estimates of North American Indian Populations," pp. 243-88. Sources and techniques for determining population estimates are discussed in the individual essays, while a bibliography compiled by Denevan lists literature pertaining to New World historical demography.

15-20 DeVorsey, Louis, Jr. THE INDIAN BOUNDARY IN THE SOUTHERN COLONIES, 1763-1775. Chapel Hill: University of North Carolina Press, 1966. xii, 267 p. Maps, notes, bibliog., index.

The evolution of the southern Indian boundary in the southern colonies is traced from the close of the French and Indian War in 1763 to the outbreak of the revolutionary war in 1775, utilizing documentary and cartographic sources primarily from the British Museum and the Public Record Office. The delineation and demarcation of the boundary is examined in each colony (Virginia, North and South Carolina, Georgia, and East and West Florida) in the context of an expanding European frontier moving westward at the expense of the various Indian nations (Cherokee, Creek, and Choctaw). The boundary as finally established, which was intended to limit further westward expansion, was distinctly different from the general concept expressed in the treaty ending the French and Indian War.

15-21 Doran, Michael F. "Negro Slaves of the Five Civilized Tribes." AAG ANNALS 68 (September 1978): 335-50. Maps, tables, notes.

Doran examines the extent and nature of Negro slavery among the Five Civilized Tribes (Cherokee, Choctaw, Chickasaw, Creek and Seminole nations), an institution the Indians had adopted in the Southeast before their removal to the Indian Territory. Through the use of manuscript and published records of the Bureau of Indian Affairs and the 1860 manuscript census schedules, he was able to determine the number, distribution and characteristics of Negro slaves in the Indian Territory. Other articles by Doran pertaining to the Indian Territory include "Antebellum Cattle Herding in the Indian Territory," GEOGRAPHICAL REVIEW 66 (January 1976): 48-58, and "Population Statistics of Nineteenth Century Indian Territory," CHRONICLES OF OKLAHOMA 53 (Winter 1975-76): 492-515.

15-22 Goodwin, Gary C. CHEROKEES IN TRANSITION: A STUDY OF CHANGING CULTURE AND ENVIRONMENT PRIOR TO 1775. Department of Geography Research Paper, No. 181. Chicago: University of Chicago, Department of Geography, 1977. ix, 207 p. Paper. Maps, diagrs., tables, notes, bibliog.

The changing cultural ecology of the Cherokees in the southern Appalachians during the seventeenth and eighteenth centuries is examined in terms of pre- and post-European contact. After establishing pre-contact settlement patterns and plant and animal associations, Goodwin describes the more exploitative man-land relationships that developed as the Cherokees adjusted to the British and American domination.

15-23 Hewes, Leslie. OCCUPYING THE CHEROKEE COUNTRY OF OKLAHOMA. University of Nebraska Studies: New Series, No. 57. Lincoln: University of Nebraska, 1978. x, 77 p. Paper. Maps, photos., tables, notes.

In reconstructing the settlement of the Cherokee nation in northeastern Oklahoma during the nineteenth century, Hewes concentrates on the initial occupation of the reserve prior to the Civil War, the reconstruction and expansion of settlements after the Civil War, and the effects of a changing land tenure system at the end of the nineteenth century prior to allotment. Themes which are emphasized include settlement patterns in relation to woodland and prairies, population, and economy. Much of the research is based on reports of the Commissioner of Indian Affairs, diaries, Cherokee laws and censuses, and late nineteenth-century township survey plats and field notes. Hewes's 1940 dissertation and several other articles about the Cherokees are listed in the footnotes on pages 66 and 74.

15-24 Jacobs, Wilbur R. DISPOSSESSING THE AMERICAN INDIAN: INDIANS AND WHITES ON THE COLONIAL FRONTIER. New York: Charles Scribner's Sons, 1972. xiv, 240 p. Maps, illus., photos., notes, index.

Each chapter in this history of early Indian-white relations was originally a separate essay written over a fifteen-year period. Although this study emphasizes the eastern woodland Indian and the Anglo-American pioneer of the eighteenth century, Jacobs does attempt to draw parallels between this experience in North America and the native-white contacts in other parts of the world, principally Australia and New Guinea. His focus on the cultural changes resulting from the different uses of the land and its resources provides a basis for this contrast. The need to examine Indian-white relations from the Indian viewpoint is discussed by Jacobs in "The Indian and the Frontier in American History—A Need for Revision," WESTERN HISTORICAL QUARTERLY 4 (January 1973): 43-56. The latter article is also reprinted in entry 12-33.

15-25 Jennings, Francis. THE INVASION OF AMERICA: INDIANS, COLONIALISM, AND THE CANT OF CONQUEST. Chapel Hill: University of North Carolina Press, for the Institute of Early American History and Culture, Williamsburg, 1975. xvii, 369 p. Maps, illus., notes, bibliog., index.

Jennings presents an interpretive essay concerning Indian-European relationships along the colonial Atlantic seaboard. He develops a framework that examines these cultural contacts in the context of two different civilizations (not "savagery" versus "civilization").

He also applies this interpretation to seventeenth-century New England, stressing the conquest ideology of the Puritans and the varying responses of the natives.

15-26 Moodie, D.W., and Kaye, Barry. "The Northern Limit of Indian Agriculture in North America." GEOGRAPHICAL REVIEW 59 (October 1969): 513-29. Maps, notes.

The northern expansion of Indian agriculture (corn-bean-squash-pumpkin complex) from the upper Missouri to northern Minnesota and southern Manitoba is traced through late eighteenth- and early nineteenth-century narrative accounts.

15-27 Wishart, David J. "The Dispossession of the Pawnee." AAG ANNALS 69 (September 1979): 382-401. Maps, photos., diagrs., table, notes.

The disintegration of a traditional buffalo hunting and horticultural society is observed from 1830 to 1874 as the Pawnee Indians of central Nebraska gradually cede their lands, are relegated to a reservation, and finally migrate to the Indian Territory. The research is based on records of the Bureau of Indian Affairs (Commissioner's Annual Reports and letters received at the Pawnee Agency) and private papers from the Nebraska, Missouri, and New York Historical Societies.

Chapter 16

LAND SURVEY AND TENURE

Geographical and historical studies of land survey and land tenure systems are presented in the context of the precedents established in the British, French, and Spanish colonies and the rectangular survey system instituted in the U.S. public domain.

A. GENERAL

16-1 Gates, Paul W. HISTORY OF PUBLIC LAND LAW DEVELOPMENT. Washington, D.C.: Government Printing Office, 1968. xv, 828 p. Maps, illus., photos., diagrs., tables, notes, bibliog., index.

Prepared by the foremost historian of American public lands for the Public Land Law Review (authorized in 1964), this background study provides a comprehensive review of the development of public land law. A primary emphasis of the study is the functioning of the system and its effect on those seeking land. Especially useful are the chapters devoted to the various means of alienating land (private land claims, credit sales, cash sales, preemption, military bounty lands, state grants, homesteads and dry farming, timber and grazing selections). Mineral lands are discussed in a chapter prepared by Robert W. Swenson. An extensive bibliography lists published and manuscript records in the National Archives, theses and dissertations, and published books and articles (including twenty-nine by Gates). Nine of Gates's previously published essays pertaining to public land policy prior to the homestead act are published in LANDLORDS AND TENANTS ON THE PRAIRIE FRONTIER: STUDIES IN AMERICAN LAND POLICY (Ithaca, N.Y.: Cornell University Press, 1973). Gates suggests pertinent research topics in the history of public lands in "Research in the History of the Public Lands," AGRICULTURAL HISTORY 48 (January 1974): 31-50.

16-2 McEntyre, John G. LAND SURVEY SYSTEMS. New York: John Wiley and Sons, 1978. xi, 537 p. Maps, diagrs., tables, notes, bibliog., index.

Intended as a textbook for surveying students and a general refer-

ence book for practicing surveyors, this volume summarizes the
history of land surveying procedures. In particular, it emphasizes the changing acts and surveying instructions associated with
the public land survey system. Such technical topics as exterior
boundaries, subdivision of townships into sections, meandering,
surveying instruments, monumentation, computation of area,
subdivision of sections, retracement surveys, and metes and
bounds descriptions are covered.

16-3   SURVEYING AND MAPPING. Washington, D.C.: American Congress
on Surveying and Mapping, 1941-- . Quarterly.

Although the articles in this journal pertain primarily to current
problems of surveying and mapping, there are several articles
of historical interest. Articles describing land surveys in the
public land states include Walter G. Robillard, "The Big Giveaway-
Land Grants," 39 (September 1979): 249-53; Charles Whittlesey,
"Origin of the American System of Land Surveys: Justice to the
Memory of Thomas Hutchins," 37 (June 1977): 129-32; and Donald
E. Merkel, "Colonel Butler and the Public Land Survey of Florida
(1824-1849)," 34 (December 1974): 331-36. Surveys in nonpublic
land states are discussed in Ralph H. Donnelly, "The Colonial
Land Patent System in Maryland," 40 (March 1980): 51-68;
B.K. Meade, "The Mason-Dixie Mile," 36 (December 1976):
329-35; and E.D. Heppert, Jr., "Tennessee Valley Surveying
1745 to 1780," 35 (December 1975): 347-54. See also entry
1-20.

B. BRITISH, FRENCH, AND SPANISH ORIGINS

16-4   Ackerman, Robert K. SOUTH CAROLINA LAND POLICIES. Columbia:
University of South Carolina Press for the South Carolina Tricentennial
Commission, 1977. ix, 133 p. Notes, bibliog., index.

Ackerman reviews the development and implementation of the
land policies of the proprietors and the royal government during
the colonial period. These land policies were designed to en-
courage immigration (headright systems), reward services bene-
ficial to the colony, provide a return on investment in the
colony, and serve as a source of revenue (quitrents).

16-5   Carlson, Alvar W. "Long Lots in the Rio Arriba." AAG ANNALS 65
(March 1975): 48-57.

The origin of the long lot survey system along the upper Rio
Grande Valley in New Mexico is reviewed in this article.
Comments by David Hornbeck are printed in AAG ANNALS 65
(December 1975): 592-94.

16-6   Chardon, Roland.   "The Linear League in North America." AAG AN-
        NALS 70 (June 1980): 129-53. Tables, notes.

        Chardon traces the complex European origins of the league as a
        linear measure and its application in North America during the
        colonial period. He finds that seven different linear leagues
        (five land and two marine) were used primarily in the French
        and Spanish colonies. Chardon also discusses this linear meas-
        urement in "A Quantitative Determination of a Second Linear
        League Used in New Spain," PROFESSIONAL GEOGRAPHER
        32 (November 1980): 462-66.

16-7   Harris, Richard Colebrook. THE SEIGNEURIAL SYSTEM IN EARLY
        CANADA: A GEOGRAPHICAL STUDY. Madison: University of Wis-
        consin Press; Quebec: University of Laval Press, 1966. xvi, 247 p. Maps,
        diagrs., tables, notes, bibliog., index.

        Although this study pertains to the land holding system in Can-
        ada during the French regime, it provides one example of a
        historical geographer analyzing the effect of a land tenure sys-
        tem on the landscape. In this case, Harris finds that the seigneu-
        rial system, a feudal system of land tenure, did not play a dom-
        inant role in the formation of early Canadian society, and that
        it had little influence on settlement patterns, land use, or trade.
        The distinctive settlement pattern, long thin fields and straggling
        villages along the St. Lawrence River, was related to the pattern
        of rotures (the concessions of land within a seigneurie) but was
        not directly related to the seigneurial system itself.

16-8   Hornbeck, David. "Land Tenure and Rancho Expansion in Alta California,
        1784-1846." JOURNAL OF HISTORICAL GEOGRAPHY 4 (October 1978):
        371-90. Maps, tables, notes.

        Hornbeck examines the role of the rancho land grant as part of
        the land tenure system in California prior to 1846. Besides
        mapping the diffusion of the rancho land grants during the
        Spanish and Mexican occupation, he determines the number and
        size of grants on an annual basis. The subsequent patenting of
        these Mexican claims by the U.S. General Land Office is
        examined in "The Patenting of California's Private Land
        Claims, 1851-1885," GEOGRAPHICAL REVIEW 69 (October
        1979): 434-48. Another aspect of Spanish settlement in Cali-
        fornia is portrayed graphically by Hornbeck in "Mission Population
        of Alta California, 1810-1830," HISTORICAL GEOGRAPHY
        NEWSLETTER 8 (Spring 1978), supplement, 9 p. Other articles
        by Hornbeck pertaining to Spanish and Mexican settlement in
        California include "Mexican-American Land Tenure Conflict
        in California," JOURNAL OF GEOGRAPHY 75 (April 1976):
        209-21; and "A Population Map of California, 1798," CALIFOR-
        NIA GEOGRAPHER 14 (1973-74): 52-54. For articles coauthored

by Hornbeck and Mary Tucey, see "The Submergence of a People: Migration and Occupation Structure in California, 1850," PACIFIC HISTORICAL REVIEW 46 (August 1977): 471-542; and "Agriculture in Hispanic California, 1850," CALIFORNIA GEOGRAPHER 15 (1975): 52-59.

16-9   Jordan, Terry G. "Antecedents of the Long-Lot in Texas." AAG ANNALS 64 (March 1974): 70-86. Maps, notes.

Jordan plots the historical distribution of riverine long-lot surveys in Texas and traces their diffusion from Central Europe and northern France through French settlements in Quebec, Missouri, and Louisiana rather than from Spanish antecedents.

16-10   Kim, Sung Bok. LANDLORD AND TENANT IN COLONIAL NEW YORK: MANORIAL SOCIETY, 1664-1775. Chapel Hill: University of North Carolina Press for the Institute of Early American History and Culture, Williamsburg, Va., 1978. xiii, 456 p. Maps, tables, notes, bibliog., index.

The landlord-tenant relationship is the main focus of this study of manorial tenancy in colonial New York. Of the approximately thirty great manors that dominated the landscape, Kim examines the rise, structure, and fuctioning of the four largest (Rensselaerwyck, Livingston, Cortland, and Philipsburgh). This colonial historian provides a revisionist interpretation, suggesting that because the language of real estate law (laws and lease contracts) masks the reality of the situation, the landlord-tenant relationship was not as exploitative and undemocratic as previously supposed. Eighteen maps portray the boundaries and subdivision of these manorial land grants.

16-11   Stiverson, Gregory A. POVERTY IN A LAND OF PLENTY: TENANCY IN EIGHTEENTH-CENTURY MARYLAND. Maryland Bicentennial Studies. Baltimore: Johns Hopkins University Press, 1977. xv, 187 p. Maps, tables, notes, bibliog., essay, index.

From proprietary manor papers, probate and land records, assessment lists, and court records, this historian reconstructs the life of eighteenth-century Maryland tenants, who accounted for almost half the colony's heads of household. Through his intense analysis of eight propriety manors, which were selected for variations in their regional location and ethnic composition, he concludes that there was a high degree of poverty and stability among the proprietary tenants. He also observed that variations in the tenants' economic mobility depended on the quality of natural resources that were available to them.

C. PUBLIC DOMAIN

16-12 Bowen, Marshall. "The Kinkaid Act and the Southern Sheridan County Sandhills of Nebraska." ROCKY MOUNTAIN SOCIAL SCIENCE JOUR-NAL 9 (January 1972): 39-49. Maps, diagrs., notes.

General Land Office tract books provided the basis for evaluating the effects of the Kinkaid Act of 1904 on land disposal in one county in the Nebraska Sand Hills during the beginning of the twentieth century. This was the first act to permit homestead entries of 640 acres instead of 160 acres, but it applied only to thirty-seven counties in central and western Nebraska.

16-13 Crazier, Lola. SURVEYS AND SURVEYORS OF THE PUBLIC DOMAIN, 1785-1975. Washington, D.C.: Government Printing Office, 1976. 234 p. Paper. Maps, illus., photos., notes, index.

This Bureau of Land Management publication is used as a training aid for cadastral surveyors. It summarizes the history of the public land surveys with particular emphasis on individual sur-veyors and individual surveys of particular geographic areas. Included are numerous historical photographs recording surveying activities during the early twentieth century.

16-14 Indiana American Revolution Bicentennial Symposium. THIS LAND OF OURS: THE ACQUISITION AND DISPOSITION OF THE PUBLIC DO-MAIN. Indianapolis: Indiana Historical Society, 1978. 126 p. Paper. Maps, illus., photos., notes.

Papers presented at the third American Revolution Bicentennial Symposium, held at Purdue University, April 1978, are contained in this volume. There is one paper by a geographer, Hildegard B. Johnson, "Perceptions and Illustrations of the American Land-scape in the Ohio Valley and the Midwest," pp. 1-38, in which the works of surveyors and cartographers, landscape painters, folk painters, and topographic artists are used to portray the landscape in this area. The other papers were presented by historians Malcolm J. Rohrbough, "The Land Office Business in Indiana," pp. 39-59; Reginald Horsman, "Changing Images of the Public Domain: Historians and the Shaping of Midwest Frontiers," pp. 60-86; Dwight L. Smith, "The Land Cession Treaty: A Valid Instrument of Transfer of Indian Title," pp. 87-102; and Paul W. Gates, "The Nationalizing Influence of the Public Lands: In-diana," pp. 103-26.

16-15 Johnson, Hildegard Binder. ORDER UPON THE LAND: THE U.S. REC-TANGULAR LAND SURVEY AND THE UPPER MISSISSIPPI COUNTRY. Andrew H. Clark Series in the Historical Geography of North America. New York: Oxford University Press, 1976. 268 p. Maps, illus., photos., diagrs., table, notes, index.

Johnson provides an interpretation of the effect of the U.S.

rectangular survey system on the historical-geographical development of one region, the upper Mississippi River hill country
(southeast Minnesota, northeast Iowa, and northwest Wisconsin)
during the nineteenth and twentieth centuries. Using a wide
variety of government, literary, and artistic sources (township
survey plats and field notes; tract, abstract and deed books;
diaries; county histories, atlases, and land ownership maps; and
field observations), she examines the presurvey settlement patterns
that followed the physical landscape; the nineteenth century or post
survey settlement patterns that paralleled the geometry of the survey
system; and the twentieth-century settlement patterns that show significant departures from the rectangular pattern primarily as a result
of new soil conservation practices. A constant theme is the tension
between the strict geometric pattern of the survey system and the
hilly character of the physical landscape of this region. Earlier articles by Johnson dealing with the U.S. rectangular survey system
include: "Rational and Ecological Aspects of the Quarter Section:
An Example from Minnesota," GEOGRAPHICAL REVIEW 47 (July
1957): 330-48; and "A Historical Perspective on Form and Function
in Upper Midwest Rural Settlement," AGRICULTURAL HISTORY 48
(January 1974): 11-25. See also entry 12-6.

16-16 McIntosh, C. Barron. "Patterns from Land Alienation Maps." AAG AN-
NALS 66 (December 1976): 570-82. Maps, notes.

Land entry and land patent data that record the initial disposal
of lands in the public domain were used to map the land alienation process in the Nebraska Sand Hills from 1873 until the early
twentieth century. Besides describing the pertinent records from
the former General Land Office, McIntosh demonstrates how
these land alienation records can be used to develop the historical settlement geography of a region. Other articles by
McIntosh which pertain to the disposal of the public lands in
Nebraska are "Forest Lieu Selections in the Sand Hills of Nebraska," AAG ANNALS 64 (March 1974): 87-99; and "Use and
Abuse of the Timber Culture Act," AAG ANNALS 65 (September 1975): 347-62.

16-17 Oubre, Claude F. FORTY ACRES AND A MULE: THE FREEDMEN'S
BUREAU AND BLACK LAND OWNERSHIP. Baton Rouge: Louisiana
State University Press, 1978. xv, 212 p. Maps, tables, notes, bibliog.,
index.

In the context of the supposed promise of "forty acres and a mule,"
this historical study examines the blacks' inability to become substantial landowners during the Reconstruction period. The research
concentrates primarily on the Freedmen's Bureau, congressional
confiscation acts, and the Southern Homestead Act, all of which
were designed to assist the freedmen in obtaining land.

16-18 Pattison, William D. BEGINNINGS OF THE AMERICAN RECTANGULAR
LAND SURVEY SYSTEM, 1784-1800. Department of Geography Research
Paper No. 50. Chicago: University of Chicago, Department of Geography,
1957. vii, 248 p. Paper. Maps, notes, bibliog.

The origins of the American rectangular survey system are discussed in three contexts. Initially, Pattison examines the conceptual and legal origins that resulted in the Land Ordinance
of 1785. Secondly, he reviews and analyzes the implementation
of the system with the initial surveying of Ohio's Seven Ranges.
Finally, he explores the modification of the survey system with
the continued rectangular surveying by private land companies,
the passage and content of the Land Act of 1796, and the nature
of the federal surveys following the passage of the act up until
1800. Much of the research was based on township plats, field
notes, and correspondence from the records of the General Land
Office, now in the National Archives. In addition, legislative
records pertaining to the passage of the Land Ordinance and
Land Act were used extensively. Other articles by Pattison
pertaining to the beginning of the rectangular survey system
include: "The Survey of the Seven Ranges," OHIO HISTORI-
CAL QUARTERLY 68 (April 1959): 115-40; and "The Original
Plan for an American Rectangular Land Survey," SURVEYING
AND MAPPING 21 (September 1961): 339-45. See also entries
9-9 and 12-6.

16-19 Rohrbough, Malcolm J. THE LAND OFFICE BUSINESS: THE SETTLE-
MENT AND ADMINISTRATION OF AMERICAN PUBLIC LANDS, 1789-
1837. New York: Oxford University Press, 1968. xiii, 331 p. Maps,
notes, bibliog., index.

The administrative history of the bureaucracy that was created
for the disposal of the public domain is the focus of the study.
The establishment of land offices and the implementation of
the various legislative acts for the alienation of land are emphasized. Six reconstructed maps show the locations of land
offices and the extent of the respective land districts, particularly in the Old North West (Ohio, Indiana, Illinois, Missouri,
Michigan, and Wisconsin) and the South (Florida, Alabama,
Mississippi, Louisiana, and Arkansas). The research is based
primarily on records of the General Land Office in the National
Archives.

16-20 Swierenga, Robert P. PIONEERS AND PROFITS: LAND SPECULATION
ON THE IOWA FRONTIER. Ames: Iowa State University Press, 1968.
xxviii, 260 p. Maps, illus., photos., diagrs., tables, notes, index.

Through a quantitative analysis of original land entry books and
resale registers, which had been abstracted and tabulated for an

Indian claims case, Swierenga makes a thorough study of land
speculation in central and southcentral Iowa. Numerous tables
and maps summarize his findings. The introductory chapter reviews
the historical literature on frontier land investment and speculation.

16-21 Thrower, Norman J.W. ORIGINAL SURVEY AND LAND SUBDIVISION:
A COMPARATIVE STUDY OF THE FORM AND EFFECT OF CONTRASTING
CADASTRAL SURVEYS. Association of American Geographers Monograph
Series, No. 4. Chicago: Rand McNally and Company, 1966. xxii, 160 p.
Maps, photos., diagrs., tables, notes, bibliog., index.

Thrower compares the effects of two different surveying systems
on the administration (county and township), property, field
unit, and transportation lines by examining two areas in western
Ohio in 1875 and 1955. The selected areas represent the metes
and bounds or unsystematic surveys of the Virginia Military District and the rectangular or U.S. Public land surveys of northwestern Ohio. The basic archival sources were land survey
and disposal records in the Ohio State Auditor's Office and
in county clerk's and engineer's offices.

16-22 Westphall, Victor. THE PUBLIC DOMAIN IN NEW MEXICO, 1854-1891.
Albuquerque: University of New Mexico Press, 1965. xvi, 212 p. Maps,
diagrs., tables, notes, bibliog., index.

The survey and disposal of the public domain in New Mexico
during the last half of the nineteenth century is the subject of
this study. Particular attention is paid to the various methods
of land disposal (donation claims, homestead, timber-culture,
desert-land, and mineral entries). Although the narrative focuses
on the administrative background, several appendices provide a
tabular accounting of the acreages associated with the various
types of entries. In addition, nineteen maps show the geographical and temporal distribution by township of entries related to
the various types of land disposal. See also Westphall, "The
Public Domain in New Mexico, 1854-1891," SURVEYING AND
MAPPING 37 (December 1977): 329-48.

Chapter 17

ECONOMIC ACTIVITIES

This chapter on economic activities is divided into three sections: agriculture, manufacturing, and transportation and communication. Although geographers have produced a number of studies on past agricultural patterns, the first section also includes a number of selections by agricultural historians. Historical-geographical literature pertaining exclusively to manufacturing-industrialization and transportation-communication is not as extensive. Instead, these topics are usually discussed in connection with urbanization. Publications dealing with these interrelated activities are listed in the following chapter.

A. AGRICULTURE

17-1   AGRICULTURAL HISTORY. Davis: University of California, Agricultural History Center, 1927-- . Quarterly.

The Agricultural History Society's journal consists primarily of articles, book reviews, and newsnotes pertaining to the history of American agriculture. Also included are papers presented at the society's annual symposium and a yearly list of books on the history of agriculture. Historical geographers have participated widely in this publication; articles by geographers, not listed elsewhere in this bibliography, include John J. Winberry, "The Sorghum Syrup Industry, 1854-1975," 54 (April 1980): 343-52; L. Carl Brandhorst, "The North Platte Oasis: Notes on the Geography and History of an Irrigated District," 51 (January 1977): 166-72; Stephen C. Jett, "History of Fruit Tree Raising Among the Navajo," 51 (October 1977): 681-701; Paul B. Frederic "Geography and Living Historical Farm Sites," 48 (January 1974): 5-10; Hildegard B. Johnson, "A Historical Perspective on Form and Function in Upper Midwest Rural Settlement," 48 (January 1974): 11-25; John A. Jakle, "A Historical Perspective on Rural Settlement: Comment," 48 (January 1974): 26-30; and P.J. Perry, "Agricultural History: A Geographer's Critique," 46 (April 1972): 259-68. There are numerous articles by historians which are of geographic interest; a few of these are Diane Lindstrom, "Southern Dependence upon Interregional Grain Supplies: A

Review of Trade Flows, 1840-1860," 44 (January 1970): 101-13; Morton Rothstein, "The Cotton Frontier of the Antebellum South: A Methodological Battleground," 44 (January 1970): 149-65 (reproduced in entry 12-33); Rothstein, "Antebellum Wheat and Cotton Exports: Contrast in Marketing Organization and Economic Development," 40 (April 1966): 91-100; and Robert F. Berkhofer, Jr., "Space, Time, Culture, and the New Frontier," 38 (January 1964): 21-30 (reproduced in entry 12-33).

17-2   Agricultural History Center and U.S. Department of Agriculture, Economic Research Service, Agricultural History Group. BIBLIOGRAPHIES ON AMERICAN AGRICULTURAL HISTORY. 26 vols. Davis: University of California, Agricultural History Center, 1963-80.

By July 1980, twenty-six paperback bibliographies had been issued on various general and specific topics relevant to the history of American agriculture. Some of the more comprehensive bibliographies in terms of geographical coverage include: THE HISTORY OF AGRICULTURE IN THE UNITED STATES, 1790-1840, compiled by Douglas E. Bowers, (1969); THE HISTORY OF THE FARMER AND THE REVOLUTION, 1763-1790, compiled by Douglas E. Bowers (1971); THE HISTORY OF BLACK AMERICANS IN AGRICULTURE, 1619-1974, compiled by Joel Schor (1975); THE HISTORY OF AGRICULTURE IN THE SOUTHERN UNITED STATES, 1865-1900, compiled by Helen H. Edwards (1971); THE HISTORY OF AGRICULTURE IN THE MOUNTAIN STATES, compiled by Earl M. Rogers (1972); THE HISTORY OF AGRICULTURE IN THE MIDWEST, 1840-1900, compiled by Douglas E. Bowers and James B. Hoehn (1973); and THE HISTORY OF AGRICULTURE IN THE GREAT PLAINS, compiled by Earl M. Rogers (1976).

17-3   Aiken, Charles S. "The Evolution of Cotton Ginning in the Southeastern United States." GEOGRAPHICAL REVIEW 63 (April 1973): 196-224. Maps, photos., diagrs., table, notes.

The development of cotton ginning is described in terms of three periods, each represented by significant technological changes: the antebellum period, which was highlighted by the contribution of Eli Whitney's cotton gin; the period following the Civil War in which the number of gins declined and allied businesses developed; and the final period beginning in the 1940s, which was represented by the mechanical harvesting of cotton. See also Aiken, "An Examination of the Role of the Eli Whitney Cotton Gin in the Origin of the United States Cotton Regions," AAG PROCEEDINGS 3 (1971): 5-9. The disintegration of the cotton region since World War II is described by Aiken and Merle C. Prunty in "The Demise of the Piedmont Cotton Region," AAG ANNALS 62 (June 1972): 283-306.

17-4   Clark, Andrew H. "Suggestions for the Geographical Study of Agricultural Change in the United States, 1790-1840." AGRICULTURAL HISTORY 46 (January 1972): 155-72. Notes.

Clark's suggestions for the geographical study of agricultural development in the period 1790 to 1840 include the role of regional and ethnic origins in influencing settlement and land use; the diffusion, distribution, and nature of crop and livestock systems; agricultural productivity; and the interrelationships of "subsistence" and "commercial" farming in a frontier context. This article is reproduced in entry 12-33.

17-5   Conzen, Michael P. FRONTIER FARMING IN AN URBAN SHADOW: THE INFLUENCE OF MADISON'S PROXIMITY ON THE AGRICULTURAL DEVELOPMENT OF BLOOMING GROVE, WISCONSIN. Madison: State Historical Society of Wisconsin, 1971. xviii, 235 p. Maps, illus., diagrs., tables, notes, bibliog., index.

The spatial structure of economic behavior is investigated for one township (Blooming Grove adjacent to Madison, Dane County, Wisconsin) from 1835 to 1880. The general themes that Conzen examines are the transformation of this small area from a frontier situation into a commercial production unit integrated within a regional economic system, and the impact of an urban center (Madison) on agricultural development with respect to farm production and social groups. Specific topics include land ownership (federal land sales and land ownership change), social and demographic characteristics (spread of settlement, demographic structure, occupation, persistence, and ethnicity), indexes of agricultural growth (farm size, labor, mechanization, and farm value), changing agricultural production, and changing market connections. His research was based on federal and state population and agricultural censuses, General Land Office tract books and township plats, county records, and county histories.

17-6   Earle, Carville V. "A Staple Interpretation of Slavery and Free Labor." GEOGRAPHICAL REVIEW 68 (January 1978): 52-65. Notes.

Earle uses the economics of staple crops and labor costs to explain the geography of slavery and free labor in pre-1860 United States. He suggests that northern farmers rejected slavery because of its inefficiency for wheat production rather than because of a moral-ideological repugnance. His conclusions are based on examples of two areas where staple crops were changing: the tobacco-to-wheat transition on Maryland's Eastern Shore during the eighteenth century and the wheat-to-corn transition in the antebellum lower Midwest (southern and central Ohio, Indiana, and Illinois). See also Earle and Ronald Hoffman, "The Foundation of the Modern Economy: Agriculture and the Costs of Labor in the United States and England, 1800-60," AMERICAN HISTORICAL REVIEW 85 (December 1980): 1055-94.

17-7   Fisher, James S. "Negro Farm Ownership in the South." AAG ANNALS 63 (December 1973): 478-89. Maps, diagrs., tables, notes.

Fisher reviews the extent of Negro farm ownership in the southern states from 1900 to 1969, based on agricultural census statistics. After peaking between 1910 and 1920, Negro ownership declined throughout the remainder of the study period.

17-8   Hewes, Leslie. THE SUITCASE FARMING FRONTIER: A STUDY IN THE HISTORICAL GEOGRAPHY OF THE CENTRAL GREAT PLAINS. Lincoln: University of Nebraska Press, 1973. xv, 281 p. Maps, photos., diagrs., tables, notes, bibliog., index.

Hewes examines the role of suitcase farmers (nonresident farmers mainly from the wheat growing areas of central Kansas) in the transformation of the semi-arid grasslands of western Kansas and eastern Colorado from stock raising and general farming to mainly wheat farming from 1920 to 1950. In analyzing the spatial patterns and environmental relationships in this change, he finds that a combination of factors continue to characterize this region: variable precipitation, extremely variable yields, absentee ownership, and suitcase farming. His research is based on records of the Agricultural Stabilization and Conservation Service in the Federal Records Centers in Denver and Kansas City, newspaper files, and the annual reports of county assessors and county farm agents. See also Hewes, "Early Suitcase Farming in the Central Great Plains," AGRICULTURAL HISTORY 51 (January 1977): 23-37.

17-9   Hilliard, Sam B. HOG MEAT AND HOECAKE: FOOD SUPPLY IN THE OLD SOUTH, 1840-1860. Carbondale: Southern Illinois University Press, 1972. xi, 296 p. Maps, diagrs., tables, notes, index.

Whereas the usual emphasis of studies of the agricultural economy in the South is the development of regional agricultural specializations (tobacco, rice, cotton, sugar cane), this study focuses on the role of food production in the total agricultural system. In addressing the general theme of southern food self-sufficiency, Hilliard examines the regional production of various food sources (hogs, cattle, poultry, sheep, goats, corn, wheat, sweet potatoes, garden crops, orchards); the food habits, cultural attitudes, and food consumption among various groups; and the foodstuff trade (intraregional, Mississippi waterway, and Gulf and Atlantic ports). Other articles by Hilliard pertaining to southern agriculture include "Site Characteristics and Spatial Stability of the Louisiana Sugar Cane Industry," AGRICULTURAL HISTORY 53 (January 1979): 254-69; "The Tidewater Rice Plantation: An Ingenious Adaptation to Nature," GEOSCIENCE AND MAN 12 (1975): 57-66; "Pork in the Ante-Bellum South: The Geography of Self-Sufficiency," AAG ANNALS 59 (September 1969): 461-80; and "Hog Meat and Cornpone: Food Habits in the Ante-Bellum South," PROCEEDINGS OF THE AMERICAN PHILOSOPHICAL SOCIETY 113 (February 1969): 1-13. See also entries 12-6 and 12-10.

17-10 Jordan, Terry G. "Early Northeast Texas and the Evolution of Western Ranching." AAG ANNALS 67 (March 1977): 66-87. Maps, illus., tables, notes.

> The development of open-range cattle ranching is examined in northeast Texas during the first half of the nineteenth century. The origins of ranching in this area are traced to Anglo traditions which were derived from the upper South and the Carolinas. As settlers from this area moved westward, they came in contact with Spanish ranching practices, producing a ranching complex that was characteristic of much of western America. The research is based on tax lists, manuscript census schedules, registers of brands and marks, and local histories. Other articles by Jordan pertaining to ranching in Texas include: "Texan Influence in Nineteenth-Century Arizona Cattle Ranching," JOURNAL OF THE WEST 14 (July 1975): 15-17; "The Origin and Distribution of Open-Range Ranching," SOCIAL SCIENCE QUARTERLY 53 (June 1972): 105-21; and "The Origin of Anglo-American Cattle Ranching in Texas: A Documentation of Diffusion From the Lower South," ECONOMIC GEOGRAPHY 45 (January 1969): 63-87.

17-11 Leaman, J. Harold, and Conkling, E.C. "Transport Change and Agricultural Specialization." AAG ANNALS 65 (September 1975): 425-32. Maps, tables, notes.

> In order to test the hypothesis that regional agricultural specialization increased as transportation costs decreased, this study analyzes agricultural land use in western New York state from 1840 to 1860, a period that experienced major transportation innovations with the development of canal and railroad networks. The research is based on federal agricultural censuses.

17-12 McQuillan, D. Aidan. "Farm Size and Work Ethic: Measuring the Success of Immigrant Farmers on the American Grasslands, 1875-1925." JOURNAL OF HISTORICAL GEOGRAPHY 4 (January 1978): 57-76. Maps, diagrs., tables, notes.

> In assessing the relationship between farm size and financial success, McQuillan compares the agricultural experience of three immigrant groups (Mennonites, French-Canadians, and Swedish) in central Kansas. He finds that the intensity of farming as represented by value of farm real estate and capital investments provides a better index of agricultural success than farm size. As expected, the Mennonites were the most successful, but the French-Canadians, contrary to expectations, were more successful than the Swedish. Another article by McQuillan is "The Mobility of Immigrants and Americans: A Comparison of Farmers on the Kansas Frontier, AGRICULTURAL HISTORY 53 (July 1979): 576-96. See also entry 12-10.

17-13   Peet, J. Richard. "The Spatial Expansion of Commercial Agriculture in the Nineteenth Century: A von Thunen Interpretation." ECONOMIC GE-OGRAPHY 45 (October 1969): 283-301. Diagrs., tables, notes.

In applying J. Heinrich von Thunen's theory of agricultural location to the formation and diffusion of commercial agricultural regions on a continental and world-wide basis, Peet views nineteenth-century Great Britian, Western Europe, and north-eastern North America as a "World City" surrounded by a series of large concentric agricultural zones pushing into the vacant continental interiors. This dynamic model is based on increasing central market demand and rapidly changing transportation costs. See also Peet, "Von Thunen Theory and the Dynamics of Agri-cultural Expansion," EXPLORATIONS IN ECONOMIC HISTORY 8 (Winter 1970-71): 181-201.

17-14   Schapsmeier, Edward L., and Schapsmeier, Frederick H. ENCYCLOPEDIA OF AMERICAN AGRICULTURAL HISTORY. Westport, Conn.: Greenwood Press, 1975. xii, 467 p. Index.

Definitions for a variety of terms pertaining to the history of American agriculture (personalities, organizations, journals and newspapers, legislative acts, regions, technology, equipment, crops, pests, and diseases) are included in this reference work. Many entries list a few books pertinent to the subject.

17-15   Schlebecker, John T. BIBLIOGRAPHY OF BOOKS AND PAMPHLETS ON THE HISTORY OF AGRICULTURE IN THE UNITED STATES, 1607-1967. Santa Barbara, Calif.: American Bibliographical Centers, Clio Press, 1969. vii, 183 p. Index.

Over two thousand books and pamphlets relating to the history of American agriculture are listed in this bibliography. The entries, which are arranged alphabetically by author, cover a wide range of topics, including means of production (land, labor, capital, management, and markets), rural social history (life on the farm), political and government activity relating to agri-culture, and agricultural technology and science. A substantial index lists titles, subjects, and geographical places. Books pub-lished after 1967 are listed in the bibliography of Schlebecker's history of American agriculture, WHEREBY WE THRIVE: A HIS-TORY OF AMERICAN FARMING, 1607-1972 (Ames: Iowa State University Press, 1975).

17-16   Spencer, Joseph E., and Horvath, Ronald J. "How Does an Agricultural Region Originate?" AAG ANNALS 53 (March 1963): 74-92. Notes.

In this exploratory essay, authors examine the origins, develop-ment, and change of three agricultural regions including the midwestern corn belt. They identify six cultural processes that are instrumental in this regional formation: psychological, po-litical, historical, technologic, economic, and agronomic.

B. MANUFACTURING

17-17 LeBlanc, Robert G. LOCATION OF MANUFACTURING IN NEW ENG-
LAND IN THE 19TH CENTURY. Geography Publications at Dartmouth,
No. 7. Hanover, N.H.: Dartmouth College, Geography Department,
1969. x, 173 p. Maps, diagrs., tables, notes, bibliog.

The explanation of the changing geographic patterns of manufacturing in New England during the nineteenth century is the
objective of this study. LeBlanc uses an 1831 census of manufacturers (the McLane Report) to reconstruct the localization of
various types of manufacturing (cotton and wool textiles, boots
and shoes, tanning, and primary and secondary metals). He
also uses employment statistics from the subsequent federal censuses of manufactures to analyze the changing location of manufactures from 1850 to 1900. In an appendix he discusses the
utility, limitations, and availability of the censuses of manufactures.

17-18 Walsh, Margaret. THE MANUFACTURING FRONTIER: PIONEER IN-
DUSTRY IN ANTEBELLUM WISCONSIN, 1830-1860. Madison: State
Historical Society of Wisconsin, 1972. xvi, 263 p. Maps, tables, notes,
bibliog., index.

Based on six sample counties (including Milwaukee), Walsh analyzes the process of industrial growth and change in the early
development of Wisconsin. She reviews industrial development
in terms of processing industries (flour milling, lumbering, building materials, brewing, leather processing, and meat packing),
household-craft consumer industries (shoes, clothing, blacksmiths,
and furniture), agricultural industries (implements and wagons),
and mineral processing (iron and lead). In an appendix she discusses
the use of 1840 to 1860 manuscript census schedules and Dun and
Bradstreet reports as quantitative and qualitative sources for
industrial development. Other articles by Walsh pertaining to
industrial development in the Midwest are "Pork Packing as a
Leading Edge of Midwestern Industry, 1835-1875," AGRICULTURAL
HISTORY 51 (October 1977): 702-17; and "The Spatial Evolution of a Mid-Western Pork Industry, 1833-75," JOURNAL OF
HISTORICAL GEOGRAPHY 4 (January 1978): 1-22.

17-19 Warren, Kenneth. THE AMERICAN STEEL INDUSTRY, 1850-1970: A
GEOGRAPHICAL INTERPRETATION. Oxford: Clarendon Press, 1973.
xvi, 337 p. Maps, photos., tables, notes, index.

The U.S. steel industry is examined in its geographical and historical setting from 1850 to 1970. Warren analyzes the shifting
locations of the steel industry resulting from changing physical
factors of resources and human factors of market, organization,
technology, and government policy.

C. TRANSPORTATION AND COMMUNICATION

17-20 Burghardt, Andrew F. "The Origin and Development of the Road Network of the Niagara Peninsula, Ontario, 1770-1851." AAG ANNALS 59 (September 1969): 417-40. Maps, notes.

An analysis of the development of the road network in southern Ontario shows that Indian trails did not predetermine the location of roads although town growth did exert a strong influence. The sequence of development does not agree with the model proposed by Taafe, Morrill, and Gould (see entry 17-25).

17-21 Francaviglia, Richard V. "Some Comments on the Historic and Geographic Importance of Railroads in Minnesota." MINNESOTA HISTORY 43 (Summer 1972): 58-62. Photos., notes.

The development of Minnesota's railroads is reviewed in this short article.

17-22 Langdale, John V. "The Growth of Long-Distance Telephony in the Bell System: 1875-1907." JOURNAL OF HISTORICAL GEOGRAPHY 4 (April 1978): 145-59. Map, diagrs., tables, notes.

Langdale traces the growth of long-distance telephone networks from 1875 to 1895, when the Bell system gained dominance over a number of independent telephone companies. The study is based primarily on published and manuscript records of the Bell system, the Federal Communications Commission, and the Bureau of the Census.

17-23 Quastler, I.E. "Some Major Unanswered Questions about the Historical Geography of American Railroads." HISTORICAL GEOGRAPHY NEWS-LETTER 8 (Spring 1978): 1-10. Notes.

In addition to reviewing the secondary literature that is pertinent to the historical geography of American railroads, Quastler also identifies two areas for potential research: the development of railroad networks and the spatial implications of differential rate structures. He also reviews the primary sources that are available for these studies. Other articles by Quastler include, "A Descriptive Model of Railroad Network Growth in the American Midwest, 1865-1915," JOURNAL OF GEOGRAPHY 77 (March 1978): 87-93; "The Geography of Rail Passenger Services in California and Nevada, 1900-1970," CALIFORNIA GEOGRAPHER 18 (1978): 55-83; "Interrailroad Territorial Nonaggression Agreements in the Nineteenth Century United States," AAG PROCEEDINGS 8 (1976): 65-70; and "The Areal Distribution of Railroad Abandonments in California Since 1920," CALIFORNIA GEOGRAPHER 11 (1970): 34-42.

17-24 Ray, John B. "Trade Patterns Along Zane's Trace, 1797-1812." PRO-
FESSIONAL GEOGRAPHER 22 (May 1970): 142-45. Maps, notes.

The construction of Zane's Trace in southern Ohio facilitated
the overland movement of cattle eastward to Philadelphia and
Baltimore, while the shipment of foodstuffs downstream to New
Orleans utilized the road only as a feeder to navigable streams
and rivers.

17-25 Taaffe, Richard J.; Morrill, Richard L.; and Gould, Peter R. "Transport
Expansion in Underdeveloped Countries; A Comparative Analysis."
GEOGRAPHICAL REVIEW 53 (October 1963): 503-29. Maps, diagrs.,
notes.

Although based on an examination of the emergence of transportation networks in Nigeria and Ghana during the first half of
the twentieth century, this article presents a model of transportation development that relates urban growth to the improvement
and expansion of transportation networks from coastal ports to
interior portions of a country. Examples of historical geographers
applying this model to other undeveloped areas are found in
entries 17-20 and 17-26.

17-26 Trindell, Roger T. "Transportation Development and Hinterland Piracy:
An Example from Colonial North America." JOURNAL OF TRANSPORT
HISTORY 7 (November 1966): 205-17. Map, tables, notes.

Trindell applies the model of transportation development described
by Taafe, Morrill, and Gould (see entry 17-25) to colonial North
America. His case study involves the ascendancy of Philadelphia
over two New Jersey ports on the lower Delaware River. His
research is based on Customs and Naval Officer statistics from
the British Public Record Office.

Chapter 18

HISTORICAL URBAN GEOGRAPHY

There is a wide variety of literature pertaining to historical urban geography. The first section includes general urban studies by both historical geographers and historians. The next section focuses on the external relations of cities, including such topics as the development of regional urban systems, the interrelations of urban growth and industrialization, and the application of central place and mercantile models to the interdependence of urban growth and trade. The third section deals with the internal structure of individual cities, treating such topics as physical growth, residential patterns and immigrant areas, industrial and commercial districts, and urban architectural types. Studies illustrating the application of historical urban research to historic preservation and urban planning are listed in the final section.

A. GENERAL

18-1   Glaab, Charles N., and Brown, A. Theodore. A HISTORY OF URBAN
        AMERICA. 2d ed. New York: Macmillan, 1976. xi, 350 p. Bibliog,
        index.

>   Although not intended to be a textbook, this publication does
>   examine numerous themes relevant to American urban history
>   such as everyday life and culture, the complexity of changing
>   urban population and technology, local government, bosses
>   and reformers, federal urban policy, emergence of metropolises,
>   and growth of suburbs. Originally published in 1967, this edition
>   was expanded from ten to fifteen chapters. Suggestions for fur-
>   ther reading are listed for each chapter.

18-2   Goheen, Peter G. "Interpreting the American City: Some Historical
        Perspectives." GEOGRAPHICAL REVIEW 64 (July 1974): 362-84.
        Notes.

>   In reviewing the historical and geographical studies of nineteenth-
>   and twentieth-century cities, Goheen illustrates the development
>   of two perspectives for interpreting the American city. One
>   theme focuses on the internal structure of the city as the context

for cultural change (industrialization, social and geographic mobility, and suburbanization), while the other theme adopts the wider perspective of examining the role of the city in influencing national ideas and institutions. Suggestions for new interpretations of the American city are also offered. Goheen discusses the relationship of population growth, industrial productivity, and transportation technology in "Industrialization and the Growth of Cities in Nineteenth-Century America," AMERICAN STUDIES 14 (Spring 1973): 49-65.

18-3   Schnore, Leo F., ed. THE NEW URBAN HISTORY: QUANTITATIVE EXPLORATIONS BY AMERICAN HISTORIANS. Princeton, N.J.: Princeton University Press, 1975. xi, 284 p. Maps, diagrs., tables, notes, index.

Reprinted in this volume are papers presented at a three-day conference held in Madison, Wisconsin, in June 1970, and sponsored by the Mathematical Social Science Board and the University of Wisconsin. The papers, which were presented by historians, geographers, and economists, are organized under three topics: "The Growth and Function of Cities," "Accommodation to the Urban Environment," and "Economic Analysis of Urban-Historical Phenomena." Papers of geographic interest include Allan R. Pred, "Large-City Interdependence and the Pre-Electronic Diffusion of Innovations in the United States," pp. 51-74; Martyn J. Bowden, "Growth of the Central Districts in Large Cities," pp. 75-109; and Kathleen Neils Conzen, "Patterns of Residence in Early Milwaukee," pp. 145-83.

18-4   URBANISM PAST AND PRESENT. Milwaukee: University of Wisconsin, Department of History, Winter 1975-- . Biannual.

As the successor to the American Historical Association's URBAN HISTORY GROUP NEWSLETTER, this publication addresses a wider audience of historians, sociologists, political scientists, geographers, architects, and city planners. It consists of scholarly articles, news of current research and conferences, descriptions of major data sources for the study of urbanism, and an extensive current bibliography, which includes numerous references by geographers. One article of geographic interest is Peter O. Muller, "The Evolution of American Suburbs: A Geographical Interpretation," no. 4 (Summer 1977), pp. 1-10 (reprinted in entry 12-33).

18-5   Vance, James E., Jr. THIS SCENE OF MAN: THE ROLE AND STRUCTURE OF THE CITY IN THE GEOGRAPHY OF WESTERN CIVILIZATION. New York: Harper's College Press, 1977. xx, 437 p. Maps, illus., photos., notes, index.

In this textbook survey of western urbanization, Vance is concerned with two aspects of urban morphogenesis: the role of cities in western society and the processes involved in creating and changing the physical structure of those cities. Using examples from Western Europe and North America, he describes the growth and structure of the classical, medieval, mercantile, and industrial cities. This study is a synthesis of Vance's thoughts after teaching and writing on urban morphogenesis for twenty-five years.

18-6 Ward, David. CITIES AND IMMIGRANTS: A GEOGRAPHY OF CHANGE IN NINETEENTH-CENTURY AMERICA. Andrew H. Clark Series in the Historical Geography of North America. New York: Oxford University Press, 1971. xv, 164 p. Maps, illus., photos., diagrs., tables, notes, bibliog., index.

The historical geography of urban growth is examined in terms of both external relations and internal structure of U.S. cities from 1820 to 1920, a period of mass immigration. By reviewing secondary literature from the fields of economic and urban history and geography, Ward develops generalizations and models which describe the effects of regional economic development and immigration on urbanization. In addition, he also examines the internal differentiation of cities in terms of the growth of central business districts as locations of urban employment, immigrant residential patterns and the formation of ghettos, and the development of intra-urban transportation networks which resulted in suburban expansion. This book is a key source for studies in historical urban geography because the footnotes and bibliography list a wide range of related secondary literature. In addition, the various models were proposed to stimulate further research.

18-7 Warner, Sam Bass, Jr. THE URBAN WILDERNESS: A HISTORY OF THE AMERICAN CITY. New York: Harper and Row, 1972. xvii, 303 p. Maps, illus., photos., notes, bibliog., index.

Warner presents a broad canvas of American urban history concentrating on three time periods: 1820-70, characterized by the development of commerce, canals, and sweatshops in New York City; 1870-1920, characterized by the development of factories, railroads, and skyscrapers in Chicago; and 1920 to present, characterized by the development of bureaucracy, racism, and automobiles in Los Angeles. More contemporary topics include immigrant neighborhoods, housing, and health care. A bibliographical essay is included.

B. EXTERNAL RELATIONS

18-8 Barton, Bonnie. "The Creation of Centrality." AAG ANNALS 68 (March 1978): 34-44. Map, diagrs., notes.

Barton discusses the role of exchange and the entrepreneur in achieving centrality, utilizing data on economic activities and town growth in colonial New England.

18-9   Berry, Brian J. L. GEOGRAPHY OF MARKET CENTERS AND RETAIL
        DISTRIBUTION. Foundations of Economic Geography Series. Englewood
        Cliffs, N.J.: Prentice-Hall, 1967. x, 146 p. Paper. Maps, diagrs.,
        tables, notes, index.

        Berry uses central place theory as the basis for understanding
        the geography of retail and service business. Since these activ-
        ities are clustered in market centers an explanation of their
        location, size, and spacing also provides the theoretical basis
        for much of urban and transportation geography. The develop-
        ment of market centers and service activities in an area in south-
        western Iowa (focusing on Omaha and Council Bluffs) is used as
        a historical example to introduce the concepts of central place
        theory.

18-10   Borchert, John R. "American Metropolitan Evolution." GEOGRAPHICAL
        REVIEW 57 (July 1967): 301-32. Maps, diagrs., tables, notes.

        Borchert reviews the differential growth of American cities from
        1790 to 1960 utilizing five size categories and four time periods,
        which are based on changing industrial and transportation tech-
        nologies (1790-1830, sail and wagon; 1830-70, iron horse; 1870-
        1920, steel rail; and 1920-- , automobile and air). This article
        is reprinted in SYSTEMS OF CITIES: READINGS ON STRUCTURE,
        GROWTH, AND POLICY, edited by L.S. Bourne and J.W.
        Simmons, pp. 101-25 (New York: Oxford University Press,
        1978). Borchert discusses more recent changes in American metro-
        politan regional structure in "America's Changing Metropolitan
        Regions," AAG ANNALS 62 (June 1972): 352-73.

18-11   Conzen, Michael P. "The Maturing Urban System in the United States,
        1840-1910." AAG ANNALS 67 (March 1977): 88-108. Maps, diagrs.,
        table, notes.

        Urban hinterlands and hierarchies are mapped and analyzed using
        bank correspondent accounts as an index of urban connectivity.
        As the national urban system matured, it grew from a primate
        order dominated by New York City to a four-level hierarchy
        with high-level interdependencies among the various rising re-
        gional centers. This article is reprinted in entry 12-33. See
        also Conzen, "Capital Flows and the Developing Urban Hierarchy:
        State Bank Capital in Wisconsin, 1854-1895," ECONOMIC GE-
        OGRAPHY 51 (October 1975): 321-38.

18-12   _____. "A Transport Interpretation of the Growth of Urban Regions: An
        American Example." JOURNAL OF HISTORICAL GEOGRAPHY 1 (Octo-
        ber 1975): 361-82. Maps, tables, notes.

        The development of urban regions around the major cities in the
        Midwest during the second half of the nineteenth century is studied
        using stagecoach and railroad passenger frequency patterns in

1850, 1872, 1890, and 1908. Conzen finds that the development of an urban hierarchy follows Vance's mercantile model (see entry 18-21) with the major centers developing first, followed by the lower levels of the central place system.

18-13 Earle, Carville V. "The First English Towns in North America," GEOGRAPHICAL REVIEW 67 (January 1977) 34-50. Maps, diagrs., tables, notes.

The origins and early growth of the initial towns in the seventeenth-century British North American colonies are reviewed in the context of a monopolist-migration model rather than a mercantile model. The location and frequency of towns was the result of monopoly or company colonization (one town per colony) and the viability of the towns was related to the migration of free-family units (as opposed to nonfree males) which was influenced by religious persecution and economic depressions. See also Earle, "Reflections on the Colonial City," HISTORICAL GEOGRAPHY NEWSLETTER 4 (Fall 1974) 1-17.

18-14 Earle, Carville V., and Hoffman, Ronald. "Staple Crops and Urban Development in the Eighteenth-Century South." PERSPECTIVES IN AMERICAN HISTORY 10 (1976): 7-78. Maps, notes.

The development of three urban systems in eighteenth-century Maryland, Virginia, and North and South Carolina is viewed in the context of the staple crops that were produced in and exported from the respective regions: wheat in Maryland's eastern shore and Maryland and Virginia's Piedmont and Great Valley areas; tobacco in the Chesapeake Tidewater; and rice in Charleston's hinterland. See also Earle and Hoffman, "The Urban South: The First Two Centuries," in THE CITY IN SOUTHERN HISTORY: THE GROWTH OF URBAN CIVILIZATION IN THE SOUTH, edited by Blaine A. Brownell and David R. Goldfield, pp. 23-51 (Port Washington, N.Y.: Kennikat Press, 1977).

18-15 Ernst, Joseph A., and Merrens, Harry Roy. "'Camden's Turrets Pierce the Skies!': The Urban Process in the Southern Colonies during the Eighteenth Century." WILLIAM AND MARY QUARTERLY, 3d ser., 30 (October 1973): 549-74. Notes.

In studying urban development in the southern colonies, these two authors advocate that the functional origins of towns, as well as their position in an urban system and a regional economy, should be considered. While Camden, South Carolina, is used as a case study, the urban process in North Carolina, Virginia, and Maryland is also reviewed. This article is reprinted in entry 12-33.

18-16   Gilchrist, David T., ed. THE GROWTH OF THE SEAPORT CITIES, 1790-1825. Charlottesville: University Press of Virginia for the Eleutherian Mills-Hagley Foundation, 1967. xvi, 227 p. Diagrs., tables, notes, index.

The proceedings of a conference on the comparative growth of the seaport cities (Boston, New York, Philadelphia, and Baltimore) held at the Eleutherian Mills Historical Library, Greenville, Delaware, March 1966, are printed in this volume. In the introductory paper, "Urban Growth and Regional Development," pp. 3-21, Julius Rubin discussed the broad problem of the relationship between seaport cities and their hinterlands. Other speakers examined the role of population, foreign trade, trade and manufactures, financial institutions, and economic thought in the varied growth of these cities.

18-17   Lampard, Eric E. "The Evolving System of Cities in the United States: Urbanization and Economic Development." In ISSUES IN URBAN ECONOMICS, edited by Harvey S. Perloff and Lowdon Wings, Jr., pp. 81-138. Baltimore: Johns Hopkins University Press, 1968.

The development of regional urban systems is reviewed in terms of location and growth theories.

18-18   Muller, Edward K. "Regional Urbanization and the Selective Growth of Towns in North American Regions." JOURNAL OF HISTORICAL GEOGRAPHY 3 (January 1977): 21-39. Notes.

Muller presents a model of selective urban growth in a newly settled region and considers the model in relation to previous works on regional urbanization. This model distinguishes three periods of development based on changing characteristics of circulation and export activity. Also taken into account are the effects of settlement expansion and the changing functional basis of urban centers from commercial to manufacturing activities. The footnotes provide a guide to the secondary literature on regional urbanization. The basis for this model is found in Muller's earlier work on urban development in southwestern Ohio and southeastern Indiana, which is reported in "Selective Urban Growth in the Middle Ohio Valley, 1800-1860," GEOGRAPHICAL REVIEW 66 (April 1976): 178-99 (also reprinted in entry 12-33). The major sources for this study were the published volumes and manuscript schedules from the various U.S. population and manufacturing censuses between 1800 and 1860. A summary of urbanization in the Ohio Valley, based on a review of secondary literature, is found in "Early Urbanization in the Ohio Valley: A Review Essay," HISTORICAL GEOGRAPHY NEWSLETTER 3 (Fall 1973): 19-30.

18-19 Pred, Allan R. THE SPATIAL DYNAMICS OF U.S. URBAN-INDUSTRIAL
GROWTH, 1800-1914: INTERPRETIVE AND THEORETICAL ESSAYS.
Cambridge: MIT Press, 1966. ix, 225 p. Maps, diagrs., tables, notes,
index.

> The three theoretical essays published in this volume deal with
> the spatial dynamics of urban-industrial growth during the nine-
> teenth and early twentieth centuries. The first essay explains
> the role of industrialization and initial advantage in the differen-
> tial growth of cities, 1860-1914, by developing a model that views
> urban growth as a circular and cumulative process. The second
> essay focuses on the spatial component of industrial invention
> and innovation in urban growth (using Patent Office data). The
> third essay examines the effect of industry on the growth structure
> on the primarily commercial cities of the period, 1800-1840.
> These ideas were also presented in "Manufacturing in the Ameri-
> can Mercantile City: 1800-1840," AAG ANNALS 56 (June
> 1966): 307-38; and "Industrialization, Initial Advantage, and
> American Metropolitan Growth," GEOGRAPHICAL REVIEW 55
> (April 1965): 158-85 (reproduced in entry 12-33).

18-20 _____. URBAN GROWTH AND THE CIRCULATION OF INFORMATION:
THE UNITED STATES SYSTEM OF CITIES, 1790-1840. Cambridge: Harvard University Press, 1973. xiv, 348 p. Maps, diagrs., tables, notes,
index.

> In this sequel to the previous work, Pred investigates the inter-
> relationships between information circulation and certain aspects
> of the interdependent growth of large cities, 1790 to 1840.
> Specific types of pre-telegraphic long distance information cir-
> culation with which he is concerned are newspapers, postal
> service, interurban commodity flows (domestic trade), and inter-
> urban travel. The use of newspaper information in the creation
> of time-lag surface maps is illustrated by Pred in "Urban Sys-
> tems Development and the Long-Distance Flow of Information
> through Pre-Electronic Newspapers," ECONOMIC GEOGRAPHY
> 47 (October 1971): 498-524. Similar articles by Pred are listed
> in entries 12-7 and 18-3.

18-21 Vance, James E., Jr. THE MERCHANT'S WORLD: THE GEOGRAPHY
OF WHOLESALING. Foundations of Economic Geography Series. Englewood Cliffs, N.J.: Prentice Hall, 1970. viii, 167 p. Paper. Maps,
diagrs., tables, notes.

> After defining and discussing the nature of wholesaling, Vance
> reviews the development, distribution, and organization of
> wholesaling activities, primarily in nineteenth- and twentieth-
> century United States. In addition, he presents a mercantile
> model of settlement and trade, which stresses the influence of
> external ties (long distance or transoceanic wholesaling) on
> urban growth as opposed to central place theory, which stresses
> the influence of internal forces and retail trade.

C. INTERNAL STRUCTURE

18-22 Adams, John S. "Residential Structure of Midwestern Cities." AAG ANNALS 60 (March 1970): 37-62. Diagrs., notes.

Housing construction statistics from 1889 to 1960 are used to construct a model of urban residential age structure. The model, which is tested with data from Minneapolis, reflects six building cycles and four urban transportation eras.

18-23 Archdeacon, Thomas J. NEW YORK CITY, 1664-1710: CONQUEST AND CHANGE. Ithaca, N.Y.: Cornell University Press, 1976. 197 p. Maps, diagrs., tables, notes, bibliog., index.

Archdeacon applies the techniques associated with the historical studies of New England communities (see entry 19-23) to research on a major colonial city. He focuses on New York City during the aftermath of the English takeover from the Dutch, a period of basic social, economic and political changes. Specifically he examines population origins (Dutch, English, and French Huguenots), mercantile activity, social geography (residential and social patterns), and the political implications of these patterns. In a bibliographical essay he discusses a variety of city and local records (tax assessment lists, census rolls, church records, wills, and inventories).

18-24 Bastian, Robert W. "Architecture and Class Segregation in Late Nineteenth-Century Terre Haute, Indiana." GEOGRAPHICAL REVIEW 65 (April 1975): 166-79. Maps, photos., tables, notes.

Urban house types are used as an indicator of late nineteenth-century occupational class segregation in Terre Haute. House types (stylistic versus nonstylistic) are correlated with occupational distributions, which are derived from 1879, 1884, 1889, 1894, and 1900 city directories.

18-25 Beirne, D. Randall. "Residential Growth and Stability in the Baltimore Industrial Community of Canton during the Late Nineteenth Century." MARYLAND HISTORICAL MAGAZINE 74 (Spring 1979): 39-51. Map, tables, notes.

Using census and company records, the author examines the phenomenon of residential stability in the industrial neighborhood of Canton in Baltimore from 1880 to 1930. The exceptional stability of this community was primarily a result of industrial linkages, although other factors such as ethnicity were important stabilizing forces.

18-26 Blumin, Stuart M. THE URBAN THRESHOLD: GROWTH AND CHANGE IN A NINETEENTH-CENTURY AMERICAN COMMUNITY. Chicago: University of Chicago Press, 1976. xiv, 298 p. Maps, tables, notes, bibliog., index.

> The growth and development of a smaller city (Kingston, New York, on the Hudson River) is examined from 1820 to 1860. The completion of the Delaware and Hudson Canal provided the impetus for the transformation of this terminal port from a rural village into an active commercial city. Blumin is particularly interested in the effect of the city's growth on the social and cultural integration of the community.

18-27 Bowden, Martyn J. "Downtown though Time: Delimitation, Expansion, and Internal Growth." ECONOMIC GEOGRAPHY 47 (April 1971): 121-35. Maps, notes.

> By mapping San Francisco's central business district in 1850, 1906, and 1931, Bowden was able to observe its expansion and internal growth. His reconstruction of the morphological and functional structure of the central business district was based on fire insurance maps, city directories, building and panoramic views, and newspapers. Other articles by Bowden pertaining to San Francisco are listed in entries 12-6 and 18-3, as well as "Reconstruction Following Catastrophe: The Laissez-Faire Rebuilding of Downtown San Francisco After the Earthquake and Fire of 1906," AAG PROCEEDINGS 2 (1970): 22-26.

18-28 Conzen, Kathleen Neils. IMMIGRANT MILWAUKEE, 1836-1860: ACCOMMODATION AND COMMUNITY IN A FRONTIER CITY. Cambridge: Harvard University Press, 1976. x, 300 p. Maps, diagrs., tables, notes, index.

> The accommodation of German immigrants in Milwaukee during the first twenty-five years of its existence is examined in this historical study. The findings show that the ghetto process does. not apply to this large immigrant group settling in a mid-nineteenth-century frontier city. Specific topics that are discussed are population origins, demographic characteristics, occupational structure, residential patterns and ethnic areas, social and religious institutions, and political activity. The data are derived from federal manuscript census schedules, city directories, newspapers, and early city histories. Milwaukee's retailing activities are examined by Kathleen Neils Conzen and Michael P. Conzen in "Geographical Structure in Nineteenth-Century Urban Retailing: Milwaukee, 1836-90," JOURNAL OF HISTORICAL GEOGRAPHY 5 (January 1979): 45-66. See also entry 18-3.

18-29 Deskins, Donald R. RESIDENTIAL MOBILITY OF NEGROES IN DETROIT,
1837-1965. Michigan Geographical Publication, No. 5. Ann Arbor:
University of Michigan, Department of Geography, 1972. xx, 297 p.
Paper. Maps, diagrs., tables, notes, bibliog.

Deskins examines the residential mobility of major occupational
groups by race in Detroit from 1837 to 1965. Numerous maps and
tables display the results of his quantitative study. He concludes
that structurally the city shifted from a preindustrial pattern
(workers with high skills living near the central business district)
to an industrial pattern (workers with the lowest skills living near
the city center). Although the Negro subcommunity exhibited
similar structural changes, Negroes were less residentially mobile.
See also Deskins, "Race, Residence, and Workplace in Detroit,
1880 to 1965," ECONOMIC GEOGRAPHY 48 (January 1972):
79-94.

18-30 Groves, Paul A., and Muller, Edward K. "The Evolution of Black Residential Areas in Late Nineteenth-Century Cities." JOURNAL OF HISTORICAL
GEOGRAPHY 1 (April 1975): 169-91. Maps, diagrs., tables, notes.

Black residential patterns in late nineteenth-century Washington,
D.C., and Baltimore are studied on a micro-level using the 1880
manuscript census schedules. These two border cities developed
sizeable black residential concentrations (ghettos) between 1880
and 1920, a process which did not begin in northern cities until
the early twentieth century. Other articles by Groves pertaining
to black residential patterns in Washington, D.C., are: "The
'Hidden' Population: Washington Alley Dwellers in Late Nineteenth Century," PROFESSIONAL GEOGRAPHER 26 (August
1974): 270-76, and "The Development of a Black Residential
Community in Southwest Washington, 1860-1897," RECORDS OF
THE COLUMBIA HISTORICAL SOCIETY, 1973-74, (Washington,
D.C.: 1976): 260-75.

18-31 Hoffecker, Carol E. WILMINGTON, DELAWARE: PORTRAIT OF AN IN-
DUSTRIAL CITY, 1830-1910. Charlottesville: University Press of Virginia
for the Eleutherian Mills-Hagley Foundation, 1974. xvi, 187 p. Maps,
illus., photos., tables, notes, bibliog., index.

This urban biography of Wilmington, Delaware, examines the social consequences of industrialization in a medium-sized city.
In contrast to studies of Philadelphia, the author finds that in
Wilmington, industrialization strengthened community spirit and
social institutions. Although this study does not have a strong
spatial orientation, it does emphasize the development of industry, institutions, and organizations.

18-32 Jakle, John A., and Wheeler, James O. "The Changing Residential
Structure of the Dutch Population in Kalamazoo, Michigan." AAG ANNALS
59 (September 1969): 441-60. Maps, photos., table, notes.

Dutch residential locations are mapped for 1873, 1910, 1939,

and 1965, utilizing city directories and county plat book maps.
The changing residential patterns are related to differences in
acculturation.

18-33 Kellogg, John. "Negro Urban Clusters in the Postbellum South." GEO-
GRAPHICAL REVIEW 67 (July 1977): 310-21. Maps, tables, notes.

The formation of small Negro enclaves (urban clusters) on the
periphery of four southern cities (Lexington, Ky.; Atlanta, Ga.;
Durham, N.C.; and Richmond, Va.) during the last half of the
nineteenth century is attributed to Negro migration into the cities
in the 1860s and 1870s. By comparing the residential patterns
of the 1880s with 1970, Kellogg shows that a second stage in
Negro community development was the outward growth of a
single, large Negro sector.

18-34 Knights, Peter R. THE PLAIN PEOPLE OF BOSTON, 1830-1860: A
STUDY IN CITY GROWTH. New York: Oxford University Press, 1971.
xx, 204 p. Maps, tables, notes, bibliog., index.

The growth of antebellum Boston is examined primarily in terms
of population characteristics. Specifically, Knights focuses on
population trends from 1830 to 1860, sources of Boston's population, population mobility and redistribution, wealth trends,
and out-migration. Two of his appendixes, which are reproduced
in HISTORICAL METHODS NEWSLETTER (see entry 8-13), discuss
the utility and limitations of city directories and manuscript census schedules. See also Knights and Leo F. Schnore, "Residence
and Social Structure: Boston in the Ante-Bellum Period," pp.
247-57, and Knights, "Population Turnover, Persistence, and
Residential Mobility in Boston, 1830-1860," pp. 258-74, in
NINETEENTH-CENTURY CITIES: ESSAYS IN THE NEW URBAN
HISTORY, edited by Stephan Thernstrom and Richard Sennett
(New Haven: Yale University Press, 1969).

18-35 Muller, Edward K., and Groves, Paul A. "The Emergence of Industrial
Districts in Mid-Nineteenth Century Baltimore." GEOGRAPHICAL RE-
VIEW 69 (April 1979): 159-78. Maps, diagrs., tables, notes.

Through the use of city directories and the 1860 census of
manufactures, Baltimore's industrial activities were mapped for
1833 and 1860. The 1833 patterns were representative of the
traditional mercantile model where small artisan shops and processing activities not only focused on the central business area
but were also widely dispersed throughout the city. In 1860 this
mercantile pattern persisted, but there were also the emergence
of six separate industrial districts which resulted from the localiz-
ing tendencies of several large firms. Consequently, Baltimore's
mid-nineteenth-century industrial geography was transistional

between the early nineteenth-century mercantile city and the late nineteenth-century industrial city. Another article by these authors pertaining to the industrial geography of nineteenth-century Baltimore is "The Changing Location of the Clothing Industry: A Link to the Social Geography of Baltimore in the Nineteenth Century," MARYLAND HISTORICAL MAGAZINE 71 (Fall 1976): 403-20. Muller also reviews several secondary works pertaining to mid-nineteenth-century cities in "Sharpening the Focus on Mid-Nineteenth Century Urban Life: A Review Essay," HISTORICAL GEOGRAPHY NEWSLETTER 8 (Fall 1978): 1-16.

18-36 Olson, Sherry H. BALTIMORE: THE BUILDING OF AN AMERICAN CITY. Baltimore: Johns Hopkins University Press, 1980. xii, 432 p. Maps, illus., photos., notes, index.

The history of the physical growth of Baltimore from the mid-eighteenth century until the present is recorded in this volume, which is well illustrated with historical maps, prints, and photographs. The tempo and pattern of city growth is related to a rhythm of boom and bust investment. Olson also examines the effects of this long-swing rhythm of urban investment on the morphology and internal structure of nineteenth-century Baltimore in "Baltimore Imitates the Spider," AAG ANNALS 69 (December 1979): 557-74.

18-37 Radford, John P. "Race, Residence, and Ideology: Charleston, South Carolina in the Mid-Nineteenth Century." JOURNAL OF HISTORICAL GEOGRAPHY 2 (October 1976): 329-46. Maps, tables, notes.

Based on a 10 percent systematic sample of the 1860 and 1880 manuscript census schedules, Radford maps the racial residential patterns in Charleston. Relating these residential patterns to the racial ideology of the planter-dominated city rather than to a competitive housing market, he finds no movement toward a macroscale segregation during the Civil War and Reconstruction. This article is reproduced in entry 12-33. Radford also examines Charleston's internal structure in "Testing the Model of the Pre-Industrial City: The Case of Ante-bellum Charleston, South Carolina," INSTITUTE OF BRITISH GEOGRAPHERS TRANS-ACTIONS, new series, 4 (1979): 392-410. See also entry 12-30.

18-38 Rickert, John E. "House Facades of the Northeastern United States: A Tool of Geographic Analysis." AAG ANNALS 57 (June 1967): 211-38. Illus., tables, notes.

By determining the chronology of changing house facades in a particular region, Rickert developed a useful tool for the spatial and temporal analysis of urban residential land use. Although his analysis was based on an urban sample, he suggests this method can be applied to suburban and rural areas.

18-39 Rubin, Barbara. "A Chronology of Architecture in Los Angeles." AAG
ANNALS 67 (December 1977): 521-37. Photos., notes.

In this study of urban architecture, Rubin reviews the chronology
of domestic architecture in the Los Angeles area from the 1880s
to the present. She finds that changes in architectural form and
style reflect changes in economic and social conditions, population pressures, and cost and availability of construction materials,
technology, and design options. Rubin examines the influence
of late nineteenth-century World's Fair amusement zones on
urban commercial architecture in "Aesthetic Ideology and Urban
Design," AAG ANNALS 69 (September 1979): 339-61. Both
articles utilize a large number of historical photographs.

18-40 Swauger, John. "Pittsburgh's Residential Pattern in 1815." AAG ANNALS
68 (June 1978): 265-77. Maps, tables, notes.

The mapping of residential patterns in preindustrial Pittsburgh
as derived from an 1815 city directory shows that the residential
location of all social classes except the elite conforms to the
model for the nonindustrial city. However, many of the elite
chose residences that were peripheral to the city core, a situation which is more characteristic of the later nineteenth-
century industrial city.

18-41 Thernstrom, Stephan. THE OTHER BOSTONIANS: POVERTY AND PROG-
RESS IN THE AMERICAN METROPOLIS, 1880-1970. Cambridge: Harvard
University Press, 1973. xvi, 345 p. Tables, notes, index.

The common people of Boston are studied in terms of social structure and processes from 1880 to the present. Specific themes
include population growth, sources of migrants, turnover, economic opportunity, and occupational structure. The research is
based on federal census records, city directories, and local tax
records. Thernstrom explored similar issues in his study of New-
buryport, Massachusetts, 1850 to 1880, in POVERTY AND
PROGRESS: SOCIAL MOBILITY IN A NINETEENTH CENTURY
CITY (Cambridge: Harvard University Press, 1964). Population
mobility is the subject of another study by Thernstrom and Peter
R. Knights, "Men in Motion: Some Data and Speculation about
Urban Population Mobility in Nineteenth Century America," in
ANONYMOUS AMERICANS: EXPLORATIONS IN NINETEENTH-
CENTURY SOCIAL HISTORY, edited by Tamara K. Hareven,
pp. 17-47, (Englewood Cliffs, N.J.: Prentice-Hall, 1971).

18-42 Vance, James E., Jr. GEOGRAPHY AND URBAN EVOLUTION IN THE
SAN FRANCISCO BAY AREA. Institute of Government Studies. Berkeley
and Los Angeles: University of California Press, 1964. 89 p. Paper.
Maps, tables, notes.

Vance sketches the broad outlines of the evolution of urban
growth in the San Francisco Bay area from mid-nineteenth

century to the present. He describes the physical structure of the region as well as the processes that shaped the region. He emphasizes the city's establishment as an entrepot (warehousing), changes in transportation technology (maritime, railroad, trolley, automobile), and land use segregation (development of functional districts).

18-43   Ward, David. "Victorian Cities: How Modern?" JOURNAL OF HISTORI-CAL GEOGRAPHY 1 (April 1975): 135-51. Notes.

Based on a review of recent literature relating to the social geography of nineteenth-century American and British cities, Ward assesses the modern characteristics of the Victorian (nineteenth-century) city. He suggests that the distinct residential differentiation characteristic of the modern industrial city was not readily apparent in the American city until the late nineteenth century; rather, the more homogeneous residential patterns of the early and mid-nineteenth century were transistional in character. See also entry 12-10 and "the Victorian Slum: An Enduring Myth," AAG ANNALS 66 (June 1976): 323-36. Other articles by Ward pertaining to the internal spatial structure of nineteenth-century cities include: "The Internal Spatial Structure of Immigrant Residential Districts in Late Nineteenth Century," GEO-GRAPHICAL ANALYSIS 1 (October 1969): 337-53; "The Emergence of Central Immigrant Ghettoes in American Cities: 1840-1920," AAG ANNALS 58 (June 1968): 343-59; "The Industrial Revolution and the Emergence of Boston's Central Business District," ECONOMIC GEOGRAPHY 42 (April 1966): 152-71; and "A Comparative Historical Geography of Streetcar Suburbs in Boston, Massachusetts and Leeds, England: 1850-1920," AAG ANNALS 54 (December 1964): 477-89. See also entry 12-6.

18-44   Warner, Sam Bass, Jr. THE PRIVATE CITY: PHILADELPHIA IN THREE PERIODS OF ITS GROWTH. Philadelphia: University of Pennsylvania Press, 1968. xiii, 236 p. Maps, illus., tables, notes, index.

Warner compares Philadelphia's growth at three intervals: 1770-1780 (an eighteenth-century town), 1830-1860 (a big city), and 1920-1930 (an industrial metropolis). His interpretation emphasizes the effects of privatism (an individual's search for wealth) on the growth of the city. Besides such traditional historical themes of political leadership and municipal institutions, he also discusses such geographical themes as industrial and spatial patterns of rapid growth. The universality of the Philadelphia situation is assessed by Warner in "If All the World Were Philadelphia: A Scaffolding for Urban History, 1774-1930," AMERICAN HIS-TORICAL REVIEW 74 (October 1968): 26-43. Warner also examines the physical growth of late nineteenth-century Boston in STREETCAR SUBURBS: THE PROCESS OF GROWTH IN BOS-TON, 1870-1900 (Cambridge: Harvard University Press and MIT Press, 1962).

D. HISTORIC PRESERVATION AND URBAN PLANNING

18-45 Ford, Larry R. "Historic Preservation and the Stream of Time: The Role of the Geographer." HISTORICAL GEOGRAPHY NEWSLETTER 5 (Spring 1975): 1-15. Photos., notes.

> Ford discusses the historical geographer's potential contributions to the planning process, particularly in the area of historic preservation. Other articles by Ford pertaining to historic preservation and preservation planning include "Historic Preservation and the Sense of Place," GROWTH AND CHANGE 5 (April 1974): 33-37; and "Continuity and Change in Historic Cities: Bath, Chester, and Norwich," GEOGRAPHICAL REVIEW 68 (July 1978): 253-73. Preservation efforts in Columbus, Ohio, are discussed by Ford and Richard Fusch in "Historic Preservation and the Inner City: The Perception of German Village by Those Just Beyond," AAG PROCEEDINGS 8 (1976): 110-14.

18-46 Haas, J. Eugene; Kates, Robert W.; and Bowden, Martyn J., eds. RECONSTRUCTION FOLLOWING DISASTER. Cambridge: MIT Press, 1977. xxxv, 331 p. Maps, diagrs., tables, bibliog., index.

> Bowden's research in historical urban geography pertaining to the reconstruction of San Francisco after the 1906 earthquake and fire (see entry 18-27) is used as a case example in this interdisciplinary study of the postdisaster reconstruction process. Other case studies utilize earthquake and flood disasters in the 1960s and 1970s (Anchorage, Alaska; Managua, Nicaragua; and Rapid City, South Dakota). The findings from this applied research will contribute to the planning process that is necessary for cities recovering from the widespread destruction following a major disaster.

18-47 Krim, Arthur J., et al. SURVEY OF ARCHITECTURAL HISTORY IN CAMBRIDGE. REPORT FIVE, NORTHWEST CAMBRIDGE. Cambridge: Cambridge Historical Commission, 1977. xii, 206 p. Paper. Maps, illus., photos., bibliog., index.

> This architectural survey, which will be used as a tool for developing a comprehensive city plan, reflects the thinking of the survey director, a historical urban geographer. The survey is not just a chronological listing of every building (residential, civic, commercial, and industrial) in a section of Cambridge, but it also emphasizes the process of landscape development. The changing land use and physical development are described as this area was transformed from an agricultural community in the colonial period to an urban fringe and residential suburb of Boston beginning in the mid-nineteenth century.

18-48 Newcomb, Robert M. PLANNING THE PAST: HISTORICAL LANDSCAPE RESOURCES AND RECREATION. Studies in Historical Geography. Folkestone, Kent: William Dawson and Sons; Hamden, Conn.: Archon Books, Shoe String Press, 1979. 255 p. Maps, photos., diagrs., tables, notes, bibliog., index.

> Based on his experience in Denmark, Great Britain, and the southwestern United States, Newcomb writes about the historical geographers' interest in the preservation of old landscapes and their use in educational and entertaining ways in the present. In the first part, he surveys current recreational uses of past landscapes and the preservation planning process. In the second section, he provides examples of landscapes that reflect rural, urban, industrial and political impacts.

Chapter 19

HISTORICAL CULTURAL GEOGRAPHY

Historical cultural geography, which deals mainly with rural settlement patterns, provides the focus of this chapter. The first section lists general interpretive studies, while the second section on culture regions and population origins emphasizes studies that use written sources to document migration, ethnic and regional origins, and the formation of cultural regions. The final section includes studies that use cultural landscape artifacts such as house types and rural settlement features to map culture areas and trace the diffusion of cultural traits.

A. GENERAL

19-1   Dunbar, Gary S. "Illustrations of the American Earth: A Bibliographical Essay on the Cultural Geography of the United States." In AMERICAN STUDIES: TOPICS AND SOURCES, edited by Robert H. Walker, pp. 50-58. Contributions in American Studies, No. 24. Westport, Conn.: Greenwood Press, 1976.

   This bibliographical essay emphasizes the works of geographers concerning the humanization and Americanization of the land. Dunbar includes a good sample of the works by historical geographers because historical explanations are necessary to explain the cultural (manmade or artificial) landscapes of the United States. This article is reprinted from AMERICAN STUDIES: AN INTERNATIONAL NEWSLETTER 12 (Autumn 1973): 3-15.

19-2   Mitchell, Robert D. "The Formation of Early American Cultural Regions: An Interpretation." In EUROPEAN SETTLEMENT AND DEVELOPMENT IN NORTH AMERICA, edited by James R. Gibson, pp. 66-90. Toronto: University of Toronto Press, 1978. Maps, diagrs., notes.

   Mitchell traces the diffusion of cultural traits and regional patterns from the initial hearth areas on the Atlantic seaboard (southern New England, southeastern Pennsylvania, Chesapeake, and South Carolina coast) to a series of interior secondary (North Carolina piedmont and Virginia's Shenandoah Valley) and tertiary (trans–Appalachian) settlement areas. Although the hearth and secondary areas were characterized by relatively distinctive traits, the tertiary areas experienced a fusion of traits from the former settlement areas so that an increasing cultural convergence was apparent.

19-3   Zelinsky, Wilbur. THE CULTURAL GEOGRAPHY OF THE UNITED STATES. Foundations of Cultural Geography Series. Englewood Cliffs, N.J.: Prentice-Hall, 1973. x, 164 p. Paper. Maps, diagrs., tables, notes, bibliog., index.

This introductory work is the first attempt to develop an overview of the cultural geography of the United States. In the first section, Zelinsky describes the American identity or culture and searches for its origins in the historical experience of settlement, immigration, and the frontier. The second section deals with how individual cultures are manifest on the landscape and how these patterns vary regionally. After defining basic cultural processes, he delimits five basic culture regions, each with a number of subregions. His annotated bibliography and footnotes provide a guide to recent literature on culture history and culture areas, including most of his earlier publications.

B. CULTURE REGIONS AND POPULATION ORIGINS

19-4   Allen, James P. "Changes in the American Propensity to Migrate." AAG ANNALS 67 (December 1977): 577-87. Diagrs., tables, notes.

Long-term trends of population mobility are assessed by developing a methodology for comparing 1940-70 mobility data derived from federal census statistics with pre-1930 mobility data derived from historical research based on city directories and unpublished census records. Allen also investigated the migration fields (source areas) of French Canadians migrating from Quebec to southern Maine during the nineteenth and early twentieth centuries in "Migration Fields of French Canadian Immigrants to Southern Maine," GEOGRAPHICAL REVIEW 62 (July 1972): 366-83. The research for this latter article is based on birthplace data recorded in biographical summaries and naturalization documents. See also "Variations in Catholic-Protestant Proportions among Maine Towns," AAG PROCEEDINGS 3 (1971): 15-18.

19-5   Conzen, Michael P. "Local Migration Systems in Nineteenth-Century Iowa." GEOGRAPHICAL REVIEW 64 (July 1974): 339-61. Maps, tables, notes.

Conzen examines two aspects of geographic mobility in nineteenth-century Iowa: the westward migration associated with the frontier and the cityward migration, which was often counter to the westward current. His research is based on birthplace data for selected counties recorded in the 1895 Iowa state census.

19-6   Crowley, William K. "Old Order Amish Settlement: Diffusion and
        Growth." AAG ANNALS 68 (June 1978): 249-64. Maps, tables, notes.

        The spread of Amish settlements from their initial entrance into
        southeastern Pennsylvania in 1717 throughout the United States
        is traced primarily from secondary sources. Ten maps depict
        these movements, as well as surviving and extinct communities.

19-7   Davis, George A., and Donaldson, O. Fred. BLACKS IN THE UNITED
        STATES: A GEOGRAPHIC PERSPECTIVE. Boston: Houghton Mifflin Co.,
        1975. xi, 270 p. Maps, photos., diagrs., tables, bibliog., index.

        The spatial distribution of blacks and the forces that have influ-
        enced the movement of blacks provide the focus of this study. Sev-
        eral historical chapters discuss pre-Civil War black migration (slave
        trade and underground railroad) and post-Civil War black migra-
        tion (rural-urban migration and central city concentrations).
        Each chapter includes a select bibliography of secondary litera-
        ture. The broad patterns of black population distribution and mi-
        gration from the colonial and antebellum periods up to the present
        are also presented in Richard L. Morrill and O. Fred Donaldson,
        "Geographical Perspectives on the History of Black America,"
        ECONOMIC GEOGRAPHY 48 (January 1972): 1-23. The
        latter article is also reprinted in entry 12-33.

19-8   Hudson, John C. "Migration to an American Frontier." AAG ANNALS
        66 (June 1976): 242-65. Maps, photos., diagrs., tables, notes.

        The migration patterns of various national, regional, and ethnic
        groups in the early settlement of North Dakota from 1875 to
        1915 are analyzed in the context of interregional and international
        migration processes. The study is based on one thousand auto-
        biographies of pioneer settlers that were collected in the 1930s by
        the North Dakota Historical Society and by the Works Progress
        Administration. This article is reproduced in entry 12-33. The
        migration fields and settlement of two Dakota counties are ex-
        plored in "Two Dakota Homestead Frontiers," AAG ANNALS
        63 (December 1973): 442-62. For more theoretical statements
        about frontier studies and the rural settlement process, see entry
        14-30 and "A Location Theory for Rural Settlement," AAG AN-
        NALS 59 (June 1969): 365-81 (based on Iowa data, 1870-1960).

19-9   Jordan, Terry G. GERMAN SEED IN TEXAS SOIL: IMMIGRANT FARMERS
        IN NINETEENTH-CENTURY TEXAS. Austin: University of Texas Press,
        1966. xiv, 237 p. Maps, photos., tables, notes, bibliog., index.

        Statistical data from the 1850 through 1880 manuscript population
        and agricultural census schedules provide the basis for Jordan's
        description of German immigrant settlement in south-central Texas.
        By comparing German agricultural practices in selected eastern

counties (Cotton Kingdom) and western counties (rim of the desert) with southern Anglo-American and Negro agricultural practices, Jordan evaluates the degree of assimilation experienced by the largest group of nineteenth-century European immigrant farmers in Texas.

19-10 _____. "Population Origins in Texas, 1850." GEOGRAPHICAL REVIEW 59 (January 1969): 83-103. Maps, tables, notes.

Based on the 1850 manuscript census schedules, Jordan plots by county the origins of Texas' population according to state, racial, and national nativity (lower and upper southerners, northerners, Negroes, Spanish, French, German, and other Europeans). A composite map is presented in "ANNALS Map Supplement Number Thirteen: Population Origin Groups in Rural Texas," AAG ANNALS 60 (June 1970): 404-5. More detailed studies of population origins and related cultural, economic, and political characteristics are discussed in "The Imprint of the Upper and Lower South on Mid-Nineteenth-Century Texas," AAG ANNALS 57 (December 1967): 667-90 (reprinted in entry 12-33); and "The Texan Appalachia," AAG ANNALS 60 (September 1970): 409-27.

19-11 Luebke, Frederick C. ETHNICITY ON THE GREAT PLAINS. Lincoln: University of Nebraska Press, 1980. xxxiii, 237 p. Maps, photos., diagrs., tables, notes, index.

The ethnic diversity of the Great Plains population and its interaction with the environment provided the focus for this interdisciplinary symposium sponsored by the Center for Great Plains Studies. Papers of geographic interest include Kathleen Neils Conzen, "Historical Approaches to the Study of Rural Ethnic Communities," pp. 1-18; Robert C. Ostergren, "Prairie Bound: Migration Patterns to a Swedish Settlement on the Dakota Frontier," pp. 73-91; Terry G. Jordan, "A Religious Geography of the Hill County Germans of Texas," pp. 109-28; and Bradley H. Baltensperger, "Agricultural Change Among Nebraska Immigrants, 1880-1900," pp. 170-89.

19-12 Meinig, Donald W. "The Mormon Culture Region: Strategies and Patterns in the Geography of the American West, 1847-1964." AAG ANNALS 55 (June 1965): 191-220. Maps, photo., notes.

In reviewing the development and expansion of the Mormon culture region in Utah since the middle of the nineteenth century, Meinig introduces the concept of core, domain, and sphere as a means of describing the intensity, extent, and boundaries of a culture region.

19-13 Meyer, Douglas K. "Southern Illinois Migration Fields: The Shawnee

Hills in 1850." PROFESSIONAL GEOGRAPHER 28 (May 1976): 151-60. Maps, tables, notes.

Utilizing 1850 manuscript census schedules for eleven counties in southern Illinois, Meyer confirms that the predominant source region for migration to this area was the Upland South (Kentucky, Tennessee, Virginia, and North Carolina). Other articles by Meyer pertaining to population and cultural origins in Illinois are "Diffusion of Upland Folk Housing to the Shawnee Hills of Southern Illinois," PIONEER AMERICA 7 (July 1975): 56-66; "Native-Born Immigrant Clusters on the Illinois Frontier," AAG PROCEEDINGS 8 (1976): 41-46; "Illinois Culture Regions at Mid-Nineteenth Century," BULLETIN ILLINOIS GEOGRAPHICAL SOCIETY 18 (Fall 1976): 3-13; and "Types of Farming on the Illinois Frontier," BULLETIN ILLINOIS GEOGRAPHICAL SOCIETY 21 (Spring 1979): 9-17.

19-14 Nostrand, Richard L. "Mexican Americans Circa 1850." AAG ANNALS 65 (September 1975): 378-90. Maps, tables, notes.

Nostrand reconstructs Mexican-American population patterns in California, New Mexico Territory, and Texas for the mid-nineteenth century, in order to establish a datum plane representing the extent of Hispanic settlement at the beginning of American political dominance of the Southwest. His major source was the 1850 manuscript census schedules. Nostrand uses the 1900 manuscript census schedules in another major study, "The Hispano Homeland in 1900," AAG ANNALS 70 (September 1980): 382-96. Other articles by Nostrand pertaining to Mexican-Americans in the Southwest include "The Hispanic-American Borderland: Delimitation of an American Culture Region," AAG ANNALS 60 (December 1970): 638-61; and "'Mexican American' and 'Chicano': Emerging Terms for a People Coming of Age," PACIFIC HISTORICAL REVIEW 42 (August 1973): 389-406.

19-15 Ostergren, Robert. "A Community Transplanted: The Formative Experience of a Swedish Immigrant Community in the Upper Middle West." JOURNAL OF HISTORICAL GEOGRAPHY 5 (April 1979): 189-212. Maps, diagrs., tables, notes.

By examining data from parish registers, tax rolls, land records, and census materials dating from 1840 to 1910, Ostergren traces the migration of approximately eighty-five households from the Swedish parish of Rattuik to Isanti County, Minnesota. The cultural elements that were most readily transplanted were those related to social organization which was influenced by strong church, village, and kinship linkages. Socioeconomic structures were transplanted to some extent, but economic activities had to be adjusted to the new environment. Ostergren also discusses Swedish migration to Minnesota in "Cultural Homogeneity and Population Stability among Swedish Immigrants in Chicago County," MINNESOTA HISTORY 43 (Fall 1973): 255-69. See also entry 19-16.

19-16 Rice, John C. PATTERNS OF ETHNICITY IN A MINNESOTA COUNTY, 1880-1905. Geographical Reports, No. 4. Umeo, Sweden: University of Umeo, Geography Department, 1973. 98 p. Maps, tables, diagrs., notes.

The spatial clustering of national, provincial and parochial groups (primarily Swedish but also Norwegian and Dutch) is investigated for six townships in Kandiyohi County, central Minnesota during the last half of the nineteenth century. The effect of the land alienation process on these settlement patterns is discussed in "The Effect of Land Alienation on Settlement," AAG ANNALS 68 (March 1978): 61-72. The agricultural practices of these different cultural groups are reviewed in "The Role of Culture and Community in Frontier Prairie Farming," JOURNAL OF HIS-TORICAL GEOGRAPHY 3 (April 1977): 155-75 (also reprinted in entry 12-33). The major sources for these three studies are federal and state censuses, church registers, land ownership records (cadastral maps and tract books), and local histories. A more general treatment of the migration process, using examples from west central Sweden, is found in Rice and Robert C. Ostergren, "The Decision to Emigrate: A Study in Diffusion," GEOGRAFISKA ANNALER, Series B, 60 B (1978): 1-15. See also 19-15.

19-17 Sutherland, Stella H. POPULATION DISTRIBUTION IN COLONIAL AMERICA. New York: Columbia University Press, 1936. Reprint. New York: AMS Press, 1966. xxxii, 353 p. Maps, tables, notes, bibliog., index.

Population distribution in the thirteen colonies during the pre-revolutionary era (1771-76) is shown on three population dot maps and discussed in relation to soil fertility and topography, racial and national origins, and economic activity. Population distributions were reconstructed from colony and county censuses and tax lists as near to 1775 as possible. The variety of sources used in this reconstruction are discussed in the text.

C. CULTURAL LANDSCAPES AND RURAL SETTLEMENT FEATURES

19-18 Denecke, Dietrich. [The Multifunctional settlement with functional relations fields outside the settlement in eastern North America in the eighteenth and nineteenth centuries. Origins, planning and development of independence upon the type and state of development of the spatial settlement pattern]. FRANKFURTER WIRTSCHAFTS-UND SOZIALGEOGRAPHISCHEN SCHRIFTEN 28 (1978): 141-69. Maps, table, notes.

While the eighteenth- and nineteenth-century development of group (town and village) and individual settlement forms in the eastern United States is the focus of this study, Denecke also examines the development of other settlement features (central places and land ownership patterns) in the Middle Colonies (Virginia, Maryland, and Pennsylvania) and New England in the following articles: [Processes of the development and locational displacement of the central places in areas of high instability of spatial-functional structure. Virginia and Maryland from the beginning colonization to today], MARBURGER GEOGRAPHISCHE SCHRIFTEN 66 (1976): 175-200, and [Tradition and adjustment of the organization of area and settlement formation in the process of settlement of eastern North America during the seventeenth and eighteenth centuries. A contribution to the problem of formgiving processes and process regulators], 40 DEUTSCHER GEOGRAPHEN-TAG INNSBRUCK. TAGUNGSBERICHT UND WISSENSCHAFT-LICHE ABHANDLUNGEN (Wiesbaden: Franz Steiner, 1975), pp. 228-55. Although published in German, these articles provide significant insights into eighteenth and nineteenth-century settlement patterns.

19-19 Fly, La Barbara Wigfall, and Fly, Everett L. BLACK SETTLEMENTS IN AMERICA. Austin, Tex.: Entourage, Inc., 1980. 10 p. Maps, diagrs.,

The historical development of black settlements from 1865 to the present is documented in ten detailed posters.

19-20 Francaviglia, Richard V. THE MORMON LANDSCAPE: EXISTENCE, CREATION, AND PERCEPTION OF A UNIQUE IMAGE IN THE AMERI-CAN WEST. New York: AMS Press, 1978. xviii, 177 p. Maps, illus., photos., diagrs., notes, bibliog., index.

In examining the role of the Mormons in creating a distinctive landscape in the West, Francaviglia describes the landscape associated with the rural-village Mormon settlement, explains how these elements vary over space and time, and discusses the primary factors in creating such a landscape. See also "The Passing Mormon Village," LANDSCAPE 22 (Spring 1978): 40-47; "Mormon Central-Hall Houses in the American West," AAG ANNALS 61 (March 1971): 65-71; and "The Mormon Landscape: Definition of an Image in the American West," AAG PROCEED-INGS 2 (1970): 59-61.

19-21 Gerlach, Russel L. IMMIGRANTS IN THE OZARKS: A STUDY IN ETH-NIC GEOGRAPHY. Columbia: University of Missouri Press, 1976. xiv, 206 p. Maps, photos., diargs., tables, notes, bibliog., index.

In studying the immigrant experience in the Ozark Highland region of Missouri, Gerlach focuses on the landscape imprint of various ethnic groups (French, Spanish, American, German with special attention to the Amish and Mennonite religious groups, and other small concentrations of Europeans including Swedish, Swiss, Polish, and Italian). Besides reviewing the settlement history, he examines the rural landscape with emphasis on contemporary agricultural and settlement patterns but with some attention to their evolution. His sources include the 1860 to 1880 manuscript census schedules, secondary historical accounts, interviews, and field mapping.

19-22 Glassie, Henry. FOLK HOUSING IN MIDDLE VIRGINIA: A STRUC-
TURAL ANALYSIS OF HISTORIC ARTIFACTS. Knoxville: University of
Tennessee Press, 1975. xiv, 231 p. Maps, illus., photos., notes,
bibliog., index.

Although the primary focus of this study is a structural analysis
of the house architecture in a small area in Louisa and Gooch-
land Counties, folklorist Glassie strongly supports the use of
artifacts (as opposed to written documents) to study the cultural
history of the common man. In particular, Glassie is interested
in interpreting the mind of the folk builder. He indicates that
his sample area is representative of a larger region that encom-
passes most of the Virginia Piedmont and Tidewater. Glassie,
whose methodology relies heavily on cultural geography, architectural history,and archaeology, studies a wider range of artifacts in the context of three broad material culture regions in
the eastern United States (North, Mid-Atlantic, and South) in
an earlier study, PATTERNS IN THE MATERIAL FOLK CULTURE
OF THE EASTERN UNITED STATES (Philadelphia: University of
Pennsylvania Press, 1968).

19-23 Isaac, Rhys. "Order and Growth, Authority and Meaning in Colonial New
England." AMERICAN HISTORICAL REVIEW 76 (June 1971): 728-37.
Notes.

In this review essay, Isaac reviews four historical studies of co-
lonial New England. Three of these are based on the demographic
and social reconstruction of individual communities: John Demos,
A LITTLE COMMONWEALTH: FAMILY LIFE IN PLYMOUTH
COLONY (New York: Oxford University Press, 1970); Philip
J. Greven, Jr., FOUR GENERATIONS: POPULATION, LAND
AND FAMILY IN COLONIAL ANDOVER, MASSACHUSETTS
(Ithaca, N.Y.: Cornell University Press, 1970); and Kenneth A.
Lockridge, A NEW ENGLAND TOWN: THE FIRST HUNDRED
YEARS, DEDHAM, MASSACHUSETTS, 1636-1736 (New York:
W. W. Norton, 1970). Although spatial relationships and set-
tlement patterns are not emphasized, two authors discuss land-
holdings: Greven, "Old Patterns in the New World: The Distribution of Land in Seventeenth-Century Andover," ESSEX IN-
STITUTE HISTORICAL COLLECTIONS 101 (April 1965): 133-48
(reprinted in entry 12-33); and Lockridge, "Land, Population
and the Evolution of New England Society, 1630-1790," PAST
AND PRESENT, no. 39 (April 1968), pp. 62-80 (reprinted in
entry 20-13). Demos's, Greven's, and Lockridge's microstudies
as well as several earlier New England town studies are reviewed
by John M. Bumsted and James T. Lemon in "New Approaches
in Early American Studies: The Local Community in New England,"
SOCIAL HISTORY: A CANADIAN REVIEW 2 (1968): 98-112.

19-24   Jackson, John B. AMERICAN SPACE: THE CENTENNIAL YEARS, 1865–
1876. New York: W.W. Norton & Co., 1972. 254 p. Maps, illus.,
bibliog., index.

Jackson, a highly articulate interpreter and critic of the American landscape, presents a series of essays that examine the
major landscape changes that occurred in the decade following
the Civil War up the American centennial. He focuses on seven
regions (Northwest, Midwest, New England, South, Plains,
California, and New York) emphasizing particular landscape
changes associated with those regions. Jackson, who views
landscape as the cumulative expression of social values and
cultural patterns, has written extensively on the American landscape; some of his writings appear in LANDSCAPE: SELECTED
WRITINGS OF JOHN B. JACKSON, edited by Ervin Zube
(Amherst: University of Massachusetts Press, 1970), and THE
NECESSITY FOR RUINS (Amherst: University of Massachusetts
Press, 1980). See also entries 19-27 and 19-28.

19-25   Jordan, Terry G. TEXAS LOG BUILDINGS: A FOLK ARCHITECTURE.
Austin: University of Texas Press, 1978. x, 230 p. Maps, illus.,
photos., notes, bibliog., index.

Jordan maps the location of various structural elements of Texas
log buildings in order to analyze the interaction of various
cultural groups with different physical environments. Log-culture
regions within Texas are delimited in the final chapter. The research is based on the Texas Log Cabin register, a collection of
notes, photographs, and sketches compiled by various field workers
under Jordan's direction and housed in the Archives of North
Texas State University. While Jordan discusses log construction
in "Log Timbering in Texas," PIONEER AMERICA 8 (January
1976): 8-18, he explores the European origins of log architecture
in "Alpine, Alemannic, and American Log Architecture," AAG
ANNALS 70 (June 1980): 154-80. An explanation of the origins of log houses in Louisiana is presented by Milton B. Newton, Jr., and Linda Pulliam-DiNapoli in "Log Houses as Public
Occasions: A Historical Theory," AAG ANNALS 67 (September
1977): 360-83.

19-26   Kniffen, Fred B. "Folk Housing: Key to Diffusion." AAG ANNALS
55 (December 1965): 549-77. Maps, photos., illus., notes.

Originally presented as an address as honorary president of the
Association of American Geographers, this article demonstrates
the use of folk housing (primarily house and barn types) in mapping the broad patterns of westward migration and cultural diffusion from the initial settlements on the Atlantic Seaboard
(New England, Middle Atlantic, and Lower Chesapeake) throughout the eastern half of the United States (Midwest, Upland South,
and Tidewater South). See also Kniffen and Henry Glassie,

"Building in Wood in the Eastern United States: A Time Place Perspective," GEOGRAPHICAL REVIEW 56 (January 1966): 40-66. Kniffen's numerous publications on settlement geography and material folk culture are listed by Gene Wilhelm in "Publications of Professor Fred B. Kniffen," PIONEER AMERICA 5 (January 1973): 16-22. In a more recent article, Kniffen discusses the settlement of the southwestern Louisiana prairies in "Material Culture in the Geographic Interpretation of the Landscape," in THE HUMAN MIRROR: MATERIAL AND SPATIAL IMAGES OF MAN, edited by Miles Richardson, pp. 252-67 (Baton Rouge: Louisiana State University Press, 1974).

19-27 LANDSCAPE. Vols. 1-17, edited by J.B. Jackson. Santa Fe, N.M.: n.p., 1951-68. Vol. 18-- , edited by Blair Boyd. Berkeley, Calif.: n.p., 1969--. Three issues per year.

Originally subtitled MAGAZINE OF HUMAN GEOGRAPHY, this publication was founded by J. B. Jackson with a focus on the human geography of the Southwest. It now addresses a wider audience of environmentalists (landscape architects, geographers, architects, city and regional planners, industrial designers, biologists, and conservationists) with an emphasis on the man-made environment in general. Selected articles of historical and geographical interest include: James Borchert, "Alley Landscapes of Washington," 23, no. 3 (1979): 3-10; Alvar W. Carlson, "Designating Historic Rural Areas: A Survey of Northwestern Ohio Barns," 22 (Summer 1978): 29-33; Karl B. Raitz, "The Barns of Barren County [Ky.]," 22 (Spring 1978): 19-26; Richard V. Francaviglia, "Main Street USA: The Creation of a Popular Image," 21 (Spring-Summer 1977): 18-22; Carl O. Sauer, "Homestead and Community on the Middle Border," 20 (Winter 1976): 44-47; Karl B. Raitz, "The Wisconsin Tobacco Shed: A Key to Ethnic Settlement and Diffusion," 20 (October 1975): 32-37; Ronald Rees, "The Scenery Cult: Changing Landscape Tastes over Three Centuries," 19 (May 1975): 39-47; Peirce F. Lewis, "Common Houses, Cultural Spoor," 19 (January 1975): 1-22 (diffusion of house types); and John W. Reps, "Downing and the Washington Mall," 16 (Spring 1967): 6-11.

19-28 Meinig, Donald W., ed. THE INTERPRETATION OF ORDINARY LANDSCAPES: GEOGRAPHICAL ESSAYS. New York: Oxford University Press, 1979. viii, 255 p. Paper. Photos., notes, index.

Nine essays, two that were previously published and seven that were presented at a series of public lectures at Syracuse University, discuss the complexity of landscape analysis and interpretation. A common theme is that landscape, as an accumulation of artifacts, is worthy of historical study (in the tradition of W.G. Hoskins) by determining the cultural processes that have produced these ordinary, everyday landscapes. Meinig contributed three essays, while the remainder were presented by Peirce

F. Lewis, Marwyn S. Samuels, Yi-Fu Tuan, David Lowenthal, David E. Sopher, and J. B. Jackson. Meinig's concluding essay provides an appreciation of the work of W.G. Hoskins and J.B. Jackson, the two foremost students of landscape study in England and America.

19-29 Miller, E. Joan Wilson. "The Ozark Culture Region as Revealed by Traditional Materials." AAG ANNALS 58 (March 1968): 51-77. Maps, diagr., tables, notes.

Miller uses oral folk materials (folk tales, folk speech, and superstitions) to document the settlement process and to define a distinct cultural region in the Ozarks of Missouri and Arkansas. These oral traditions also reveal evidence of man's use and organization of the habitat. Miller examines place names (toponyms) as part of the cultural process in "The Naming of the Land in the Arkansas Ozarks: A Study in Culture Processes," AAG ANNALS 59 (June 1969): 240-51.

19-30 Newton, Milton B., Jr. "Route Geography and the Routes of St. Helena Parish, Louisiana." AAG ANNALS 60 (March 1970): 134-52. Maps, photos., diagrs., notes.

The route system of St. Helena Parish is examined as a cultural landform representing a complex summary of the numerous factors (physical, cultural, historical, political, and economic) producing the landscape. Relic roads in an adjacent parish are examined by Newton and Raphael C. Nicholas in "Relic Roads of East Feliciana Parish, Louisiana," GEOGRAPHICAL REVIEW 61 (April 1971): 250-64. Newton describes the development of Negro and white settlement patterns in St. Helena Parish in "Settlement Patterns as Artifacts of Social Structure," in THE HUMAN MIRROR: MATERIAL AND SPATIAL IMAGES OF MAN, edited by Miles Richardson, pp. 339-61 (Baton Rouge: Louisiana State University Press, 1974).

19-31 Pillsbury, Richard. "The Urban Street Pattern as a Culture Indicator: Pennsylvania, 1682-1815." AAG ANNALS 60 (September 1970): 428-46. Maps, table, notes.

Urban street patterns are used as indicators of the Pennsylvania culture area. After examining the introduction and diffusion of four morphological types, Pillsbury concludes that their distributions were determined by culture rather than by physical or economic considerations. Comments by Michael P. Conzen are printed in AAG ANNALS 61: 204-13. Other articles by Pillsbury pertaining to the Pennsylvania culture area include "Urban Street Patterns and Topography: A Pennsylvania Case Study," PROFESSIONAL GEOGRAPHER 22 (January 1970): 21-25; "The Religious Geography of Pennsylvania: A Factor Analytic Approach," AAG PROCEEDINGS 3 (1971): 130-34; "The Con-

struction Materials of the Rural Folk Housing of the Pennsylvania Culture Region," PIONEER AMERICA 8 (July 1976): 98-
106; and "Patterns in the Folk and Vernacular House Forms of
the Pennsylvania Culture Region," PIONEER AMERICA 9 (Janaury
1977): 12-29.

19-32 PIONEER AMERICA, THE JOURNAL OF HISTORIC AMERICAN MATERIAL
CULTURE. Vols. 1-18, 1969-76. Falls Church, Va.: Pioneer America
Society. Vol. 9-- . Baton Rouge: Louisiana State University, Depart-
ment of Geography and Anthropology, 1977-- . Biannual.

Founded as the journal of the Pioneer America Society, an organization with a strong regional orientation (Potomac Valley
and the Middle Atlantic States), this publication continues to
emphasize material culture, vernacular architecture, and cultural landscape studies in the tradition of Fred Kniffen and Henry
Glassie. Articles by geographers include Marshall Bowen,
"Migration to and from a Northern Wyoming Mormon Community
1900-1975," 9 (July 1977): 208-27; Robert W. Bastian, "Indiana Folk Architecture: A Lower Midwestern Index," 9 (July
1977): 115-36; Allen G. Noble, "Barns as Elements in the
Settlement Landscape of Ohio," 9 (January 1977): 62-79;
Robert L. Janiskee, "City Trouble, the Pastoral Retreat, and
Pioneer America: A Rationale for Rescuing the Middle Land-
scape," 8 (January 1976): 1-7; Peirce F. Lewis, "The Future
of the Past: Our Clouded Vision of Historic Preservation," 7
(July 1975): 1-20; Fred B. Kniffen, "Milestones and Stumbling
Blocks," 7 (January 1975): 1-8; Albert J. Larson, "Northern Il-
linois as New England Extended: A Preliminary Report," 7 (Jan-
uary 1975): 45-51; Allen G. Noble, "Barns and Square Silos in
Northeast Ohio," 6 (July 1974): 12-21; Terry G. Jordan,
"Evolution of the American Windmill: A Study in Diffusion and
Modification," 5 (July 1973): 3-12; Gene Wilhelm, "Pioneer
Boats and Transportation on the Upper James River," 3 (January
1971): 39-47; and Kniffen, "On Corner-Timbering," 1 (Jan-
uary 1969): 1-8.

19-33 Wacker, Peter O. LAND AND PEOPLE, A CULTURAL GEOGRAPHY
OF PREINDUSTRIAL NEW JERSEY: ORIGINS AND SETTLEMENT PAT-
TERNS. New Brunswick, N.J.: Rutgers University Press, 1975. xx,
499 p. Maps, tables, notes, bibliog., index.

The cultural geography of New Jersey during the colonial period
and the immediate post-colonial period ending about 1820 is
reconstructed in this study. New Jersey, which was transitional
between the southeast Pennsylvania and New England culture
hearths, had one of the most culturally diverse populations of
the colonies, with distinct contrasts in the regional concentrations of some of the cultural groups. Themes that Wacker discusses include the natural and Indian-altered landscape, the
cultural origins and changing distribution of various European
and African groups, and land subdivision and settlement patterns.

Besides those works listed in entries 12-6, 12-14, 19-34, and 19-35, other presentations by Wacker pertaining to the cultural geography of New Jersey include "Folk Architecture as an Indicator of Culture Areas and Culture Diffusion: Dutch Barns and Barracks in New Jersey," PIONEER AMERICA 5 (July 1973): 37-47; and "The Changing Geography of the Black Population of New Jersey, 1810-1860: A Preliminary View," AAG PROCEEDINGS 3 (1971): 174-78. See also Wacker and Roger T. Trindell, "The Log House in New Jersey: Origins and Diffusion," KEYSTONE FOLKLORE QUARTERLY 14 (Winter 1969): 248-68.

19-34 _____. THE MUSCONETCONG VALLEY OF NEW JERSEY: A HISTORICAL GEOGRAPHY. New Brunswick, N.J.: Rutgers University Press, 1968. xi, 207 p. Maps, illus., photos., tables, notes, bibliog., index.

The changing cultural landscape of one watershed in northern New Jersey is studied from aboriginal occupation until the end of the eighteenth century. Individual topics include physical geography, aboriginal occupance, the settlement process (landownership patterns and population origins), agriculture, pioneer farmstead (house and barn types), charcoal iron industry, and villages, market and transportation.

19-35 Walker, H.J., and Haage, W.G., eds. MAN AND CULTURAL HERITAGE: PAPERS IN HONOR OF FRED B. KNIFFEN. Geoscience and Man, vol. 5. Baton Rouge: Louisiana State University, 1974. vii, 235 p. Maps, illus., photos., tables, diagrs., notes.

Fifteen essays, which reflect the type of research Kniffen enjoyed (cultural landscapes, settlement features, and house types), were prepared by former students and associates. The essays pertaining to historical-cultural patterns in the United States include: Theodore W. Kury, "Iron and Settlement: The New York-New Jersey Highlands in the Eighteenth Century," pp. 7-23; Eugene M. Wilson, "Form Changes in Folk Houses," pp. 65-71 (northern Alabama); John Fraser Hart, "The Spread of the Frontier and the Growth of Population," pp. 73-81; Alan K. Craig and Christopher S. Peebles, "Ethnoecologic Change among the Seminoles, 1740-1840," pp. 83-96 (Florida); Milton Newton, "Cultural Preadaptation and the Upland South," pp. 143-54; Hubert G. H. Wilhelm, "The Pennsylvania-Dutch Barn in Southeastern Ohio," pp. 155-62; Peter O. Wacker, "Traditional House and Barn Types in New Jersey: Keys to Acculturation, Past Cultureographic Regions, and Settlement History," pp. 163-76; and Henry Glassie, "The Variation of Concepts within Tradition: Barn Building in Ostego County, New York," pp. 177-235. Most of the other articles pertain to Latin America. Each essay is accompanied by a list of pertinent references.

Chapter 20

PHYSICAL ENVIRONMENT

Although past historical studies dealing with the physical environment have been associated with environmental determinism, recent literature on this topic has taken new approaches. In this chapter three themes are emphasized: man's perception and creation of images about the physical environment; man's evaluation, use, and abuse of the physical environment; and the use of documentary sources to reconstruct past physical landscapes and/or processes.

A. ENVIRONMENTAL PERCEPTION

20-1   Allen, John L. "Division of the Waters: Changing Concepts of the Continental Divide, 1804-44." JOURNAL OF HISTORICAL GEOGRAPHY 4 (October 1978): 357-70. Maps, notes.

Allen traces the changing conceptual geography of the drainage systems of the western United States during the first half of the nineteenth century by reviewing explorers' and fur traders' accounts and related maps beginning with the explorations of Lewis and Clark and ending with John C. Fremont. This perception, which was closely related to the desire to find a commercial route across the continent, started with a symmetrical or common source region, but as more accurate knowledge was obtained, developed into the concept of a linear continental divide. A similar article by Allen is listed in entry 20-9.

20-2   Bowden, Martyn J. "The Great American Desert and the American Frontier, 1800-1882; Popular Images of the Plains." In ANONYMOUS AMERICANS: EXPLORATIONS IN NINETEENTH-CENTURY SOCIAL HISTORY, edited by Tamara Hareven, pp. 48-79. Englewood Cliffs, N.J.: Prentice-Hall, 1971. Illus., tables, notes.

Bowden examined geographies and school textbooks (1800-1882), Vermont newspapers (1849-51), letters and manuscript diaries (1843-54), and travelers' and explorers' accounts to reconstruct the various conceptions of the western interior held by the American public. He found that before 1850, a desert image of the

Great Plains may have existed in the minds of some northeastern
elites, but it was not a concept shared by the common folk who
were migrating through this area. Rather, the legend of a pre-
1850 desert image was created in the histories of the 1870s.
Bowden also discusses this thesis in an essay printed in entry
20-9 as well as in "The Perception of the Western Interior of
the United States, 1800-1870," AAG PROCEEDINGS 1 (1969):
16-21. See also Bowden, "Desertification of the Great Plains:
Will it Happen?" ECONOMIC GEOGRAPHY 53 (October
1977): 397-406.

20-3   Earle, Carville. "Environment, Disease, and Mortality in Early Virginia."
        JOURNAL OF HISTORICAL GEOGRAPHY 5 (October 1979): 365-90.
        Maps, tables, notes.

        Concentrating on the early English settlement of Jamestown be-
        tween 1607 and 1624, Earle shows how seasonal changes in the
        estuarine environment (the fresh-salt transition in the James
        River) and the Virginia Company's misunderstanding of these
        changes contributed to death from waterborn diseases.

20-4   Huth, Hans. NATURE AND THE AMERICAN: THREE CENTURIES OF
        CHANGING ATTITUDES. Berkeley and Los Angeles: University of
        California Press, 1957. Reprint. Lincoln: University of Nebraska
        Press, 1972. xvii, 250 p. Paper. Illus., photos., notes, bibliog.,
        index.

        Americans' changing attitudes toward nature are recorded in this
        history. Beginning with the wasteful practices of the colonial
        and frontier eras, Huth traces the basic developments that led
        to the conservation movement at the end of the nineteenth and
        the beginning of the twentieth centuries, including the creation
        of national and city parks. A selection of sixty-four paintings
        and photographs of landscape scenes emphasize the Americans'
        appreciation and recreational use of nature.

20-5   Jackson, Richard H. "Mormon Perception and Settlement." AAG AN-
        NALS 68 (September 1978): 317-34. Maps, notes.

        Jackson examines the role of the Mormon leaders' environmental
        perception in directing the location of Mormon settlements into
        the arid southern portion of the Great Basin. Since the Mormon
        elite believed the northern areas were too cold for agriculture,
        they had to convince the settlers that the desert could be trans-
        formed through irrigation. The research is based on official
        church accounts and settlers' diaries. Other articles by Jackson
        on the Mormons' environmental perception are: "Myth and
        Reality: Environmental Perception of the Mormon Pioneers,"
        ROCKY MOUNTAIN SOCIAL SCIENCE JOURNAL 9 (January
        1972): 33-38, and "Righteousness and Environmental Change:
        The Mormons and the Environment of the West," in ESSAYS

ON THE AMERICAN WEST, 1973-74, Charles Redd Monographs in Western History, no. 5, pp. 21-42 (Provo, Utah: Brigham Young University Press, 1975). For a discussion of Mormon settlement patterns see Jackson and Robert L. Layton, "The Mormon Village: Analysis of a Settlement Type," PROFESSIONAL GEOGRAPHER 28 (May 1976): 136-41.

20-6   Kovacik, Charles F., and Rowland, Lawrence S. "Images of Colonial Port Royal, South Carolina." AAG ANNALS 63 (September 1973): 331-40. Map, table, notes.

The changing perception of the deep-water sound and numerous waterways of Port Royal, South Carolina, are considered in terms of the evolving settlement framework. Early explorers perceived the waterways as an advantage for the development of a major port, while the early settlers perceived the waterways as an obstacle which led to isolation, political fragmentation, and military insecurity.

20-7   Lewis, G. Malcolm. "William Gilpin and the Concept of the Great Plains Region." AAG ANNALS 56 (March 1966): 33-51. Maps, notes.

Lewis examines the role of William Gilpin, first governor of Colorado Territory, in the formation of the regional concept of the Great Plains, which developed during the middle of the nineteenth century. Gilpin, as an early traveler and resident in the trans-Mississippi West, promoted the region as a positive area for settlement and not as an uninhabited desert. Other articles by Lewis pertaining to the images of the plains include "Regional Ideas and Reality in the Cis-Rocky Mountain West," TRANSACTIONS OF THE INSTITUTE OF BRITISH GEOGRAPHERS 38 (1966): 135-50; "Three Centuries of Desert Concepts of the Cis-Rocky Mountain West," JOURNAL OF THE WEST 4 (July 1965): 457-68; "Early American Exploration and the Cis-Rocky Mountain Desert, 1803-1823," GREAT PLAINS JOURNAL 5 (Fall 1965): 1-11; and "Changing Emphases in the Description of the Natural Environment of the American Great Plains Area," TRANSACTIONS OF THE INSTITUTE OF BRITISH GEOGRAPHERS 30 (1962): 75-90.

20-8   Lowenthal, David. "The Bicentennial Landscape: A Mirror Held Up to the Past." GEOGRAPHICAL REVIEW 67 (July 1977): 253-67. Notes.

Using the Bicentennial celebration as a point of departure, Lowenthal reflects on Americans' changing attitudes toward artifacts and past landscapes. He also discusses the changing perception of the American landscape in "The American Scene," GEOGRAPHICAL REVIEW 58 (January 1968): 61-88 (reproduced in entry 12-33). Also see 20-9.

20-9 Lowenthal, David, and Bowden, Martyn J., eds. GEOGRAPHIES OF
THE MIND: ESSAYS IN HISTORICAL GEOSOPHY IN HONOR OF
JOHN KIRTLAND WRIGHT. New York: Oxford University Press, 1975.
263 p. Maps, illus., tables, noted, index.

The essays presented in this volume were prepared by students,
friends, and colleagues of John K. Wright and reflect his wide-
ranging interests in the study of geographic knowledge. Selections pertaining to environmental perception and related behavior
include John L. Allen, "Lands of Myth, Waters of Wonder: The
Place of the Imagination in the History of Geographic Exploration," pp. 41-61; David Lowenthal, "The Place of the Past in
the American Landscape," pp. 89-117; Martyn J. Bowden, "The
Great American Desert in the American Minds: The Historiog-
raphy of a Geographical Notion," pp. 119-47; and Wilbur
Zelinsky, "Unearthly Delights: Cemetery Names and the Map
of the Changing American Afterward," pp. 171-95. A list of
Wright's publications is included.

20-10 Nash, Roderick. WILDERNESS AND THE AMERICAN MIND. New Haven:
Yale University Press, 1967. ix, 256 p. Notes, bibliog., index.

The intellectual origins and development of the wilderness concept in the American mind are explored in this study. Specific
themes include the romantic and national concepts of wilderness, the beginnings of the preservation movement, and the role
of prominent individuals (Henry Thoreau, John Muir, and Aldo
Leopold) and significant events (the beginnings of the national
park system with the creation of Yellowstone National Park, and
the establishment of the National Wilderness Preservation System)
in the development of the preservation movement.

20-11 Owings, Loren C., ed. ENVIRONMENTAL VALUES, 1860-1972: A
GUIDE TO INFORMATION SOURCES. Man and the Environment Information Guide Series, vol. 4. Detroit: Gale Research Co., 1976. xii,
324 pp. Index.

The historical development of attitudes toward and the concern
for nature provides the general theme for this annotated bibliography. Selected categories of entries include travel reports on
scenery, American landscape painting, conservation and the
preservation of natural beauty, the idea of wilderness, and the
development of an environmental ethic.

20-12 Peters, Bernard C. "Early Perception of a High Plain in Michigan." AAG
ANNALS 62 (March 1972): 57-60. Notes.

The depiction of a "high plain" on early maps of Michigan was
based on early travelers' perception of a change in vegetation
rather than a change in landforms. Comments by John W. Pawl-
ing are printed in AAG ANNALS 62 (December 1972): 733-39.

For other articles by Peters pertaining to early images of Michigan, see entry 12-9 and "Oak Openings or Barrens: Landscape Evaluation on the Michigan Frontier," AAG PROCEEDINGS 4 (1972): 84-86.

20-13 Rosenkrantz, Barbara G., and Koelsch, William A., eds. AMERICAN HABITAT: A HISTORICAL PERSPECTIVE. New York: Free Press, 1973. xi, 372 p. Maps, illus., diagrs., notes, index.

This collection of previously published essays illustrates various themes in the history of the American perception of the environment. The organizational structure of the anthology focuses on the habitat of the American people as it was perceived, used, and valued.

20-14 Thompson, Kenneth. "Wilderness and Health in the Nineteenth Century." JOURNAL OF HISTORICAL GEOGRAPHY 2 (April 1976): 145-61. Notes.

The late nineteenth-century perception of the wilderness as a source of health (particularly as a cure for pulmonary tuberculosis) was helpful in changing pre-existing negative attitudes about the wilderness. Other articles by Thompson pertaining to the perceived relationships between environment and health in nineteenth-century California include "Negative Perception of Early California," CALIFORNIA GEOGRAPHER 18 (1978): 1-15; "Climatotheraphy in California," CALIFORNIA HISTORICAL QUARTERLY 50 (June 1971): 111-30; "The Australian Fever Tree in California: Eucalypts and Malarial Prophylaxis," AAG ANNALS 60 (June 1970): 230-44; "Irrigation as a Menace to Health in California: A Nineteenth Century View," GEOGRAPHICAL REVIEW 59 (April 1969): 195-214; and "Insalubrious California: Perception and Reality," AAG ANNALS 59 (March 1969): 50-64. The perception of agricultural resources in the Sacramento Valley is discussed by Thompson and Richard A. Eigenheer in "The Agricultural Promise of the Sacramento Valley: Some Early Views," JOURNAL OF THE WEST 18 (October 1979): 33-41, as well as by Thompson in "The Perception of the Agricultural Environment," AGRICULTURAL HISTORY 49 (January 1975): 230-37, and "Historic Flooding in the Sacramento Valley," PACIFIC HISTORICAL REVIEW 29 (November 1960): 349-60.

20-15 Tuan, Yi-Fu. TOPOPHILIA: A STUDY OF ENVIRONMENTAL PERCEPTION, ATTITUDES AND VALUES. Englewood Cliffs, N.J.: Prentice-Hall, 1974. x, 260 p. Maps, diagrs., notes, index.

In providing a general survey of environmental perception, attitudes, and values, Tuan defines topophilia as the effective bond between people and place or setting. Although this study is not intended to be historical, the definition of relevant concepts is useful for historical studies of environmental perception.

His examples are derived from various cultural and historical experiences, such as the contrast between the Spanish and Anglo attitudes in the exploration of the Southwest. Tuan also writes about environmental feelings in LANDSCAPES OF FEAR (New York: Pantheon Books, 1979).

B. MAN-LAND RELATIONS

20-16 Bahre, Conrad J., and Bradbury, David E. "Vegetation Change Along the Arizona-Sonora Boundary." AAG ANNALS 68 (June 1978): 145-65. Maps, photos., table, notes.

Photographs of boundary monuments in 1892, 1969, and 1972 are used to analyze vegetational change which was the result of culturally distinct land-use patterns along the United States-Mexican international boundary. The 1892 photographs depict the area before the boundary line was fenced and when land-use practices were relatively homogeneous on both sides of the boundary.

20-17 Birch, Brian P. "The Environment and Settlement of the Prairie-Woodland Transition Belt--A Case Study of Edwards County, Illinois." SOUTHAMPTON RESEARCH SERIES IN GEOGRAPHY 6 (1971): 3-31. Maps, tables, notes.

The land acquisition and settlement preferences of English pioneers in early nineteenth-century Edwards County, Illinois, show a predilection for prairie edge locations. Township survey plats and field notes were used to reconstruct woodland and prairie patterns at the time of initial white settlement. Other articles by Birch pertaining to this topic are listed in entries 14-25 and 14-30, as well as "Farmstead Settlement in the North American Corn Belt," SOUTHAMPTON RESEARCH SERIES IN GEOGRAPHY 3 (1966): 25-57.

20-18 Bridenbaugh, Carl. "Yankee Use and Abuse of the Forest in the Building of New England, 1620-1660." PROCEEDINGS OF THE MASSACHUSETTS HISTORICAL SOCIETY 89 (1977): 3-35. Notes.

Colonial historian Bridenbaugh reviews the various uses of timber in the early settlement of New England.

20-19 Denevan, William M. "Livestock Numbers in Nineteenth-Century New Mexico and the Problem of Gullying in the Southwest." AAG ANNALS 57 (December 1967): 691-703. Maps, notes.

An examination of livestock numbers (particularly sheep) in relation to vegetation cover and climate in the upper Rio Grande Valley during the nineteenth century provides a new perspective on the role of overgrazing in causing increased gullying during the 1880s.

20-20 Durrenberger, Robert W. ENVIRONMENT AND MAN: A BIBLIOGRAPHY. Palo Alto, Calif.: National Press Books, 1970. x, 118 p. Paper.

This alphabetical listing includes books and articles published primarily in the 1960s that discuss the relationship of man and environment. Although the subject index does not include a specific category for historical geography, items of historical interest may be found under such headings as agriculture, climatic change, conservation, environmental and landscape change, environmental perception, land use, population, settlement geography, and man-environment relations.

20-21 Fahl, Ronald J. NORTH AMERICAN FOREST AND CONSERVATION HISTORY: A BIBLIOGRAPHY. Santa Barbara, Calif.: Clio Press for Forest History Society, 1977. 408 p. Index.

Secondary works (forest industry trade journals, professional forestry journals, conservation magazines, government documents and reports, state and local histories, and doctoral dissertations and master's theses) pertaining to man's exploitation, utilization, and appreciation of forest resources in the United States and Canada are listed in this bibliography. The entries are arranged alphabetically by author and there is also a subject index.

20-22 Graf, William. "Mining and Channel Response." AAG ANNALS 69 (June 1979): 262-75. Maps, photos., diagrs., tables, notes.

This study in historical geomorphology uses a series of historical photographs to determine that man-induced vegetation changes were a contributing factor in the erosion of a valley floor and subsequent formation of gullies and arroyos in the Central City, Colorado, gold mining district, from 1864 to the present.

20-23 Jordan, Terry G. "Between the Forest and the Prairie." AGRICULTURAL HISTORY 38 (October 1964): 205-16. Maps, tables, notes.

A major theme in the settlement history of the midwestern United States is the selection of woodland over prairie environments as preferred settlement sites. In analyzing the settlement of twenty-four sites in the Old Northwest (Ohio, Indiana, Illinois, Michigan, and Wisconsin), Jordan finds that mixed woodland-prairie sites were the preferred choice of settlers with different origins (northerners, southerners, English, and Germans) during a wide time range (1817-48). This article is reprinted in entry 12-33. Another article by Jordan concerning vegetational perception and the choice of settlement sites in Texas is included in entry 12-6.

20-24 Knox, James C. "Human Impacts on Wisconsin Stream Channels." AAG ANNALS 67 (September 1977): 323-42. Maps, photo., diagrs., tables, notes.

Field notes and plats from the original 1832-33 township surveys are used to reconstruct the vegetative and hydrologic characteristics of the Platte River watershed in Grant County, Wisconsin. This reconstruction provides an initial datum point for studying the impact of land clearance and cultivation on erosion, sedimentation, and stream channel adjustments.

20-25 Kollmorgen, Walter M. "The Woodsman's Assaults on the Domain of the Cattleman." AAG ANNALS 59 (June 1969): 215-39. Maps, notes.

The land utilization of the Great Plains is examined in the context of the competing goals of the woodsman settlers coming from the East and the cattleman migrating northward from Texas. The land alienation laws, which favored the woodsman, were not based on the reality of the geographic environment. In order to adjust to this dilemma, the farmers attempted rainmaking (by tree planting), irrigation, and dry farming. This article is reproduced in entry 20-13.

20-26 McManis, Douglas R. THE INITIAL EVALUATION AND UTILIZATION OF THE ILLINOIS PRAIRIES, 1815-1840. Department of Geography Research Paper, No. 64. Chicago: University of Chicago, Department of Geography, 1964. x, 109 p. Paper. Maps, illus., tables, notes, bibliog.

McManis evaluates the hypothesis that prairies were initially considered a negative area for settlement by studying the settlement process on the Illinois prairies from 1815 to 1840. Contemporary written sources (travel accounts, diaries, family papers, and correspondence) are used to determine the early settlers' evaluation or perception of the prairies in terms of healthiness, availability of materials, suitability for agriculture and livestock, and accessibility to markets. In contrast, land entry tract books and field survey notes are used to determine when the wooded or prairie lands were sold while contemporary written accounts reflect how the prairies were utilized. He concludes that the initial settlement represented a period of trial and error with regard to the prairies, with early settlers often selecting sites that capitalized on both the woodland and prairie environments.

20-27 Olson, Sherry H. THE DEPLETION MYTH: A HISTORY OF RAILROAD USE OF TIMBER. Cambridge: Harvard University Press, 1971. xvi, 228 p. Maps, illus., photos., diagrs., tables, notes, index.

As a case study of the long-term changes in the pattern of use of one major natural resource, the focus of this study is the use of timber by the railroads from 1870 to the present. The major emphasis is the late nineteenth and early twentieth centuries when the concern for the depletion of forest resources coincided with the railroads' peak use of timber (primarily cross ties, but also bridges, railroad cars, telegraph lines, and accessory buildings). Her sources include publications of the railway engineering societies, the Association of American Railroads, and the U.S. Forest Service. The Burlington Northern Railroad is used as an example.

20-28 Parry, Martin L. CLIMATIC CHANGE, AGRICULTURE AND SETTLEMENT. Studies in Historical Geography. Folkestone, Kent: William Dawson and Sons; Hamden, Conn.: Archon Books, Shoe String Press, 1978. 214 p. Maps, illus., photos., diagrs., tables, notes, bibliog., index.

Despite the failure of studies from the 1920s to adequately assess the influence of climate on historical developments, this study focuses on the role of climatic change in the agricultural history of vulnerable areas. Although most of the examples are confined to Great Britain and Northwestern Europe, Parry does mention the United States, particularly the Great Plains. In developing the theme that agriculture and settlement in marginal areas are susceptible to long-term climatic changes, he discusses the process and chronology of climatic change and the significance of climatic change in terms of harvest yields, harvest failures, and the limits of agriculture.

20-29 Speth, William W. "Carl Ortwin Sauer on Destructive Exploitation." BIOLOGICAL CONSERVATION 11 (February 1977): 145-60. Notes.

Sauer's publications pertaining to the theme of destructive exploitation of the earth are reviewed in this essay.

20-30 Thomas, William L., Jr., ed. MAN'S ROLE IN CHANGING THE FACE OF THE EARTH. Chicago: University of Chicago Press, 1956. xxxviii, 1193 p. Maps, photos., diagrs., tables, notes, index.

This classic compendium of essays on man's role in changing his physical environment is the result of an international and inter-disciplinary symposium held in June 1955 at Princeton. The symposium was organized by Carl O. Sauer, Marston Bates, and Lewis Mumford and was funded by the Wenner-Gren Foundation for Anthropological Research and the National Science Foundation. The fifty-three contributions are grouped under three broad topics: "Retrospect," "Process," and "Prospect." Articles pertaining to man's impact on physical-biological environments in the historical-geographical context of the United States include James C. Malin, "The Grassland of North America: Its Occupation and the Challenge of Continuous Reappraisals," pp. 350-66 (reproduced in entry 20-13); John T. Curtis, "The Modification of Mid-Latitude Grasslands and Forests by Man," pp. 721-36; and Andrew H. Clark, "The Impact of Exotic Invasion of the Remaining New World Mid-Latitude Grasslands," pp. 737-62.

20-31 Trimble, Stanley W. MAN-INDUCED SOIL EROSION ON THE SOUTHERN PIEDMONT, 1700-1970. Ankeny, Iowa: Soil Conservation Society of

America, 1974. viii, 180 p. Maps, illus., photos., diagrs., tables, notes, bibliog.

Trimble describes the spatial and chronological aspects of erosive land use and consequent erosion in the southern piedmont (Virginia, North and South Carolina, Georgia, and Alabama). He identifies four periods of erosive land use: pre-1700, limited erosion associated with aboriginal settlement; 1700-1860, increased erosion associated with European agricultural settlement; 1860-1920, period of greatest erosive land use; and 1920 to present, a time of decline in erosion. His research is based on agricultural censuses and Department of Agriculture and Soil Conservation Service published reports, soil surveys, and archival materials. See also "The Alcovy River Swamps: The Result of Culturally Accelerated Sedimentation," BULLETIN OF THE GEORGIA ACADEMY OF SCIENCE 28 (September 1970): 131-41.

C. RECONSTRUCTION OF PHYSICAL LANDSCAPES AND PROCESSES

20-32 Alexander, Charles S., and Nunnally, Nelson R. "Channel Stability on the Lower Ohio River." AAG ANNALS 62 (September 1972): 411-17. Maps, notes.

Radiocarbon dating, township survey plats (1809), topographic maps (1958), and aerial photographs (1938 and 1965) are used to study channel stability on the lower Ohio River (Illinois and Indiana).

20-33 Dolan, Robert, and Bosserman, Kenton. "Shoreline Erosion and the Lost Colony." AAG ANNALS 62 (September 1972): 424-26. Maps, notes.

Coastal charts prepared by the Coast and Geodetic Survey and the Army Corps of Engineers since the mid-nineteenth century were used to calculate erosion trends on Roanoke Island, North Carolina. By extending these trends backwards, the authors suggest that the inability to locate the site of Sir Walter Raleigh's 1585 settlement may be a result of shoreline erosion.

20-34 Johannessen, Carl L., et al. "The Vegetation of the Willamette Valley." AAG ANNALS 61 (June 1971): 286-302. Maps, illus., photos., notes.

Vegetation patterns (prairie versus woodland and tree species) are reconstructed for the Willamette Valley, Oregon, during the 1850s using explorers' and settlers' accounts and township survey plats and field notes. In order to assess change, these patterns were compared with aerial photographs and field surveys from the 1960s.

20-35 Lawson, Merlin P. THE CLIMATE OF THE GREAT AMERICAN DESERT: RECONSTRUCTION OF THE CLIMATE OF WESTERN INTERIOR UNITED STATES, 1800-1850. University of Nebraska, new series, no. 46. Lincoln: University of Nebraska Press, 1974. viii, 134 p. Paper. Maps, illus., diagrs., tables, notes, bibliog.

In attempting to assess the contrasting images (either desert or garden) of the Great Plains, Lawson reconstructs climatic conditions for 1849, because image creation would be strengthened by extensive migrations, which occurred that year. His reconstruction is based on dendrochronological (tree ring) evidence, fort records (meteorological observations), diaries and letters, and deductive models of long-period climatic change. Whereas previous historical interpretations have assumed that the climate was unchanging, Lawson shows that 1849 was a particularly wet year in a fifty-year wet period. Other studies by Lawson pertaining to the reconstruction of climatic conditions include NEBRASKA DROUGHTS: A STUDY OF THEIR PAST CHRONO-LOGICAL AND SPATIAL EXTENT WITH IMPLICATIONS FOR THE FUTURE (Lincoln: University of Nebraska, Department of Geography, 1971); and "A Dendroclimatological Interpretation of the Great American Desert," AAG PROCEEDINGS 3 (1971): 109-14.

20-36 Strahler, Alan. "Forests of the Fairfax Line." AAG ANNALS 62 (December 1972): 664-84. Maps, diagrs., tables, notes.

Witness trees as recorded in the 1746 survey of the Fairfax Line (connecting the headwaters of the Rappahannock and Potomac Rivers) are compared to current vegetational patterns. Despite extensive human destruction of the original forests, there is general agreement in the two distributions.

ADDENDUM

ADDENDUM

When the first draft of this guide was submitted to the editors in the early
part of 1981, I had no intention of compiling an addendum of 1980 publications
that I had missed or 1981 publications that had appeared during the editorial
process. However, several significant items have come to my attention which
should not be omitted in a work of this nature. The most significant of these
new developments were the release of the 1910 manuscript census schedules
(entry 21-10) and the publication of a directory of historical geographers (entry
21-4). The emphasis of this addendum is on publications that describe cartographic and archival sources, as well as works by several authors that continue
topics mentioned in the previous chapters. Periodical literature for 1981 was
not considered for inclusion in this addendum.

21-1 Baer, Christopher T. CANALS AND RAILROADS OF THE MIDATLANTIC
      STATES, 1800-1860. Wilmington, Del.: Regional Economic History Re-
      search Center, Eleutherian Mills, Hagley Foundation, 1981. iv, 51 p.
      Paper. Maps, diagrs., tables, bibliog.

> As part of its large-scale investigation of transportation in the
> Middle Atlantic states, the Regional Economic History Research
> Center sponsored this study, which resulted in the compilation
> of five maps showing the development of canal and railroad
> networks in the Middle Atlantic states (northern Virginia and
> West Virginia, Maryland, Delaware, Pennsylvania, New Jersey,
> New York, and western Connecticut) in 1800, 1815, 1830,
> 1845, and 1860. Also included are detailed maps of the
> transportation networks in the Pennsylvania anthracite coal
> regions and the four major cities (New York, Philadelphia,
> Baltimore, and Washington, D.C.) and organizational and
> mileage tables. A lengthy bibliography lists state and federal
> legislative documents, newspapers, maps, corporations' annual
> reports, and secondary works.

21-2 Cobb, David A. NEW HAMPSHIRE MAPS TO 1900: AN ANNOTATED
      CHECKLIST. Hanover: University Press of New England for New
      Hampshire Historical Society, 1981. xv, 106 p. Paper. Bibliog., index.

Addendum

Pre-1900 maps in twenty-two institutions are listed. The 516 entries, which are arranged chronologically, pertain primarily to published maps, although five significant collections of manuscript maps are described briefly. Appendixes list U.S. Geological Survey topographic quadrangles and Sanborn fire insurance maps for New Hampshire.

21-3 Conzen, Michael P. "Historical Geography: North American Progress during the 1970s." PROGRESS IN HUMAN GEOGRAPHY 4 (1980): 549-59.

Conzen reviews the research output in the historical geography of Canada and the United States during the 1970s. He also provides a brief analysis of research trends and relates the growth of this research interest to the increased number of publications and growing membership in professional organizations. A list of key references is included.

21-4 _____, comp. NEW GEOGRAPHIES OF THE PAST: A REGISTER OF RESEARCH INTERESTS IN AND RECENT PUBLICATIONS ON AMERICAN AND RELATED HISTORICAL GEOGRAPHY. Chicago: University of Chicago, Department of Geography for the Historical Geography Specialty Group of the Association of American Geographers, 1981. iv, 56 p. Paper. Index.

The research interests and recent publications of over three hundred geographers are listed in this directory. The information is based on questionnaires mailed to the members of the Historical Geography Specialty Group of the Association of American Geographers. The directory will be useful for recent publications not included in the present guide.

21-5 Heynen, William J., comp. PRELIMINARY INVENTORY OF THE CARTO-GRAPHIC RECORDS OF THE SOIL CONSERVATION SERVICE. Preliminary Inventory, 195. Washington, D.C.: National Archives and Records Service, 1981. viii, 139 p. Paper. Maps, index.

Approximately 241,000 maps, plans, charts, profiles, and aerial photographs, which comprise the cartographic records of the Soil Conservation Service in the National Archives, are described. These records date from 1903 to 1974, but they primarily document soil surveys, soil erosion and land utilization studies, and resettlement programs from the 1930s to mid-1950s. These records will be most useful for studying changes in land utilization and the physical landscape during the twentieth century.

21-6 James Ford Bell Library. THE JAMES FORD BELL LIBRARY: AN ANNOTATED CATALOG OF ORIGINAL SOURCE MATERIALS RELATING TO THE HISTORY OF EUROPEAN EXPANSION, 1400-1800, UNIVERSITY OF MINNESOTA. Boston: G.K. Hall, 1981. iv, 493 p.

Started as a private collection, the James Ford Bell Library at the University of Minnesota collects original materials emphasizing the mercantile aspects of pre-1800 European expansion. Related subject coverage includes discovery, exploration, navigation, astronomy, cartography, laws governing international maritime trade, commerce, and travel. This catalog, which is arranged alphabetically by main entry, presents a record of the library's holdings at the end of 1980. There is no subject or geographical index, but annotations briefly describe the contents of each item.

21-7 Jordan, Terry G. TRAILS TO TEXAS: SOUTHERN ROOTS OF WESTERN CATTLE RANCHING. Lincoln: University of Nebraska Press, 1981. xv, 220 p. Maps, photos., tables, notes, bibliog., index.

In the context of cultural diffusion, Jordan examines the development of open-range cattle herding in Texas. Specifically, he concentrates on the Anglo herding practices transferred from the South (South Carolina) and their amalgamation with Hispanic traditions in three areas in eastern Texas. It was these hybrid practices that eventually diffused into the Great Plains. Earlier articles on this topic are listed in entry 17-10.

21-8 Judd, Carol M., and Ray, Arthur J., eds. OLD TRAILS AND NEW DIRECTIONS: PAPERS OF THE THIRD NORTH AMERICAN FUR TRADE CONFERENCE. Toronto: University of Toronto Press, 1980. ix, 337 p. Maps, diagrs., tables, notes, bibliog.

The proceedings of the multidisciplinary Third North American Fur Trade Conference, which was held in Winnipeg, Manitoba, in May 1978, are recorded. Although most of these presentations deal with Canadian topics, the following are of interest: G. Malcolm Lewis, "Indian Maps," pp. 9-23 (see entry 2-16); Richard I. Ruggles, "Hudson's Bay Company Mapping," pp. 24-36 (see entry 6-9); James R. Gibson, "The Russian Fur Trade," pp. 217-30 (see entry 13-10); Arthur J. Ray, "Indians as Consumers in the Eighteenth Century," pp. 255-71 (see entry 15-15); D.W. Moddie, "Agriculture and the Fur Trade," pp. 272-90 (see entry 15-26); and Irene M. Spry, "Innis, the Fur Trade, and Modern Economic Problems," pp. 291-307.

21-9 Moffat, Riley Moore. PRINTED MAPS OF UTAH TO 1900: AN ANNOTATED CARTOBIBLIOGRAPHY. Western Association of Map Libraries Occasional Paper, no. 8. Santa Cruz, Calif.: Western Association of Map Libraries, 1981. xvi, 176 p. Paper. Bibliog., index.

The first chapter summarizes the history of mapping in Utah, while the remaining six chapters list approximately three hundred published maps of Utah dated from 1778 to 1899. The maps are found in the Library of Congress, the Bancroft Library, and nine map collections within the state of Utah.

Addendum

21-10 National Archives and Records Service. THE 1910 FEDERAL POPULATION
CENSUS: A CATALOG OF MICROFILM COPIES OF THE SCHEDULES.
Washington, D.C.: National Archives Trust Fund Board, 1982. xii,
44 p. Paper.

> The microfilm copies of the 1910 manuscript census schedules,
> name indexes, and enumeration district descriptions are listed
> in this catalog. Ordering instructions are also included.
> Catalogs for the microfilm of the 1790-1900 manuscript census
> schedules are described in entries 8-17 and 8-18.

21-11 Pred, Allan R. URBAN GROWTH AND CITY-SYSTEMS IN THE UNITED
STATES, 1840-1860. Harvard Studies in Urban History. Cambridge:
Harvard University Press, 1980. xv, 282 p. Maps, tables, diagrs.,
notes, index.

> This work complements Pred's two earlier works (see entries
> 18-19 and 18-20) by concentrating on urban growth and city-
> systems development during the pivotal years of 1840-1860.
> This was a period of rapid urban growth, as well as a period
> of transition marking the beginning of the shift from commercial
> to industrial bases for urban growth. In examining the complex-
> ity of the economic interdependence of the major U.S. cities,
> he presents case studies of six cities (Boston, Philadelphia,
> Buffalo, Cincinnati, New Orleans, and Charleston) and a
> contents analysis of a sample of antebellum newspapers.

21-12 Sauer, Carl O. SEVENTEENTH CENTURY NORTH AMERICA. Berkeley,
Calif.: Turtle Island Foundation, 1980. 295 p. Maps, bibliog., index.

> Sauer's last book, which was published posthumously, examines
> French and Spanish activities in seventeenth-century North
> America. It provides a sequel to his earlier works on the
> European discovery and exploration of North America (see
> entries 14-14 and 14-15).

21-13 Schroeder, Walter A. PRESETTLEMENT PRAIRIE OF MISSOURI.
Natural History Series, no. 2. [Jefferson City]: Missouri Department
of Conservation, 1981. 40 p. Paper. Maps, illus., photos., bibliog.

> Utilizing field notes and township plats from the original town-
> ship surveys by the General Land Office, Schroeder maps the
> extent of the presettlement prairie in Missouri. Nine regional
> maps depict the details of this reconstruction.

21-14 Stephenson, Richard W. THE CARTOGRAPHY OF NORTHERN VIRGINIA:
FACSIMILE REPRODUCTIONS OF MAPS DATING FROM 1608 TO 1915.
Fairfax County, Va.: Office of Comprehensive Planning, History and
Archaeology Section, 1981. v, 145 p. Paper. Maps, bibliog., index.

> Seventy maps and two atlases pertaining to northern Virginia
> are reproduced in this facsimile atlas. Although the maps

date from 1608 to 1915, the largest representation is from the eighteenth and nineteenth centuries. These maps, most of which are from the Geography and Map Division, Library of Congress, illustrate the use of cartographic materials in documenting geographic change in a local area.

INDEXES

AUTHOR INDEX

This index includes authors, compilers, editors, translators, and other contributors to the text. Alphabetization is letter by letter, and numbers refer to entry numbers.

Author Index

Bedini, Silvio 1-20
Beirne, D. Randall 12-22, 18-25
Ben-Arieh, Yehoshua 12-28
Bennett, Sari 5-4
Bennion, Lowell 12-19
Berkhofer, Robert F. 17-1
Berry, Brian J.L. 18-9
Bertrand, Kenneth J. 14-6
Billington, Ray Allen 14-21
Birch, Brian P. 12-28, 14-25, 14-30, 20-17
Birdsall, Stephen S. 5-5
Birmingham (Alabama). Public Library 3-9
Black, Jeannette D. 2-3, 2-26
Blake, Janice G. 3-10
Bliss, Carey S. 1-24
Block, Robert H. 12-28
Bloom, John Porter 6-37
Blouet, Brian W. 12-3, 12-4
Blouin, Francis X., Jr. 6-12
Blumin, Stuart M. 18-26
Boer, G. De. See DeBoer, G.
Borchert, James 19-27
Borchert, John R. 13-1, 18-10
Bosserman, Kenton 20-33
Bouman, Lane J. 9-1
Boume, L.S. 18-10
Bowden, Martyn J. 12-3, 12-6, 12-24, 13-4, 18-3, 18-27, 18-46, 20-2, 20-9
Bowen, Marshall E. 12-11, 12-28, 16-12, 19-32
Bowen, William A. 12-24, 12-28, 12-31, 13-8
Bowers, Douglas E. 17-2
Bowling, Kenneth R. 6-39
Bowman, Jacob N. 9-2
Bradbury, David E. 20-16
Bradford, John 10-37
Brahm, William G. De. See DeBrahm, William G.
Brand, Donald D. 14-6
Brandhorst, L. Carl 17-1
Brayshay, Mark 6-2
Bredeson, Robert C. 7-2
Bridenbaugh, Carl 20-18
Brigham, Clarence S. 7-17
Brinkman, Leonard W. 12-30
British Museum. See Great Britain. British Museum

Brodeur, David D. 12-25
Brooks, Philip C. 6-14
Brower, Philip P. 9-12
Brown, A. Theodore 18-1
Brown, Anne S.K. 2-22
Brown, Lloyd A. 3-1
Brown, Ralph H. 13-2, 13-3
Brown, Robert H. 12-1
Brownell, Blaine A. 18-14
Browning, Clyde E. 11-11, 11-22
Brun, Christian 1-33, 2-27
Brune, Basel H. 12-22
Brunn, Stanley D. 12-8
Bryant, Pat 5-35, 9-3
Bufkin, Don 5-57
Bumsted, John M. 19-23
Burch, Franklin W. 12-6
Burghardt, Andrew F. 12-20, 17-20
Burns, Elizabeth K. 12-2
Burrill, Robert M. 15-17
Butler, Ruth L. 6-38
Butzer, Karl W. 10-7, 13-4

C

California, University of. Berkeley. Bancroft Library 1-27, 6-30
Campbell, Ann M. 6-36
Campbell, Tony 1-13
Cappon, Lester J. 2-4, 5-1, 5-6
Capps, Marie T. 2-5
Carlson, Alvar W. 15-1, 16-5, 19-27
Carr, A.P. 1-6
Carr, Lois Green 6-20
Carrington, David K. 1-28
Carson, Jane 7-3
Carver, Fred E. 5-31
Cassara, Ernest 11-12
Chandler, Tertius 12-13
Chardon, Roland 16-6
Chatterjee, S.P. 12-18
Child, Sargent B. 6-28
Chorley, Richard J. 11-9
Christopher, A.J. 12-28
Clark, Andrew H. 11-1, 11-2, 12-3, 12-6, 12-10, 17-4, 20-30
Clark, David Sanders 2-6, 2-7, 3-11
Clark, Thomas D. 3-12, 7-4

Author Index

E

Eakins, Rosemary 10-29
Earle, Carville V. 5-4, 11-7, 12-28, 13-9, 17-6, 18-13, 18-14, 20-3
Eastin, Roy B. 6-24
Easton, William W. 1-19
Edwards, Helen H. 17-2
Ee, Patricia Molen van. See Van Ee, Patricia Molen
Ehrenberg, Ralph E. 1-14, 2-2, 2-29, 2-30, 4-17, 4-18, 6-3, 7-13, 12-6
Eigenheer, Richard A. 20-14
Emmons, David M. 12-3
Engerman, Richard W. 1-24
Engerrand, Steven W. 12-27
Entrikin, J. Nicholas 12-28
Ernst, Joseph A. 6-4, 12-30, 18-15
Esposito, Vincent J. 5-9
Estes, John E. 10-42
Etulain, Richard W. 14-31
Evans, Frank B. 6-36
Evans, Hilary 10-17
Evans, Mary 10-17
Ewers, John C. 10-2

F

Fahl, Ronald J. 20-21
Farmer, Judith A. 5-42
Farrell, Richard T. 7-18
Feller, Irwin 12-5
Fellman, Jerome D. 11-18
Fields, Dale 4-34
Finberg, H.P.R. 11-4
Finster, Jerome 6-37
Fishbein, Meyer H. 6-37, 8-7, 12-6
Fisher, James S. 17-7
Fite, Emerson D. 2-10
Florin, John W. 5-5, 12-30, 14-23
Fly, Everett L. 19-19
Fly, La Barbara Wigfall 19-19
Fogelson, Raymond D. 15-2
Ford, Larry R. 12-2, 12-20, 18-45
Fox, Edward W. 5-10
Francaviglia, Richard V. 12-1, 17-21, 19-20, 19-27

Franklin, W. Neil 8-8
Frassanito, William A. 10-18
Frazier, Arthur H. 1-20
Frederic, Paul B. 17-1
Freeman, Archibald 2-10
Freeman, Donald B. 15-15
Freidel, Frank 6-17, 11-15
French, Carolyn 12-12
Friis, Herman R. 1-8, 1-14, 2-28, 2-31, 3-3, 4-17, 5-11, 5-28, 6-37, 7-13, 12-3, 12-6, 14-6
Fullard, Harold 5-8
Fuson, Robert H. 12-24

G

Galneder, Mary 5-2
Garry, Robert J. 14-6
Gates, Paul W. 16-1, 16-14
Gaustad, Edwin S. 5-12
Gentilcore, R. Louis 1-2, 12-28
Gentry, Daphne 9-4
Gerasimov, I.P. 12-17
Gerlach, Larry R. 6-41
Gerlach, Russel L. 12-20, 19-21
Gibb, Hugh R. 6-40
Gibson, James R. 12-10, 12-28, 12-31, 13-10, 19-2, 21-8
Gibson, Lay James 4-1
Gilbert, Martin 5-13
Gilchrist, David T. 18-16
Gjerde, Jon 12-21
Glaab, Charles N. 18-1
Glassen, Robert 12-27
Glassie, Henry 19-22, 19-26, 19-32, 19-35
Goetzman, William H. 10-3, 14-7
Goheen, Peter G. 18-2
Gohstand, Robert 12-17
Goins, Charles R. 5-49
Goldfield, David R. 18-14
Goodrum, Charles A. 6-34
Goodwin, Gary C. 15-22
Gottmann, Jean 13-11
Gouger, James B. 12-30
Gould, Peter R. 17-25
Graf, William 20-22
Grant, Eric G. 12-28
Great Britain. British Museum 1-41
Great Britain. Public Record Office 1-29

Author Index

L

Lackey, Richard S. 9-12
Ladd, Richard S. 2-40
Lambert, Patricia 12-29
Lampard, Eric E. 18-17
Lamprecht, Sandra J. 11-13
Landing, James E. 12-16
Langdale, John V. 17-22
Langton, John 6-1
LaRose, Bruce L. 12-24
Larson, Albert J. 19-32
Laws, Kevin J. 12-27
Lawson, Merlin P. 12-3, 12-11, 20-35
Laxton, Paul 12-28
Layton, Robert L. 20-5
Leaman, J. Harold 17-11
Lebeder, Dimitri M. 14-6
LeBlanc, Robert 12-24, 17-17
Lee, Charles E. 3-23
LeFurgy, William G. 4-31
LeGear, Clara Egli 1-16, 1-30, 1-31, 2-41
Lehr, John C. 11-10
Leighly, John 12-1, 12-26
Lemon, James T. 12-10, 13-13, 19-23
Lewis, Carolyn B. 14-30
Lewis, G. Malcolm 2-16, 12-3, 12-4, 20-7, 21-8
Lewis, George K. 13-1
Lewis, Peirce F. 13-1, 13-4, 19-27, 19-28, 19-32
Lewis, Thomas R. 12-23
Lewthwaite, Gordon R. 12-24, 12-28
Library of Congress 6-19, 7-21
Library of Congress. Census Library Project 8-14, 8-15
Library of Congress. General Reference and Bibliography Division 11-19
Library of Congress. Geography and Map Division 1-11, 1-32, 4-4
Library of Congress. Prints and Photographs Division 10-22, 10-23
Lindstrom, Diane 17-1
Lockmann, Ronald F. 3-5
Lockridge, Kenneth A. 19-23
Long, John H. 5-6, 5-20

Lord, Clifford L. 5-16, 5-21
Lord, Elizabeth H. 5-21
Louder, Dean 12-19, 12-24
Lowenthal, David 19-28, 20-8, 20-9
Loy, William G. 5-46
Luebke, Frederick C. 12-4, 19-11
Lyons, Thomas R. 10-38

M

McCauley, Lois B. 4-23
McCorkle, Barbara B. 14-17
McDermott, John Francis 7-8, 7-13, 14-28
McDonald, Archie P. 2-41
McDonald, Donna 6-13
McEntyre, John G. 16-2
McGovern, Carolyn G. 12-29
McIntire, Elliot G. 12-1
McIntosh, C. Barron 16-16
McLane, Alvin R. 1-24
McLaughlin, Patrick D. 2-17, 2-42
McManis, Douglas R. 11-20, 12-13, 13-14, 14-9, 20-26
Macpherson, Alan G. 12-28
McQuillan, D. Aidan 12-10, 12-28, 17-12
McReynolds, Edwin C. 5-49
Maddox, Jerald C. 10-16
Main, Gloria L. 6-20
Malan, Nancy E. 10-24
Malin, James C. 20-30
Malone, Dumas 3-28
Margary, Harry 2-18
Marks, Bayly Ellen 12-22
Marshall, Douglas W. 1-33, 2-18, 2-19
Marston, Thomas E. 2-24
Martin, Calvin 15-14
Martin, Lawrence 1-16
Marzio, Peter C. 10-14, 10-25
Mason, Sara Elizabeth 3-9
Mather, E. Cotton 13-1
Mathien, Francis Joan 10-38
Matthews, William 7-9
Maule, Elizabeth Singer 4-14
Maxwell, Richard S. 9-8
May, Betty 1-5
Mayer, Harold M. 10-26

Author Index

Meade, B.K. 16-3
Mealor, W. Theodore, Jr. 12-1
Meinig, Donald W. 6-5, 11-7, 12-10, 12-17, 13-1, 13-6, 13-7, 13-15, 13-16, 13-17, 13-20, 19-12, 19-28
Melody, Michael E. 15-2
Melville, Annette 6-34
Merk, Frederick 14-29
Merkel, Donald E. 16-3
Merrens, Harry Roy 6-4, 6-6, 6-7, 6-8, 11-8, 12-6, 12-30, 13-18, 18-15
Mesinger, Jonathan S. 12-29
Meyer, David R. 12-5, 12-28, 13-4
Meyer, Douglas K. 12-28, 19-13
Meyer, Judith W. 12-8, 12-23
Meyer, Robert J. 12-24
Michigan, University of. William L. Clements Library 1-33, 6-35
Miles, William 3-21
Miller, David E. 5-47
Miller, David H. 14-30
Miller, E. Joan Wilson 19-29
Miller, Ruby M. 3-22
Miller, Theodore R. 5-22
Mills, Robert 3-23
Miltudson, Charles 1-1
Mishara, Brian 12-24
Mitchell, Robert D. 12-10, 12-22, 12-25, 12-28, 13-19, 14-23, 19-2
Moak, Jefferson M. 2-43
Modelski, Andrew M. 1-19, 2-44
Moffat, Riley Moore 21-9
Mohr, Carolyn Curtis 6-38
Moodie, D.W. 6-9, 11-10, 12-28, 15-26, 21-8
Moody, Eric N. 4-5
Moore, Conrad T. 12-24
Morgan, Dale L. 6-30
Morgan, John 12-27
Morgan, Michael A. 6-10
Morison, Samuel Eliot 14-10
Morrill, Richard L. 17-25, 19-7
Morris, Gerald E. 5-48
Morris, John W. 5-49
Mottaz, Stan 5-50
Muller, Edward K. 8-16, 12-13, 12-22, 12-28, 13-4, 18-18, 18-30, 18-35

Muller, Peter O. 18-4
Mumford, Lewis 20-30
Muntz, A. Philip 1-34, 2-45, 12-14

N

Naef, Weston J. 10-15
Nash, Roderick 20-10
National Archives and Records Service 1-34, 2-45, 6-21, 6-36, 6-37, 8-17, 8-18, 21-10
National Archives and Records Service. Office of Educational Programs 10-27
National Geographic Society 14-11
Nebenzahl, Kenneth 2-20, 2-21
Nelki, Andra 10-17
Nelson, Howard J. 12-2
Nelson, Thomas 11-13
Newberry Library 3-4, 6-38
Newcomb, Robert M. 10-39, 12-2, 18-48
Newhall, Beaumont 10-28
Newson, Linda A. 12-28
Newton, Milton B., Jr. 19-25, 19-30
Newton, Milton S. 19-35
New York (City). Public Library. Map Division 1-35
Nicholas, Raphael C. 19-30
Nichols, Michael L. 6-41
Nimmo, Sylvia 5-51
Noble, Allen G. 12-20, 19-32
Noe, Barbara R. 1-36
Norris, Darrell A. 12-28
Norris, Frank 12-28
Nostrand, Richard L. 12-20, 12-28, 13-4, 19-14
Novak, Barbara 10-6
Novotny, Ann 10-29
Nunnally, Nelson R. 20-32

O

Ohrn, Karin Becker 10-30
O'Keefe, Doris 12-29
Olson, Sherry H. 18-36, 20-27
Orme, Anthony R. 12-28
Osborne, Brian S. 7-20, 14-30

Spear, Dorothea N. 4-33
Spencer, Joseph E. 17-16
Speth, William W. 20-29
Spillman, Robert C. 12-29
Spry, Irene M. 12-3, 21-8
Spurr, Richard E. 10-41
Stanley, William A. 1-40
Steffen, Jerome O. 14-30
Stenzel, Franz 10-9
Stephenson, Charles 6-39
Stephenson, Richard W. 1-12, 1-15, 1-16, 1-21, 1-28, 2-49, 4-26, 5-2, 9-16, 21-14
Stevens, Stanley D. 1-19, 1-24, 4-2
Stewart, Ian R. 11-13
Stiverson, Gregory A. 16-11
Storm, Colton 1-7, 6-38
Strahler, Alan 20-36
Stroup, Theodore G. 2-5
Stuart, Merrill M. 11-22
Sturtevant, William C. 15-6
Sublett, Pirie 14-17
Sutherland, Stella H. 8-22, 19-17
Sutton, Imre 15-9
Swanson, Duane P. 6-40
Swauger, John 18-40
Swenson, Robert W. 16-1
Swierenga, Robert P. 12-15, 16-20
Syracuse University. Department of Geography 12-29

T

Taaffe, Richard J. 17-25
Taft, Robert 10-10, 10-35
Tanner, Helen Hornbeck 15-2
Tatum, Charles E. 12-20
Taylor, Charles E. 10-41
Taylor, Hugh A. 10-11
Thernstrom, Stephan 18-34, 18-41
Thomas, Joe D. 10-27
Thomas, Samuel W. 4-27
Thomas, William L., Jr. 20-30
Thomason, Michael 10-36
Thompson, John H. 13-20
Thompson, Kenneth 20-14
Thompson, Stephen I. 14-30
Thrower, Norman J.W. 1-22, 2-26, 9-17, 16-21

Tinney, Larry R. 10-42
Tobin, Gregory M. 13-21
Tooker, Elisabeth 15-2
Tooley, Ronald Vere 1-12, 1-13, 1-41
Towner, Lawrence W. 2-13
Trachtenberg, Alan 10-27
Tracie, C.J. 12-3
Treftz, Walter H. 12-24
Treude, Mai 9-18
Trimble, Stanley W. 12-16, 12-28, 20-31
Trindell, Roger T. 6-11, 17-26
Truettner, William H. 10-12
Tuan, Yi Fu 19-28, 20-15
Tutorow, Norman D. 6-36
Tyacke, Sarah 1-41
Tyler, David B. 14-18
Tyler, Ronnie C. 10-14
Tyman, John L. 12-3

U

U.S. Bureau of the Census 8-14, 8-21, 8-22
U.S. Department of Agriculture 17-2
U.S. Geological Survey 5-28
U.S. Historic American Building Survey 6-32
U.S. National Historical Publications and Records Commission 6-21, 6-22
U.S. National Ocean Survey 2-50
U.S. Smithsonian Institution 15-5
U.S. War Department 2-51
University of California, Bancroft Library (Berkeley). See California, University of. Berkeley. Bancroft Library
University of Michigan. William L. Clements Library. See Michigan, University of. William L. Clements Library
Unrau, William E. 15-2
Unruh, John D., Jr. 14-34
Upchurch, John C. 12-30

V

Vance, James E., Jr. 12-5, 13-1, 13-4, 18-5, 18-21, 18-42

Author Index

Z

Zandt, Franklin K. van. See Van-
    Zandt, Franklin K.

Zelinsky, Wilbur 11-10, 12-1, 12-
    8, 13-4, 19-3, 20-9
Zoegner, Lothar 1-23
Zube, Ervin 19-24

TITLE INDEX

This index includes titles of books cited in the text as well as the titles of geographical, historical, and archival journals for which there are main entries in the text (all references to a particular journal are included although the main entry is underlined). In some cases, titles of books have been shortened. Titles of articles within journals or collections of essays are not listed. Alphabetization is letter by letter, and numbers refer to entry numbers.

A

Advance of Frontier Settlement in Pennsylvania, The 14-23
Aerial Photographs in the National Archives 10-41
Aerial Remote Sensing Techniques in Archeology 10-38
Afro-American History 6-37
Agricultural History 6-36, 7-18, 13-13, 13-19, 15-16, 16-1, 16-15, 17-1, 17-4, 17-8, 17-9, 17-12, 17-18, 20-14, 20-23
Agricultural Maps in the National Archives 2-34
A. Hoen on Stone 4-23
Aids to Geographical Research 11-17
A La Carte 1-15, 1-16
America: History and Life 15-4
America Explored 14-8
America in Maps 2-15
American Architecture and Art 10-8
American Archivist 2-17, 4-8, 6-12, 6-15, 6-28, 10-11, 10-33
American Atlas, The 2-14
American Campaigns of Rochambeau's Army, The 2-22

American Cartographer 1-8, 5-6
American City, The 11-13
American Diaries in Manuscript 7-9
American Expansion 5-26
American Geography 11-2
American Habitat 20-13
American Heritage Pictorial Atlas of United States History 5-18
American History Atlas 5-13
American Image, The 10-27
American Landscape 10-12
American Light 10-13
American Maps and Map Makers of the Revolution 2-12
American Newspapers 7-19
American Painting 10-5
American Population before the Federal Census of 1790 8-9
American Printmaking before 1876 10-14
American Revolution, 1775-1783, The 2-11
American Space 19-24
American State Papers 2-48, 6-15
American Steel Industry, The 17-19
American Studies: Topics and Sources 19-1

Title Index

H

Q

R

S

Title Index

SUBJECT INDEX

This index includes references to geographic places (primarily states and there-under by city or county), selected topics pertinent to historical geography, types of source material, libraries and archival repositories, and persons cited as subjects in the annotations. All agencies of the federal government (except the Library of Congress and the National Archives) are listed under U.S. State and foreign institutions are listed under the name of the appropriate governing body. Libraries associated with universities are listed under the name of the university. Alphabetization is letter by letter, and references are to entry numbers.

A

Acculturation. See Cultural geography, acculturation
Aerial photographs 4-18, 4-19, 10-37, 10-38, 10-39, 10-40, 10-41, 10-42, 14-10, 20-32, 20-34
Agriculture 5-18, 5-21, 5-24, 5-33, 12-4, 12-16, 12-19, 13-6, 13-8, 13-13, 13-14, 13-18, 13-20, 14-21, 14-23, 14-24, 14-27, 14-29, 14-30, 14-31, 16-8, 17-1 through 17-16, 19-9, 19-11, 19-13, 19-16, 19-34, 20-14, 20-20, 20-28, 20-31
    bibliography 11-19, 11-20, 17-2, 17-14, 17-15, 20-20
    domestication 12-26
    farm land abandonment 12-1
    food supplies 13-10, 17-9
    historical sources 2-34, 2-35, 6-3, 6-10, 6-36, 6-37,

7-17, 7-18, 8-27, 10-29. See also U.S. Bureau of the Census, agricultural censuses
    irrigation 12-14, 17-1, 20-5, 20-14, 20-25
    regional specialization 12-28, 17-9, 17-11, 17-13, 17-16, 18-14
    sharecropping 12-12
    staple crops 12-28, 13-12, 17-6, 18-14
    See also Indians, agriculture; and individual crops or products
Alabama 3-9, 5-39, 8-10, 9-10, 12-24, 16-19, 19-35, 20-31,
    Mobile 10-36
Alaska 3-5, 12-10, 13-10, 15-10
Alden, James Madison 10-9
American Antiquarian Society 4-33, 6-29, 7-17
American Geographical Society 1-23, 1-26, 10-31, 11-14

Subject Index

F

Family papers 6-8, 6-18, 6-29,
    6-30
Farming. See Agriculture
Field notes. See U.S. General Land
    Office, field notes
Fillmore Millard 1-12
Fire insurance atlases-maps 1-30,
    1-31, 1-32, 1-33, 3-13,
    3-17, 3-22, 4-1, 4-2, 4-
    3, 4-4, 4-5, 4-6, 4-7,
    4-9, 4-10, 8-3, 18-27,
    21-2
Flathead Indians 10-2
Florida 7-12, 12-1, 12-6, 12-16,
    12-25, 12-30, 14-15,
    14-30, 15-20, 16-3, 16-19,
    19-35
Food stuffs. See Agriculture, food
    supplies
Force, Peter 1-15
Forest resources 6-16, 8-22, 10-6,
    13-14, 13-18, 20-18, 20-
    21, 20-27
France, Bibliotheque nationale 1-23,
    1-38
Franklin, Benjamin 1-10
Fremont, John C. 3-6, 6-21, 14-11,
    20-1
French and Indian War 2-7, 2-9
French Canadian immigrants 12-10,
    12-25, 17-12, 19-4
French colonies in North America
    12-10, 13-2, 13-3, 13-4,
    14-24, 16-6, 16-7, 16-9,
    19-21
French exploration 14-6, 14-9,
    21-12
French mapping in North America
    1-12, 1-13, 1-38, 2-12,
    2-22, 3-5
Frontier
    early settlement of an area 12-22,
        12-24, 12-25, 13-6, 13-8,
        13-19, 14-24, 14-26,
        14-32, 16-20, 17-4, 17-5,
        19-8, 19-11, 19-13, 20-17.
        See also Colonization
    general studies 12-28, 14-20,

    14-21, 14-22, 14-25,
    14-27, 14-28, 14-29,
    14-30, 14-31, 14-33,
    15-24
    hypothesis 14-21, 14-27, 14-
        28, 14-31
    urbanization 12-2, 12-5, 12-28,
        14-20, 14-23, 14-26, 14-
        27, 14-28, 14-31
    westward expansion of settlement
        3-2, 3-15, 5-26, 5-52,
        12-33, 14-19, 14-23,
        14-29, 14-33, 14-34, 14-
        35, 15-20, 19-5, 19-35.
        See also Fur trade; Indians
        relations with Europeans
Fur trade 5-42, 6-9, 10-2, 12-3,
    12-10, 13-10, 13-15,
    14-7, 14-15, 14-27, 14-28,
    14-30, 14-31, 15-12, 15-
    13, 15-14, 15-15, 15-16,
    21-8

G

Genealogical Society of the Church
    of Jesus Christ of Latter-
    Day Saints 4-29, 6-18,
    6-41
Geographic mobility. See Migra-
    tion-immigration. See also
    Urban geography, internal
    structure, geographic mobil-
    ity
Georgia 3-10, 5-35, 6-12, 7-12,
    9-3, 12-10, 12-27, 15-20,
    18-33, 20-31
German immigrants 12-8, 18-28,
    19-9, 19-11, 19-21
Government reports 6-8, 6-15,
    6-24, 7-12, 7-13, 7-14,
    7-15
Grain. See wheat
Grand Canyon 1-19
Grassland-woodland settlement. See
    Perception, prairie-woodland
    preference
Great Basin 15-6
Great Britain, British Museum 1-
    41, 6-22, 7-12, 8-24

Subject Index

Subject Index